# Impossible Organizations

**Recent Titles in
Contributions in Sociology**

# IMPOSSIBLE ORGANIZATIONS

## Self-Management and Organizational Reproduction

YOHANAN STRYJAN

Contributions in Sociology, Number 83

GREENWOOD PRESS
New York • Westport, Connecticut • London

**Library of Congress Cataloging-in-Publication Data**

Stryjan, Yohanan.
   Impossible organizations : self-management and organizational
reproduction / Yohanan Stryjan.
     p.  cm. — (Contributions in sociology, ISSN 0084-9278 ; no.
83)
   Bibliography: p.
   Includes index.
   ISBN 0-313-26795-2 (lib. bdg. : alk. paper)
   1. Management—Employee participation.  2. Employee ownership.
3. Producer cooperatives.  I. Title.  II. Series.
HD5650.S835  1989
658.3′152—dc20       89-2186

British Library Cataloguing in Publication Data is available.

Library of Congress Catalog Card Number: 89-2186
ISBN: 0-313-26795-2
ISSN: 0084-9278

First published in 1989

Greenwood Press, Inc.
88 Post Road West, Westport, Connecticut 06881

Printed in the United States of America

The paper used in this book complies with the
Permanent Paper Standard issued by the National
Information Standards Organization (Z39.48-1984).

10 9 8 7 6 5 4 3 2 1

# CONTENTS

# FIGURES AND TABLES

**Figures**

**Tables**

# FOREWORD

This is a book about a specific way of organizing human activity. It is also about a specific way of considering organizations in general. My theoretical interest in cooperative organizations has its roots in an old frustration, generated upon entering university after ten years of organizational experience with self-management and encountering the organization theory of that day. I have never been brought closer to admitting my own impossibility than I was then. It was an Alice-in-Wonderland experience that I am not likely to forget.

The situation has improved considerably since then. A number of outstanding books on self management and alternative organizations have been published and have gained recognition, and organization theory is no longer the straitjacket it seemed to be those days. Nevertheless, there is still a need for an integrated perspective that would do justice both to self-managed organizations and to organization theory. A bridge is called for between what can be observed in such organizations and what is being taught in mainstream courses in organizational theory. An approach that shows ways to bend theory to accommodate new realities can be of benefit for both organizational scientists striving to understand practice, and practitioners of self management seeking a way of understanding and accounting for what they are actually doing. With the recent explosive growth of worker-ownership in the United States, and of new cooperation in the Soviet Union and Eastern Europe, this challenge is more topical than ever. I hope that this book goes some way toward meeting it.

Many helped along the road. Particular thanks are due to Tom R. Burns for his invaluable advice and support. Casten von Otter helped to pilot the project through some of its most critical moments. Sven Åke Böök, the director of the Swedish Cooperative Institute at the time, provided an institutional haven in which to complete the work. This work could hardly ever been completed without their support.

Anthony Giddens and Barbara Czarniawska-Joerges commented on the manuscript, and helped hammer it into a book. Their encouragement made the task feel worth the while. Valuable comments were made by Ulf Erik Andersson, Torben Bager, Chris Conforth, Edmund Dahlström, Ann-Britt Hellmark, Ove Jobring, Anders Olsson, Menachem Rosner, Per Ove Rökholt, Richard Saltman, Mårten Söder, Roger Spear and Danny Zamir, and others too numerous to thank.

The work has generously been supported by the Swedish Council for Coordination of Research (FRN), the Cooperative Council's Development Programme (Basprogrammet), and the Swedish Cooperative Institute.

# Impossible Organizations

# 1

# INTRODUCTION

## 1.1 A STATEMENT OF AIM

The aim of this work is to outline a new theoretical perspective on self-managed organizations. Existing research on such organizations has, thus far, tended to apply paradigms and test hypotheses generated during research on other organizational forms, testing, as it were, the applicability of "general truths" to a specific type. Useful as this approach may have been in enriching mainstream theory, it does not do self-management justice nor generate knowledge that is specifically relevant to it. Self-managed organizations represent change. Research has stressed just those points when an effort at change was aborted and indirectly reinforced conventional characteristics.

The point of departure here is that special organizations may need to conduct themselves in special ways. A theory of the self-managed organization should thus best proceed from organizational practices, as they are applied in such organizations, to theory, rather than the other way around. The new insights that such a theory may generate can, in turn, enrich established theory.

Attention to practice presupposes that a body of practitioners is delimited as an object for study. Primarily, the examples used in this work are worker cooperatives. Two closely related clusters of organizations, worker-owned enterprises and Israeli kibbutzim are also included.

A considerable deal of research tends to see self-managed organizations as basically conventional organizations owned, or otherwise controlled by their workforce. This view may be consciously adopted on theoretical grounds (e.g. Abrahamsson, 1986). Often, however, it is simply a side effect of the unreflexive adoption of conceptual frameworks constructed to fit research in other types of organizations (Robinson,

1981a). The theoretical stance adopted here rests, instead, on a literal interpretation of the democratic model, seriously assuming that the self-managed organization's "superiors" do indeed permanently reside at and shape the organization from its "bottom".

The emerging model of the self-managed organization that the approach applied here suggests centres around the reproduction, through its members' daily practice, of an organization that reproduces its membership and thus also its mode of organization. Such an organization, through being self-managed, would deviate from the generally accepted norm of organizational conduct. As is generally the case with deviant organizations, it would also be exposed to pressures to "step back in line". Observable, real-life organizations would thus represent different forms of *modus vivendi* between principle and constraint. This presents more of a problem for the theorist, seeking regularities, than for the organization member, for whom such complexities would constitute a part of everyday reality.

A considerable portion of self-management research (briefly presented in section 1.2.1, below) has addressed itself to the issue of this organization form's alleged unviability. This thesis is not discussed here. Two tacit assumptions are made in this work, about such organizations' existence and performance: first, that such organizations are not inherently impossible (Jones, 1976); second, that to the extent comparison is possible, such organizations can perform at least as efficiently (MAC MAREV, 1982) or even outperform (Melman, 1970, 1971) comparable conventional ones. Assumptions of this sort are normally considered self-evident in research of other, "mainstream" organization forms. They obviously need to be restated in our case. Stating that self-managed organizations are in principle possible, does not amount to claiming that the existence of any single one is guaranteed. As is the case with all endeavours, deviant and conventional alike, some self-managed organizations would succeed, and others would not. One of this work's main aims is to understand the ways of, and preconditions for, successful self-management rather than to chart failures.

Being a study of organizations, this work is formulated in the language of organization theory, as far as the choice of conceptual accounting tools and "bibliographical pedigree" is concerned. When dealing with the relationship between (individual) members and their organization, an undeveloped area of organization theory, this apparatus will be augmented by application of the perspective developed by Alfred O. Hirschman.

Self-management is a deviant organization form. Immediately, this places some limitations on the applicability of conventional organizational concepts to the study of self-managed organizations (see 1.2.2). Dealing with deviant organizations, in trying to construct a (by implication) deviant theory, is anything but unproblematic. The problems a deviant organization encounters in its relation to a conventional environment (problems dealt with in chapters 5 and 6 of this book) are reflected, in a fashion, on the theoretical level. Organizational theory is, by its nature, geared to deal with the accepted rather than the exceptional. It offers no conceptual tools suitable for accounting for phenomena that fail to keep the standards it sets. The understanding of individual conduct within self-managed organizations, of the meaning of deviance and the way it is maintained, and, finally, of such organizations' positioning in macro systems, would presuppose a frame of reference of a higher order, where the established order of things is a subject for research rather than a taken-for granted reality. Such a frame of reference is provided by Anthony Giddens' theory of structuration. Some of the linkages of this work to the theory of structuration are briefly discussed in section 1.2.3.

The phenomenon addressed in this work is self-management, "an unusual way to organize and control the work we do as human beings" (Gunn, 1984). The focus is on a *mode* of organization rather than on one concrete organization *form* (as, for instance, the cooperative). A useful definition in this vein that focuses attention on aspirations rather than on practices is suggested by David Stodolsky[1]: "Self-management is a method of workplace organization based on an asymptotic attempt for direct and comprehensive democracy" (1985:40). The definition employed by Yohanan Stryjan (1983b), for the case of the self-managed enterprise was: "As a self managed enterprise can be regarded any enterprise that is managed democratically by its workers by virtue/right of their labour" (p.244). The view taken in this work is somewhat more generalized; labour is treated as one specific condition of membership. The organizations that we shall be dealing with do, as a rule, require that their members be working within them. Some of them may, as we shall see, impose additional conditions of membership. The definition quoted above can, in fact, be seen as one specific application of a members' organization, that is, an organization whose activities are carried by, and controlled by its members.

A variety of organizational forms have been tried historically in pursuit of these aspirations. The concrete organizational population dealt with, and used here as a source of empirical material, consists of three groups of organizations, each of them presented in the existing literature as reflecting, to some degree, the basic properties of self-management: worker-owned enterprises, worker cooperatives, and Israeli kibbutzim. All three organization types fulfill, in broad terms, the following conditions:

a. All of the organizations have a clear, formally defined body of members.

b. All members take part, actually or potentially, in decision-making and implementation.

c. The locus for all decisions is situated within the organization.

These conditions considerably simplify the task of constructing a reproduction model, as we shall see in chapter 3.

It is intuitively clear that none of these groups (nor, indeed, any concrete, real-life organization) could lay claim to representing "true and unabased" self-management. None of these organizations is perfect, nor should any one be expected to be so. Local deviations abound. Considerable variation exists between organizations within the groups, due in part to human fallibility, and in part to the need to adjust organizations' external appearances to environmental demands that would vary from one case to the next. "Operational" definitions are therefore used here as convenient guidelines for material collection and not as a standard evaluating specific organizations or populations.

**Worker-owned enterprises**, or enterprises owned by their workforce, have been a matter of considerable political and scientific interest in the course of the past two decades, often in conjunction with takeovers of closing plants (see Coates, 1976). In dealing with worker-owned enterprises, the definition applied here is Åke Gabrielsson's (1980):

> a company with *at least* five employees who are also joint-owners, where *at least* half of the employees directly or indirectly own *at least* half of the share/deposit capital. The ownership should also be *somewhat* evenly spread among the employed joint-owners. (Lindkvist and Svensson 1982; Italics mine)

As the definition implies, this (sub)population is highly heterogeneous in terms of internal ownership arrangements and of internal organization, the common denominator being that of *ownership*. The discussion of such enterprises in chapter 2 centres, accordingly, on the concept of ownership and its relevance for self-management research. Two clusters of cases are examined: Swedish personnel-owned companies (personalägda företag) and American Employee Stock Ownership Plans (ESOPs). The discussion of Swedish enterprises draws extensively on a number of thorough surveys (Gabrielsson, 1980; Jansson, 1983) and builds on the analysis of EDLA[2] survey's data presented in Stryjan and Hellmark (1985).

**Worker cooperatives** represent a tradition dating from the 1840s (Pollard, 1967). There is, however, no universally accepted definition for such cooperatives (Abell, 1983:73)[3]. Derek Jones' definition (1976:35) captures most of the essentials of this organization form:

i)     the establishment is autonomous
ii)    employees are able to become members of the
       enterprise by nominal holdings of share
       capital, usually £5 or less
iii)   The principle of "one-member-one-vote" prevails
iv)    formal provision exists for direct employee
       participation in decision making at all levels
       within the enterprise
v)     employees share in profits.

Article iii of the definition (nominal membership shares) is relaxed here to accommodate the American plywood cooperatives and the Mondragon cooperatives in the sample. There is general agreement about the cooperative character of these two groups, though neither of them conforms to the definition on this point.

Finally, the third group of cases, **kibbutzim,** are a  particular Israeli form of rural collective settlement. Kibbutzim differ from the other two organization forms in their stronger communal emphasis. Democratic principles are applied in these organizations to a considerably broader scope of activities, including consumption and municipal services. The first kibbutz was established 1910. In 1986 the movement had a population of 126,700 (Maron, 1988), in approximately 300 member kibbutzim. The kibbutz organizational population is clearly defined geographically, historically, and in terms of affiliation with distinct kibbutz federations, so as to make an operational definition superfluous[4].

Because of the kibbutz' communal character, its inclusion in typologies of cooperative or self-managed organizations has been a matter of some controversy (see Bergmann, 1980, for cooperatives and Ben Ner and Neuberger, 1979a, for self-managed organizations, respectively)[5]. Difficulties in generalizing from kibbutz material are not substantially different from those encountered in comparative studies of self-management (see Stryjan 1985b). They are well outweighted, for research purposes, by the fact of the kibbutzim being one of the biggest and most long-lived and best documented self-managed organization forms now in existence[6]. Although its stability may be threatened at present by dramatic turbulence in its environment, the abundant material collected in nearly eight decades of existence remains invaluable.

## 1.2 THEORETICAL COUPLINGS

### 1.2.1    THE RESEARCH TRADITION:
### ON THE IMPOSSIBILITY OF SELF-MANAGED ENTERPRISE

Systematic research of "associations of producers", at least where English-speaking culture is concerned, can be said to have started in 1891 with Beatrice Potter's (married Webb) "Cooperative Movement in Great Britain". Webb's study claims to cover the whole contemporary population of such associations, 54 of them[7]. With eight dutifully noted exceptions, all dismissed by Webb as being either too new or too small to matter, the study's results are summed up as "a dismal record of repeated failure" (1891:149). The budding association, confronting "the real world" and its demands, would, it is claimed, invariably end by giving up either its principles or its very existence.

For the Webbs, the 1891 study had grounded an irrevocable judgment. Changes in the actual population of self-managed enterprises notwithstanding, this judgment remained firm and was repeated by them time and again, sometimes verbatim, during their nearly 50-year political, public, and scientific career.

The Webbsian judgment has set a quasi-paradigmatic imprint on nearly a century of self-management research. It would be too simple to attribute its diffusion merely to the Webbs' personal authority, formidable as it was at the time[8]. Its strength lies, instead, in organizing commonsense observations to match a seemingly self-evident conclusion, namely, "since cooperatives keep failing, they must be impossible". It could well be that Webb-like conclusions were reached also by others, researchers and politicians alike, independently of the Webbs' work. We would then be dealing with a research archetype of sorts, with the Webbs' work probably its most craftfully wrought manifestation.

What does this "Webbsian legacy" consist of? We ought to distinguish here between concrete, empirical findings and (purported) universally valid conclusions.

On the empirical side, Webb provided a poignant analysis of cooperative deficiencies underlying the observed trail of failure. These are "want of capital, want of custom and absence of administrative discipline" (1891:149)[9]. These observations, representing, in all likelihood, the earliest application of an organizational ecology model (see sections 6.2-6.3), have maintained their salience to this day. However, in the Webbs' interpretation, these are not the *reasons* for cooperative failure, but its symptoms or, in other words, ways for the inherent impossibility of this organization form to manifest itself by (Clarke, 1981). As Webb herself put it: "It is the very form of associations of producers that is ill adapted to survive" (1891:156)[10].

The roots of self-management's inherent impossibility lie, supposedly, in an impossible union between capital and labour and in an
entirely unrealistic organization principle. The first, workers' ownership,
would never gain acceptance since "the workers prefer, if they have a
choice, that the severance between the capitalist and workers should be
complete" (Webb, 1891:130). The unstable union between capital and
labour is thus bound to drift out of hand: The workers would end up
either being disowned or as an association of small masters.

The second, the principle of shop-floor industrial democracy, would
simply never work. "Profitable administration of property", a *sine qua
non* for an enterprise in a capitalist environment, is "a condition which
cannot be fulfilled by a self-governing body of workers". (Webb,
1891:128)[11].

These two elements together spring, according to Webb, an inescapable trap, neatly presented as follows: "While government by the
workers proved a potent cause of commercial failure, commercial success promptly destroyed this form of government, /. . / by substituting
(with or without the workers' leave) the outside capitalist for the working shareholder" (1891:131)

A great deal of the empirical foundations for the Webbs' conclusions, regarding choice of research population, definitions employed,
and actual prognoses for the studied organizations, have been substantially questioned since[12]. In spite of these substantial inroads, their
seductive power never waned. The basic tensions between ownership
and labour, between democracy and efficiency, and between the
demands of the market and moral principles came to constitute the core
of the self-management problematique[13]. These tensions are said (in
what is probably the earliest processual model ever developed in
organizational theory) to give rise to *cooperative degeneration*.

The position of any future advocates of self-management has not
been made any easier by the specific twists of logic the Webbs introduced, and which came to plague the SM debate:

a. The market is considered, simultaneously, as basically immoral and
debasing and as an arbiter of rational functioning.

b. Direct democratic principles of organization are both dismissed as
unrealistic and employed as a standard by which to measure organizational failures.

Letting this perspective guide the discussion has led SM organizations to enjoy the notoriety once reserved to two-headed calves and
other freaks of nature, fit to be examined to better see how "normal"
organisms operate, but not to be considered seriously in their own right.
Within other branches of organizational and management research the

tacit assumption seems to be that an organizational form, if studied, must indeed exist and therefore is also possible. This licence was, however, never fully extended to SM research. Advocates of self-management for nearly two generations have argued their point from a position of basic illegitimacy that has effectively inhibited the emergence of a common frame of reference. Coupled with the tendency to use the field as a testing ground for diverse theories and loaned approaches, this has led to a confusing proliferation of terms and definitions.

The case strongly reminds one of the century-old dispute about whether machines that are heavier than air can fly. The winning argument at that time was to present a machine that did fly. In our case, however, the opponents' covert demand was to present a machine that would stay in the air indefinitely. This impossible demand was, perhaps unconsciously, accepted; a great deal of research effort carried out by supporters of self-management ideas came to be devoted to disproving various impossibility theorems, to proving SM's mere possibility (most often through comparative twin studies) or to documenting it through surveys and descriptive studies[14].

Despite the image of failure, there is no evidence that self-managed organizations are more failure prone than other organizations (Abell, 1983; Jones, 1976). What is true, however, is that cases of failure do, as Webb (1891) suggested, show generalizable regularities. The commonly encountered tendency, pioneered by Webb, to see this as a proof for some fatal faults intrinsic to the self-managed organization is somewhat simplistic. An equally plausible explanation, that would be adopted here, is that such regularities should be attributed to regularities in the environment, and in the organization-environment relation. Success would require ingenuous use of (often time, or place-specific) opportunities and would, thus, be highly idiosyncratic. Failures, on the other hand, would be regular, predictable, and more accessible to research. To sum up with another flight allegory: already the ancients could provide a plausible explanation for Icarus' fall; understanding Dædalus' performance took considerably longer.

This work takes the existence (and thus the possibility) of self managed organizations for granted (see Stryjan 1984a). In an important sense, it attempts a renewed exploration of the Webbs' basic themes- ownership and control, environment and degeneration – though set in a new context. A state of affairs in which a manager may "stand as a servant before the [worker composed] board of directors" (Webb, 1891:152), once so abhorrent to the Webbs, is seen here as describing the core of self-management and of organizational democracy, alhough, to be sure, servitude on either side of this relation is not. Some of the links postulated in their and later work — between ownership and control, between rationality and market — are broken. Finally, the issue of degeneration is set within a broader framework of organizational reproduction, where it rightly belongs.

*1.2.2 SELF-MANAGEMENT AND ORGANIZATION THEORY*

> He put his face in front of the bathroom mirror.
> I exist, said the mirror.
> What about me? said Kleinzeit.
> Not my problem, said the mirror.
> -Russell Hoban, *Kleinzeit*

Organization theories are construed so as to be relevant to mainstream organizations. The broad assortment of available organization models is geared to fit the diversity of organizations that adepts and users of organization theory consider worthy of interest. As noted, this list does not include self-management, a mode of organization whose viability is often questioned. Thus its increasing diversity notwithstanding, the models that organization theory at the moment provides are not directly applicable to self-management.

The organization models drawn upon in this work are all related to the emergent cluster of organization research that W. R. Scott (1981) classified as *open natural system models*. This is especially the case insofar as the critical attitude to rational models (Cohen et al. 1972; March and Olsen, 1976), and the stress on interaction and processes (Weick, 1969) are concerned; links to natural system models are also evident in the analysis of the organization's relationship to the environment (Meyer and Rowan, 1977; Pfeffer and Salancik 1978; Pfeffer, 1982)[15]. Considerably extending the scope of organization theory (sometimes in a demaskatory fashion), one finds that open natural models still share some desiderata and unquestioned assumptions in common with most organization-theoretical approaches. Some of the desiderata that are particularily limiting for our discussion are:

a. An inability to deal simultaneously with individuals and the organizations they constitute. As a rule, only one of these would be studied, with the other held constant (see 3.1).

b. Difficulties with simultaneous assessment of structures and processes, at least in part caused by the inability to see the organization's members as bearers, and potential modifiers, of both.

c. Where individuals' inputs to the organization are concerned, the perspective is narrowed to "attitudes" and motivation. The eventuality that individuals may consider or attempt to do something about the organization is excluded.

d. In keeping with the above, a hierarchical distribution of authority, initiative, and creativity is normally postulated, even when
such models are applied to democratic organizations (Robinson,
1981a).

The limitations listed above may not be too serious where conventional organizations are concerned. Authority and the right to exercise
initiative are, after all, hierarchically distributed in the best of organizations. Given sufficiently circumscribed freedom of action, individuals
may also find themselves decoupled from both structures and processes
in their organizations, precisely in the way that mainstream theory
would lead us to take for granted.

The claim here is not that organization theory in any way lacks relevance but rather that it addresses itself to a circumscribed universe of
organizational phenomena. Application to phenomena that lie outside
this boundary would require an extension of theory, preserving its
logical structure while removing some implicit assumptions. The result
will be a more sensitive theory and a keener distinction between the
average and the possible. The limitations of theory, in the case of self-
management, and the potential it has *if* used in a more imaginative way
are evident when dealing with issues of authority and compliance. Consider, for instance, the following passage:

> Of course, *subordinates* may know precisely what is expected of them, be per-
> fectly capable of doing it, and still not do it. /. . / Resistance /. . / is not easy
> to detect when it takes place surreptitiously. Open rebellion is much more
> visible. But people usually have to be pushed quite far before they resort to
> open disobedience /. . /; more often, when orders *from above* conflict sharply
> with their values, they quietly construe the orders in a way that makes them
> tolerable. (Kaufman, 1973:3ff; italics mine)

The author proceeds from this commonsense description and argues for
the need for administrative feedback so that superiors would know what
their subordinates actually are doing. However, once managers are seen
as decision-takers, the concept of "subordinate" disobedience easily
may be applied to cases of *managerial* disobedience. The passage above,
and much of its logical underpinnings, would still make sense when read
backwards with "officers" or "managers" substituted for "subordinates",
and "orders from above" replaced by "members' will" or "decisions of
the assembly".

The theoretical problems in an attempt to deal with self-managed
organizations with conventional tools are seldom as clear-cut as in the
example above. In their daily functioning, such organizations, regardless
of their size, would have to manage simultaneously environmental
problems, whose understanding lies within the domain of macro theory,
and those of managing a "multicephalous" organization (Rothschild-

Whitt, 1979), responsive to its members inputs, issues that normally lie within the domain of micro theory. The ways and means they are likely to employ in spanning these problems and reconciling demands would often be deviant on both counts[16]. A theoretical understanding of such an organization's behaviour, and of the limitations inherent in the application of mainstream theory to such cases, would often require a theoretical framework that spans both individuals and structures, both micro and macro domains, and is capable of dealing with the common-place as well as with the different or deviant. Giddens' theory of struc-turation (1984) provides some important insights of direct relevance for the task.

### 1.2.3 STRUCTURATION THEORY

Giddens' (1984) theory of structuration proposes to integrate the analysis of macro and micro levels, individual action (agency), and struc-ture. As such, it provides important tools for understanding of indi-viduals in organizations and organizations in environments. The insights the theory provides that are of particular relevance to the task here are:

a. A workable concept of a knowledgeable agent, *a sine qua non* for a theory of a democratic organization. At the same time, the the-ory offers an insight into the limitations of purposive action and the complexity of connections between action and its consequen-ces, adding depth to often programmatic notions of organiza-tional democracy.

b. An approach to the relationship between agent and structure, which allows for the possibility of a two-way relationship between the two. Giddens' *agent* acts within a structure. Structure is both constraining *and* enabling, setting limitations on action but also providing resources that may, in turn, be employed either within the constraints set or in order to transcend them.

c. A concept of reproduction, linking the continuity of structure to agents' actions and to action's unintended consequences.

Structuration theory does not purport to be *a* theory of organiza-tions[17]. Its main thrust is directed at linking micro and macro levels. Semi-macro levels, where organizations dwell, are left, at least for the time being, relatively untended. The nodes of structurally defined rules and resources that constitute organizations tend to melt into the grand tapestry of reproduction (cf Berger and Luckmann, 1967).

Given this limitation, no attempt will made here to apply structuration theory uncritically to organization research. However, the approach applied would, to a considerable degree, be formed by the insights the theory provides. Furthermore, it can also be argued that the study of self-managed organizations can, potentially, contribute to the theory: "It is precisely because cooperatives are anomalous, contradictory organizations that they are worth pondering. They allow social thinkers to look two ways at once" (Jackall and Levin, 1984a:11). Self-managed organizations occupy a somewhat anomalous position, being "*in* the system, but not quite *of* it". In a way, their condition reminds one of that of Harold Garfinkel's (1967) "outsiders" in providing an exceptional vantage point from which to consider society and its order. Taking advantage of this opportunity presupposes a theoretical perspective capable of looking two ways at once, a requirement amply met by structuration theory. Furthermore, distinguishing deviant organizations in the grand design may be somewhat easier than tracing out conventional ones. Intuitively, we may expect such organizations to be less integrated in the general flow and thrown back on their own resources as far as the reproduction of their own deviant mode of organization is concerned, not unlike a proud owner of a unique machine, lathing the spare parts in his own back yard. A closer look at such organizations may contribute important insights into the mechanics of reproduction.

### 1.3 AN OUTLINE OF THE WORK

The theoretical perspective to be outlined in this work was assembled from elements previously formulated within different, and often disparate, research traditions. Rather than attempting to lock the product into a formal-logical structure, a running discourse structure (Glaser and Strauss, 1967) was adopted, gradually broadening the scope of the work and adding new problem formulations. Each step presents a somewhat more complex model and thus calls for the application of new perspectives that are suitable to deal with the complexities at hand. The basic metaphor, in a sense, is a one of a journey, where each stage, though being a continuation of the former one, supplies a new venture point on the road as a whole. It may require a different gear, as the conditions of the terrain at each stage change.

Chapter 2 is largely devoted to establishing a point of departure for the work. Ownership, a traditional point of departure for a great deal of self-management research, is examined first. The limitations of worker ownership as a vehicle for self-management are explored, first through a review of some empirical evidence on worker-owned enterprises; then through a discussion of theoretical approaches to worker ownership; and, finally, through a review of property-rights theory and its application to the case at hand and to stock ownership in general. In view of the limitations inherent in the concept, a new point of departure, basing self-management on *membership*, is suggested. The objective of an organizational theory for self-management is, thus, indirectly changed; instead of outlining an organization controlled by its owners who work in it, the model would be of an organization capable of accommodating and thus, being steered by, that its members actually do.

The search for such a model begins in Chapter 3, by taking stock of available theoretical tools within organizational research that can deal with the links between individuals and organizations. Linking the notion of organizations being designed by their members, a logical corollary of self-management, to the notion of organizations enhancing their continuation over time through the shaping of their members' behaviours, basic to the research of organizational commitment, yields a rudimentary model of a reproduction loop. A broader theoretical restatement of the model is then attempted: it is claimed that self-management's core process is centred on the reproduction of the organization's active membership. Membership is seen as consisting of three elements: a corpus of members, a shared perspective, and a repertoire of action. All three elements are being reproduced. A simplified model is outlined, centring on decision-making in an organization with a stable (given) membership.

In the remainder of the work, this simplified model is expanded to approximate real-life situations through stepwise elimination of simplifying assumptions, a mode often used in economic model construction.

The first assumptions to be removed in Chapter 4, are those of error-free decision-making and implementation. Both decisions and the actions they lead to are prone to be wrong at times and have to be reversed or corrected. In applying the reproduction model to the case of the fallible organization, extensive use is made of the work of Alfred O. Hirschman. It is argued that the task of correcting inevitable and randomly occurring malfunctions and errors is borne by the organization's membership. A basic repertoire of members' inputs, consisting of voice, involvement, loyalty and exit is outlined. Personal differences between members in terms of propensity for and proficiency in different modes of input are acknowledged and are used as a point of departure for an outline of an organizational demography approach.

Questions of environmental relationships and resource dependencies are introduced in chapter 5. Three categories of resources are dealt with: (new) members, capital, and skills, respectively. The focus is on internal accommodation to uncertainties of supply and to incompatibilities in quality of available resources. The environment is largely "held constant" and treated as a turbulent, but essentially random, source of pressure. The SM organization is portrayed as living off the environment, in a hunter and gatherer fashion, rather than living in it, in a two-sided interaction.

The presentation of the model is completed in chapter 6, with the introduction of a more dynamic view of the environment and the organizations positioning in it. The environment is presented as exerting active pressure on the organization and the SM organization as engaged in coping with these pressures in order to preserve its (deviant) identity. Two theoretical perspectives on the environmental pressures that act to level populations of organizations and eliminate deviation are examined: organizational ecology and institutionalization theory. It is argued that the constraints that the environment imposes can be coped with and that deviant organizations can modify their immediate environment so as to shape preconditions for their reproduction. The chapter closes with a tentative outline of federative coping strategies and possible scenarios for societal change.

Chapter 7 goes beyond the framework of the work proper, leaving the case of self-management, to outline some of the general implications of the reproduction model developed in this book. It is argued that the insights the model provides can enrich organizational theory. Applied as a general perspective, the reproduction perspective can improve the understanding of organizations' interaction both with individuals within and the environment without.

# 2

# ON OWNERSHIP
# AND MEMBERSHIP

> In common speech we frequently speak of someone
> owning this land, that house, or these bonds. This
> conversational style undoubtedly is economical from
> the viewpoint of quick communication, but it masks
> the variety and complexity of the ownership
> relationship. (Alchian and Demsetz, 1972:17).

## 2.1. INTRODUCTION

Worker ownership occupies a central place in the conceptual framework
of self-management (SM) research. It is frequently used in operational
definitions of research populations, taken as a starting point for economic model-construction and elaborated in case descriptions[18]. A considerable portion of both the European and the American SM debate is
conducted in terms of worker ownership. This, in itself, is hardly sur-
prising, given the prominence of the ownership concept in economics,
politics, and society in general (Furubotn and Pejovich, 1974). Unfortunately, as is often the case with truly basic concepts, there is a great deal
of ambiguity in its usages. Consequently, stating that an enterprise is
"owned by its workforce" hardly specifies the actual form of ownership,
let alone its content (Perry and Davis, 1985). Not only do various researchers disagree as to the meaning of ownership. It is often unclear
what they themselves mean when employing this term. Some of this lack
of clarity will have to be settled before we can proceed to this work's
actual task.

For many SM researchers, starting with Beatrice Webb, worker ownership and self management on the plant level are indeed two aspects
of the same thing. Bengt Abrahamsson's work (1975, 1977, 1986) offers

the most lucid contemporary formulation of this approach: An organization is considered to be a tool maintained by its *mandators*. Mandatorship over an economic enterprise (a subspecies of organization) is established by ownership and manifested (in all organizations) through a constitutional prerogative to nominate and recall the executive (1975:26). As long as this requirement is formally met, the owner-mandator *ex definitio* controls the organization[19].

Abrahamsson's and similar analyses of self-management leave fairly little space to features other than ownership[20]. Starting, as I do, with the assumption that ownership is, at most, but one of possible elements constituting a self-management system, it is of prime importance that (worker) ownership's net contribution to such systems be defined. First then, would it be possible to outline the "residual", which, as I propose to demonstrate, actually constitutes such systems' nucleus.

Somewhat simplified, the hypothetical question taken up below is: Is it possible to base self-management on ownership alone? Can ownership be treated as an independent variable, with self-management as its ultimate product? In theory, a question of this sort could have been answered by a simple before-after examination of cases of ownership transfer. The problem is that *ceteris paribus* norms seldom apply to such cases. Other factors, most typically ideology and workforce mobilization (which would probably have some independent implications; see, for example, Baumgartner et al., 1978), are likely to play an important role.

Two groups of cases in which such intervening factors are kept at minimum are briefly reviewed in this chapter: wage-earner-owned firms in Swedish industry, and American Employee Stock Ownership Plans (ESOPs). Both groups may be seen as relatively "pure" examples of ownership transfer, grounded on faith in the importance of ownership and relatively free from alternative ambitions. The ESOP case, in its emphasis on individual ownership, is an extreme example of worker ownership undertaken on conventional premises. In the Swedish case, these premises are somewhat moderated by a long-standing tradition of labour organization.

The two groups can hardly be considered as representative of self-management. The ESOPs are certainly not representative of all forms of SM current in the United States, and an interesting population of alternative organizations is evident in Sweden. The examination below is intended as an illustration of a theoretical point and *not* as an empirical confirmation. The discussion is carried on two distinct levels, the one dealing with concrete organizational changes observed in worker takeovers' wake ant the other with the plausibility of explaining them by ownership or mandator change. The limitations of the ownership concept and the problems involved in the ownership-control relationship that this examination demonstrates are then taken up in a theoretical reconstruction of the ownership concept. It is argued that ownership in the way it is commonly applied to industrial property (and complex assets in general) cannot be considered a vehicle for workers' control. To fulfill this role, ownership must be modified (Ellerman, 1984) and augmented to a degree that would make a singular use of the term dubious.

## 2.2 THE SWEDISH EXPERIENCE

The first cases of worker ownership in Sweden date from the late 19th century[21]. Later waves of worker takeovers and worker cooperative formation, inspired by guild-socialist ideas or by syndicalist thought and motivated by post World War I and the great crises, can be noted in the 1920s and 1930s. With one isolated exception, a syndicalist stone quarry, none of these enterprises has survived, and no historically rooted tradition of worker ownership or self-management was ever established in Sweden.

The rise of a new wave of workertakeovers in the 1970s was first documented by Johan Bucht and associates (1976). A more recent survey was carried out by Åke Gabrielsson (1980). No data are available on the situation in the service sector, although some evidence indicates fairly rapid growth (Fast, 1986). A comprehensive register of worker-owned firms in production branches has been started by Sune Jansson and is, at present, managed by the Arbetslivscentrum (The Swedish Centre for Working-Life Research). In 1987 the register covered some 105 employee-owned industrial enterprises, conforming to the definition of "a company with no less than 5 employees, where no less than 50 percent of the employees control no less than 50 percent of the shareholder vote, and the control is evenly or close to evenly divided". (Jansson, 1983). The firms are located in different lines of business; such as printing, textile, metal, footwear, and construction. Employment totals approximately 3,500 people. As the numbers indicate, employee ownership is of marginal importance to the Swedish economy. It may, however, be of great importance to local communities, especially in declining regions with a stagnating labour market[22]. The importance of worker-owned enterprises' contribution to job-creation has declined somewhat in the overheated Swedish labour-market of the late 1980s.

Approximately 80 percent of the firms in the register were taken over during the past decade. Ideological considerations seem to have played but a minor role in the conversion to employee ownership. In a majority of cases the motive was defensive; takeover was regarded either as a means to save jobs from a threatening close down or as a means of solving owner-succession problems.

2.2.1 THE EDLA SAMPLE

A section of the Jansson register population (firms with a minimum size of 25 employees, established no later than 1982) was surveyed in 1984 within the EDLA project at the Arbetslivscentrum[23]. Apart from being somewhat larger in size, the firms within the sample are representative of the population as a whole, as far as branch spread and the background for takeover are concerned. Basic information on these firms is supplied in table 2.1.

**Table 2.1  The EDLA Sample**

| Name | year of takeover | no. of employees | no. of owners | percent | no. white collar |
|------|------------------|------------------|---------------|---------|------------------|
| BESTERS | 1982 | 112 | 81 | 72 | 12 |
| BUTEK | 1967 | 28 | 21 | 75 | 5 |
| LISTER | 1977 | 39 | 80 | 86 | 18 |
| MATEX | 1977 | 35 | 27 | 77 | 2 |
| PARSA | 1978 | 43 | 32 | 74 | 7 |
| JUNO | 1979 | 140 | 165 | 100 | 19 |
| NIKE | 1980 | 45 | 34 | 75 | 4 |
| FURMAN | 1944 | 170 | 170 | 100 | 41 |
| CLIFFS | 1979 | 48 | 48 | 100 | 6 |
| SMEDE | 1973 | 81 | 44 | 54 | 7 |
| SYDOR | 1980 | 38 | 36 | 95 | 4 |
| OVAL | 1977 | 63 | 61 | 97 | 6 |
| THUMBS | 1976 | 155 | 122 | 79 | 21 |
| WOLFS | 1979 | 45 | 30 | 67 | 3 |
| SKORE | 1972 | 110 | 93 | 85 | 16 |
| STONE | 1982 | 28 | 20 | 71 | 5 |
| LUNDEL | 1982 | 28 | 19 | 68 | 4 |
| ORSON | 1982 | 62 | 51 | 82 | 11 |
| PLYMARK | 1981 | 77 | 70 | 90 | 17 |

Source: Stryjan and Hellmark (1985)

The motive for takeover in all but one of the cases studied can be regarded as pragmatic, be it direct job saving (13 cases) or defense against the uncertainty that a sale to an unknown owner would have implied (6 cases)[24]. One enterprise was willed by the owner to the employees. A feature common to all cases is the total absence of conflict during takeover. The term buyout would, in general, appear more suitable[25]. The organizational form adopted was, without exception, that of joint-stock company. The choice of this particular ownership form is generally reported to have been smooth and perceived as a matter of course. In 14 of the cases the organization was supplemented by a second tier arrangement — a holding organization or a consortium agreement, regulating votes and traffic with shares.

The traditional stratification between blue- and white-collar groups has been preserved in most cases. Sharp conflicts between the two groups were reported in some of the cases[26]. When managers are internally recruited, which is the case in 14 of the firms, the recruitment base is usually senior staff.

A part of the collected material, consisting mainly of interviews with managers, union officers and board members, was analyzed by Ann-Britt Hellmark and me (Stryjan and Hellmark, 1985). The changes introduced in the enterprises' organization under, or after, takeover were summarized as follows:

1. **Formal decision-making**: The formal "shareholder democracy" organs appear to be somewhat more active than their conventional counterparts. This applies especially to the management boards[27]. Given the boards' composition (prominence of externally nominated members and a skewed distribution of workers' seats, favouring, as a rule, white-collar groups), this need not be a sign of increased worker influence[28]. A provision of one worker-one-vote is generally kept on the shareholder convention.

2. **Information**: The quality and accessibility of information are generally reported to have improved since takeover.

3. **Foremen**: Apart from one case in which foremen posts were introduced after takeover, the tendency seems to be toward abolishing foreman posts or replacing "non working" foremen with working ones elected by a team.

4. **Wage policies**: The outspoken tendency in most enterprises has been toward reduction of wage differentials within the blue collar group. Equalization was commonly achieved by abolishing piece-rates[29]. Equal wages were introduced in two cases. In one case the blue- and white-collar distinction has been eliminated. In another two cases it has been considerably softened.

5. **General meeting**: An accepted feature introduced in at least 12 of the enterprises. Meetings' frequency and regularity vary widely among the enterprises; general meetings may be a routine institution, assembling at regular intervals or special meetings, called for consultations pending important decisions. Unprovided for in company legislation, and therefore lacking power to form binding decisions, the assembly's opinion would probably carry a considerable weight, once expressed. This feature represents the greatest single departure from conventional company organization in the sample. However, rather than a conscious innovation, general meetings

seem, in most cases, to be a carryover from the takeover period, and their frequency in the enterprises surveyed seems to be on the decline.

The EDLA project's central paradigm presupposed a causal link between ownership change and organizational change. The surveyed changes do, indeed, seem to add up to a pattern of sorts, encompassing diffuse notions of *increased* control over the immediate work-situation as well as over long-range goals, and of equality. The collected evidence as to such a link's existence is, however, inconclusive. Most recorded changes seem to have occurred either before, or in close connection with takeover. As in the case of the worker assembly, mentioned above, they appear to be products of the selfsame process that had led to take-over, rather than its result. Their actual significance is hard to assess:

> It would perhaps be gratifying to suppose that these changes are the first steps on a new path of development, embarked upon by the act of takeover. Unfortunately, such a conclusion seems hardly plausible. For a majority of the cases we may, considering their age as employee-owned firms, speak of a single change (or set of changes) followed by a standstill. If a process at all, then it is mainly examples of arrested processes we are dealing with. Furthermore, the advances made are never fully secured. Change of manager or an economic crisis (and even more so a combination of both factors) are prone to cause regression. (Stryjan and Hellmark, 1985)

The proximity of change, when present, to the actual takeover moment suggests that we are dealing here with interregnum pheno-mena, prompted by the *fact* of change rather than by its *content*. As M. A. Gurdon, in a different takeover context, stated: "The internal structure of the organization was wide open for change during the first few months of the experiment, as traditional roles were in a state of flux, managers and supervisors being unsure of the form and content of their relationship with subordinates" (1980:304). As such, they are instructive of workforce expectations rather than of what ownership actually can deliver. Whatever these expectations are (they are discussed later in this work), they cannot be traced to stock ownership. In this particular case they may be carryovers from the nationally well-ingrained tradition of trade unionism and collective action. This explanation is strengthened on comparison with the ESOP cases reviewed in the following section, cases that are set in a national context where precisely these features are lacking.

## 2.3 THE ESOP CASE; AN AMERICAN APPROACH TO WORKER OWNERSHIP

"In the United States today, it is becoming increasingly common to read about groups of factory workers purchasing their plants or about corporations establishing employee stock ownership plans (ESOPs)" (Russell, 1984b:254). The ESOP schemes were first introduced in 1974[30]. But they had spread, by 1983, to more than 6,000 corporations (ibid.)[31]. The number of workers enrolled in such schemes was estimated in 1985 at 10 million. "At that pace, 25% or more of all US workers will own part or all of their companies by the year 2000"[32].

An ESOP provides an advantageous system for divestment of stock to collectively managed, individually accounted worker funds. The interest of ESOP schemes for our discussion lies precisely in ownership transfer coming totally divorced from any self-management-inspired "normative trimmings". As Raymond Russell demonstrated, in his historical review (1984b), the basic normative notions underlying the ESOP approach can be traced to the Homestead Act, rather than to socialist tradition, or, as C. E. Gunn (1984) remarks, to a "Horatio Alger tradition", with individualism translated, by sleight of hand, into individual stock ownership. Although the passed legislation does not exclude the possibility of workers' control, it seems that it has not done much to advance it either (Perry and Davis, 1985:290). Critical voices about the results' quality were raised at a relatively early stage of the ESOP schemes' diffusion: "In most cases so far where an employee stock ownership trust has been established, management has sought to share ownership without sharing control" (Blasi and Whyte, 1980:410).

Joseph Blasi and William F. Whyte's analysis introduces two important distinctions: between ownership and control and between management and other groups of employees. This distinction is sharpened in Russell's (1984b) thorough and critical analysis of the ESOP idea. It is questionable, stated Russell, that such schemes would lead to increased worker control. The obverse may be true, namely, that they are intended to increase control over workers: "Like technical and bureaucratic control, ownership now appears to be another effective way to encourage rank-and-file employees to do what managers would like them to do" (ibid.:265).

> Given the enormous spread of the ESOP idea, extreme cases, manifesting either a high degree of worker participation or its total absence, are to be expected. However, even the situation in mainstream schemes seems to be far from satisfying: "Workers in many employee-owned companies gain no voice in workplace decisions and lack the right to vote their stock /../ In 85% of all companies with ESOPs, studies show, worker-owners do not have voting rights"[33].

In a high percentage of cases the ESOPs are, in fact, "schemes that involve ownership with minimal control" (Gunn, 1984:173). Granted, some minority-post ESOPs may have been designed from the outset as merely a profit-sharing measure and should therefore not be measured against expectations they were never meant to deliver. Cases of take-over, involving a transfer of majority, or 100 percent, of stock do not necessarily fare better. Conversion to employee ownership is commonly done in a fashion that preserves previous governance structures (see Zwerdling 1980:58ff; Gurdon, 1980). The ESOP stocks are often voted by trustees appointed by management: "The 'employee owners' are insulated from the control of their own worklives by the trustees who exercise their votes in the 'best interests' of the worker-owners" (Eller-man, 1986:63). The forms of takeover negotiation and the agreements negotiated border, at times, on sharp practices (see also section 2.4):

> South Bend Lathe in Indiana represents one of the most dramatic examples of an ESOP gone wrong. Because the union responded to a management initiative /. . / the buy-out deal included terminating the union pension plan. The ESOP plan also prohibited employees from voting their stock. The management at south Bend Lathe has recently shifted a significant portion of the company's production to South Korea (Livingston, 1986:35)

An evidence of sharp practices does not invalidate a system. It does, however, point out its weaknesses. Similiar problems are evident also in the case of Rath Packing Co., initially a pioneering case in the attempt to establish "democratic ESOPs" (Rothschild-Whitt, 1986:76) and, cer-tainly, one of the more thoroughly prepared ESOP takeovers (Gunn, 1984). The attempt is summarized in an interview with Rath union offi-cials[34]: "Even though all the directors were selected by the ESOP parti-cipants, the employees do not control Rath Packing. We own it but we have less control than we did when we first started the thing" (Daniels et al., 1986:22).

It is important to realize that developments of the sort outlined above are perfectly compatible with a system based on capital stock ow-nership. In fact, stock ownership, as pointed out by S. E. Perry and H. C. Davis (1985), does not even give stockholders right of entry to the com-pany premises. At least one case is documented (Daniels, 1986:17) of management calling the police to evict worker-owners from "their" plant. In other words, *stock ownership*, the dominant mode of ownership of industrial assets, and *control* are far from synonymous (Levin, 1984). The gap between the two can be bridged, as will be demonstrated later in this chapter. But the measures that would need to be taken for this purpose by far exceed the limits of the ownership concept, as it is gene-rally understood.

## 2.4 OWNERSHIP AND CONTROL: MANDATORS VERSUS MANAGERS?

The identification of control with ownership, though historically sound, bears the seed of future misconceptions, inasmuch as it may lead to the expectation that all problems will solve themselves once ownership is set right. Once the ownership problem is done away with, through assumption of ownership by the workforce, a subtler case of degenerative development may however be discerned, namely, that of divorce between labour and control, with control drifting upwards to a managerial group[35].

Some extreme cases of ownership without control have been related above. In some of these cases the workforce even lacked the formal prerogative of recalling the executive. Though titular "owner", the workforce in these cases cannot qualify as a mandator after Abrahamsson's definition (see section 2.1). The situation may be virtually the same in cases in which the mandator function is formally maintained: Keith Bradley, summing up an international survey of management in worker cooperatives, stated: "although these managers were supposed to act strictly within a framework determined by workers, there is little evidence to suggest that this was the case /. . / evidence suggests the relative ease with which skilled 'professional' managers could influence company policy and unilaterally pursue particular management strategies" (1980:165).

Elimination of external ownership does not seem to result in broadened worker control. On the contrary, it may improve management's relative power position versus the workforce: "authority and legal ownership are additive. In other words, the long-term impact of employee ownership is a reinforcement of managerial status /. . / Thus, the change of ownership from an absentee to a broad employee basis, when structured in the traditional stock form, merely enhances management's status" (Gurdon 1980:302)

A managerial de facto usurpation of power may be the result of sharp negotiating practices, as in the Weirton Steel (Lynd, 1986) and Dan River (Livingston, 1986:35) cases, of managerial control over information flows (Bradley, 1980:165), or of a workforce's passive reliance on management expertise (Gurdon, 1980:307)[36]. It may also be caused by external pressures, such as outside creditors' or major customers interference (Zwerdling, 1980; Levin, 1984:253; see also section 5.4 and the JUNO case, described in Stryjan and Hellmark, 1985). In some cases such external pressures may be mobilized by management.

Two conflicting assessments of this often occurring phenomenon are discussed below: The "logic of organization" thesis, and the "managerial revolution" (Berle and Means, 1934)[37]. According to the logic of organization approach (Abrahamsson, 1986), the broad prerogatives that managers in (at least some) worker-owned enterprises enjoy are not an encroachment on but a direct expression of the manadator's will: They cannot but have been endorsed by the mandator since he controls the organization, and obviously did not choose to change the executive. In endorsing managerial control the mandator has simply bowed to a higher necessity, namely, that of maintaining efficiency. Branding such a development as degeneration is, according to Abrahamsson, simply a result of democratic standards being set impossibly high[38]. Worker-manadators' control cannot, and therefore does not, encroach on managerial prerogatives. It is, instead, enacted through a setting of broad policy guidelines, which are then implemented by management. Eventual participative measures may then be introduced, if economy permits, as a distributive measure or a "social dividend" of sorts (1986:192-193).

From a "managerial revolution" perspective, it would instead be possible to speak of the situation in terms of an actual or potential control gap between workers-shareholders and "their" enterprise. This gap is inbuilt into the joint-stock corporations' very structure (I shall return to this issue in the following section) and may be seized upon by management whenever the owner constellation permits it. The examples suggested by proponents of the approach are spread ownership and passive institutional investors.

The managerial revolution approach directly challenges the mandator approach's rational-legal base. Consequently, sharp "counter-revolutionary" attacks have been launched by proponents of the mandator model (Abrahamsson, 1986; Broström, 1982, 1984). A short review of this critique below will help clarify the two approaches' respective premises.

An important normative assumption behind the ownership-control concept is that an agent, to be considered in control, must be endowed with free will. Supposedly, corporate directors, subject to a shareholder-formulated policy, market imperatives, and monitoring by the board and shareholder convention, would not qualify as free agents (Broström 1982:56). Rather than a case of power usurpation, the executive's apparent autonomy  is a case of government by proxy. The executive's "excesses", if they indeed occur, are tolerated, as long as management supplies the goods. They can, in fact be considered a rationally calculated cost of management. This argument presupposes the existence of strong owner groups, a questionable assumption for our particular population. Implicitly, it builds upon Harold Demsetz' argument (1983), namely, that the clear and quantifiable definition of a goal in the case of the joint-stock corporation makes monitoring feasible. Even passive minority owners can participate in a fashion, through monitoring the dominant owner group's monitoring performance (Eidem, 1982:43)[39]. Control, especially where minority shareholders (in this case individual workers) are concerned, would, in this model, be exercised primarily through *exit* (see Hirschman, 1970). Indirectly, the exercise of the exit option opens a possibility of establishing a market for corporate control. In other words, dissatisfied stockholders unable to control "their" executive would be expected to sell below substance value to parts that are determined enough to have control reestablished (Hindley, 1970[40]). The resulting lowering of the share price will have a direct disciplinary effect (see Eidem, 1982:43.45).

A major weakness of this argument, when applied to the case of worker ownership, lies in the fact that worker-owners' freedom to exercise an exit option (and thus, presumably, control) is considerably smaller than the small shareholder's[41]. Furthermore, 76 percent of the ESOPs were established in closely traded companies (U.S. General Accounting Office, 1986:25). Consequently, the exit option's effect on the share's market value would be highly limited.

A somewhat more sophisticated argument is presented by Abrahamsson (1986:158ff). The developments interpreted as a managerial revolution are, according to Abrahamsson, simply a process of specialization. The traditional owner-industrialist role is being narrowed to a specialized owner role, and the actual task of running the enterprise is transferred to the executive. Abrahamsson admits that such a broadening of managerial prerogatives entails a certain risk for managerial takeover (1986:159ff)[42]. Presumably, this risk is to be held in check by an increased mandator competence.

If Abrahamsson's argument, about a growing divergence between specialized owner and manager competence indeed is right, worker takeover implies that ownership is transferred to a less specialized (and, by implication, less competent) manadator (Eidem, 1982:47). This mandator's most crucial competence fault is, precisely, a reduced ability to check "his" executive.

Furthermore, the worker *cum* mandator's interests are decidedly more complex than are his capitalist counterpart's. Monitoring the executive's performance must also become a more complex task. This task is hardly made easier by Abrahamsson's recommendation that the mandator is to restrict himself to external monitoring, at which he is incompetent, and leave internal monitoring, on which he may have considerable knowledge, entirely in management's hands[43]. Abrahamsson's optimistic scenario, of the mandator being able to advance participative measures (restricting the executive's freedom) as a part of a distributive policy, appears, in this light, as dubious. In fact, where introduced, participatory measures often seem to originate in managerial goodwill (see Long, 1978a) rather than in workforce initiative.

The control element missing in Abrahamsson's model is indirectly supplied by Sven-Erik Sjöstrand (1985:281)[44]. The executive, according to Sjöstrand, is bound by the same values as the stockholders and thus, perforce, would perform to their satisfaction. But this argument's validity is restricted to companies with conventional stockholders. There is no ground to expect a priori value correspondence between rank and file workers and managerial staff in a conventional enterprise converted to worker ownership. In the case of ESOPs, the management's and workforce's values clearly seem to diverge, and conflicts were, as already mentioned, also noted in the EDLA survey sample.

Sjöstrand's argument, however, opens an additional dimension, namely, that of societal control. Joint-stock corporations seeming vulnerability to managerial usurpation may reflect the fact that eventual countervailing forces are not an internal element of the joint-stock structure but are interposed by surrounding society and its normative and legal structures. Leaving aside the controversy about the degree to which such checks effectively protect conventional shareholders' standardized interests, it is doubtful that they would at all be geared to protect non-standard shareholders, with additional claims on the enterprise, besides the sole societally legitimated one — return on investment. To the extent a self-managed organization may count on normative control of its management, the norms that would be required would have to be internally generated and reproduced. This notion is central to the reproduction model developed in this work.

The question of the managerial revolution's claims of universal validity would be decided, as both Abrahamsson and Broström suggested, through an analysis of actual owner groups in the economy and their composition, strength, and behaviour. As such, it lies outside our field of study[45]. The question of its value as a hypothesis applied to specific owner constellations, such as worker-owned enterprises, may be resolved from case to case, independently of this macro level. A strong and increasingly specialized mandator role seems necessary to check eventual managerial appetites. The workforce's chances to maintain such a role in a worker-owned company construed along conventional lines are slim, given the limited resources at the workforce's disposal and the unlikelihood of buttressing them with societal support. In spite of assurances to the contrary, the case of self-management by worker ownership would appear, if we follow the mandator/logic of organization perspective, as a fairly illogical enterprise.

The discussion in this and the previous sections has pointed to some limitations in the application of conventional ownership constructions in self-managed organizations. A brief review of the property rights' approach to the issue of corporate stock ownership, below, will provide a closer look at the ownership concept and the role that ownership plays in the control of enterprises. Such an examination is called for before

any suggestions about possible ways of augmenting or replacing ownership as a vehicle of control can be made.

## 2.5 OWNERSHIP AND PROPERTY RIGHTS THEORY

The sweeping term ownership of common usage can be treated as a
general label for a bundle of rights: "What is owned are rights to use
resources" (Alchian and Demsetz, 1972:17) or, more generally, socially
recognized rights of action versus the "owned" asset. Jaroslav Vanek
offered the following, unilinear schematic presentation: "It is possible to
think of a maximal list of property rights consisting of *a*. the right to
manage and control, *b*. the right to appropriate product, *c*. the right to
receive income from productive capital, all the way to right *y*. to burn
property or throw it into the sea /. . / We may refer to the collection *a*
through *y* as the maximal definition" (1978:8).

Following the Roman legal tradition, it is possible to split the property rights complex into three components (Nutzinger, 1982:86;
Furubotn and Pejovich 1974:4)[46]:

*Usus*: the right to use the asset.
*Uusus fructus*: the right to appropriate returns from the asset.
*Abusus*: the right to change the asset's form and/or substance
   (processing, transport, destruction and so on) or to transfer
   ownership and to appropriate any benefits thereof.

The above list can be viewed as a basic repertoire of conceivable
rights of ownership. Being maximalistic in character, modifications and
local variations would be expressed through restrictions and omissions[47].
It is important to note that the rights in question are of a *dispositive*
character; the control they bestow is exercised primarily through
exclusion of unauthorized interference from the domain they define.
Furthermore, since it is rights rather than objects that are being owned,
such rights packets may be divisible in any number of ways between any
number of "owners". Such a division would function smoothly only as
long as the exercise of one right did not infringe on the exercise of other
rights. It becomes problematic when a single asset that is indivisible by
its nature (such as an integrated production system) is held by a number
of independent holders. Since control over assets is predominantly exercised through exclusion of "unauthorized others", the concept, as we
intuitively "know" it, suffers a breakdown once these others no longer
can be excluded. As even property rights theorists realize, the notion of
wrenching out single elements of a complex system to be used or abused
at their owner's will cannot be treated seriously[48]. Of the three compo-

nents of property rights enumerated above, only that of *usus fructus* would be (relatively) unproblematically divisible.

The practical problem is, then, that of coordinating free agents, precisely the problem property rights theory came to solve in the first place. It is solved through the introduction of an intermediary agent: the joint-stock corporation. To accommodate this concept in the property-rights framework, Demsetz chose to redefine the nature of the asset held by the "co-owners". Thus the share-owner no longer is considered to own a part in the enterprise. "What shareholders really own are their shares and not the corporation" (Demsetz, 1967).

The question of "who owns (i.e., exercises property rights over) the joint asset" is thus deftly defined away: The complex asset has found a unified "owner", and thus the coordination problem is resolved. Since the theory deals with property rights, not with the nature of owners, all remaining complications lie outside its sphere of interest. It is clear, however, that this owner (the corporation), whatever its physical manifestation may be, has the right — and duty — to exercise a great deal of the property rights surrendered by the shareholders.

To recapitulate: the corporate joint-stock structure's raison d'être is to resolve questions of coordination and not those of control. The question of coordination is resolved through abdication of control by co-owners, a fact that has given rise to the managerial revolution thesis, outlined in section 2.4.

The ESOP cases, discussed above, are a faithful replication of conventional ownership models: "In an employee-owned corporation there is no restructuring of the conventional ownership bundle; the traditional ownership rights are simply owned as property rights by the employees of the firm" (Ellerman, 1986:57). As such, they would be exposed to the same control-gap problems as conventional enterprises, being, at the same time, considerably less well equipped to check them, owing to the nature of the shareholder group and the power differential between rank and file shareholders and management shareholders. In a sense, the problems that worker-owners encounter in maintaining control over their enterprise are built into the joint-stock corporate structure. However, the joint-stock solution to the problem of corporate structure need not necessarily be exclusive .

## 2.6 RECONSTRUCTING THE SM ORGANIZATION

Abdication of control by shareholders, in the conventional enterprise, is done on the understanding that shareholders' legitimate interests (return on investment) will be met to the best of the executive's ability, subject to the shareholder's monitoring. That an arrangement of this sort is at all workable can be ascribed to the fact of the firm being primarily a means to the satisfaction of the shareholder's interests and to these interests being unambiguous enough to be guarded by way of sporadic, external monitoring (Demsetz, 1983) and legitimate enough to be safeguarded by society at large[49]. These conditions do not hold in the case of a self-managed organization or firm. A brief review of those characteristics of the self-managed enterprise that do not fit into the stock ownership model is presented below[50]:

1. Organizational structure is not a logical product independent of the owner-group composition. The fact that the mandators are in our case internal to the organization, coupled with the intensity of their commerce with the organization, bears some parallels to family business situation (see Geeraerts, 1984). It is more likely to give rise to demands for detail control. External mandators, by comparison, would tend to restrict themselves to goal setting and result monitoring.

2. The firm is a special case of an organization with external mandators. As pointed by Bjørn Gustavsen (n.d.), it is primarily an abstract construct, linking mandators and a standardized economic result. None of its elements may be considered unsubstitutable (see section 6.1). This characteristic is well captured by the French legal label for joint-stock corporations, *societé anonyme*. The self-managed enterprise, on the other hand, is, almost *ex definitio*, unique. In the concrete case of worker takeovers, the explicit reason for takeover is commonly that of preserving the enterprise. Unlike the theoretical firm, it is thus not only a means but, within boundary conditions of tolerable economic performance, also its own end.

3. The task of maintaining the joint-stock organization form is, to a considerable degree, shouldered by society at large. Shareholders' interests are guaranteed by comprehensive legislation and safeguarded by societal norms, and the risk they bear is hedged by a privilege of limited liability. No provisions of this sort exist to guarantee the maintenance of a self-managed enterprise, and the risk borne by a worker-owner exceeds, by definition, that borne by a shareholder, inasmuch it includes both capital share and employment. To maintain its form, the self-managed enterprise would thus be first and foremost thrown back on its own worker-owners' resources. In an important sense, it would have to be reproduced constantly, rather than merely maintained. Given the high price of failure for its members, it is likely that it would be able to mobilize the effort that such reproduction requires.

4. Any takeover decision requires commitment of individual economic resources for a collective end and, thus, also the creation of a system

of obligations between individual workers, as well as between them and the enterprise. In small to medium sized enterprises, such as those we deal with, these obligations, rather than formal and abstract, would tend to remain personified.

These points would, to some degree, be realized by the owner-workers. Such a realization would not add up to a clear-cut programme and is most likely to come into expression as vague notions of right and wrong. One expectation likely to be commonly shared would be that of increased control: "In certain circumstances, ownership by itself does appear to raise worker expectations that they will have more say, or will be treated with greater respect, but in instances where worker ownership does not deliver on this promise, it disappoints" (Rothschild-Whitt and Whitt, 1986:303).

Such expectations would be anchored in primitive notions of ownership, rather than in the prevailing legal structures of corporate ownership. As the case is, such notions would but seldom be consistent with accepted norms of corporate ownership conduct or, for that matter, of formal democracy. The clash between the two can be fairly sharp, as the following relation from the first shareholder convention in a newly taken over enterprise illustrates:

> In the words of one knitter, "Everyone was stunned". Another complained that "everything was set up even before you went to the meeting. I didn't want to have anything to do with the stock after that." This sentiment is revealing because it was to be translated into concrete behaviour. Only half of those who were at this gathering bothered to attend the 1977 [the following year] meeting. (Gurdon, 1980:304)

The example above deals with exercise of influence over formal policy setting. This sort of influence ought, at least in theory, to have been provided for by the ownership transfer. It is, however, important to realize that workforce notions of influence or "participation" would primarily tend to centre around work-floor issues (Long, 1982:212). Such influence, although not explicitly excluded by conventional company legislation and routines, is hardly considered mandatory.

The question of interest in this case is not whether such notions fit corporate *savoir vivre*, which they assuredly do not. It is, rather, whether expectations of this sort are indeed as unrealistic as our review this far suggests. Restated in theoretical terms, the central questions are whether the ownership concept can accommodate internal monitoring and whether it is possible to modify the ownership structure so that a workforce mandator competence could offset tendencies for managerial takeover.

Following the property rights theorists' line of reasoning, we may concede that, given the prevailing legal and cultural structure (i.e, *the institutional environment*; see section 6.4), it is clearly advantageous, even for self-managed organizations, that a complex asset be owned by some intermediate agent. As C. E. Gunn suggested, an essential component of a worker takeover would be the "establishment of a structure that will 'own' the firm in the name of its workers" (1984:175). The one crucial requirement is that this agent would be capable of concerted action, of a sort that would advance its mandators' interests. The way this agent is constituted, namely, the nature of the relationship between the agent and its mandators or constituents is an entirely different question, of secondary importance, as long as this requirement is met. The joint-stock corporation is, in this respect, but one possible solution.

Following Art Hochner's (1981:7) tentative suggestion that "different ownership statuses are basically different contexts — or organizational models", at least two basic models of organization can be outlined (figure 2.1)

**Figure 2.1 Organizational Models**

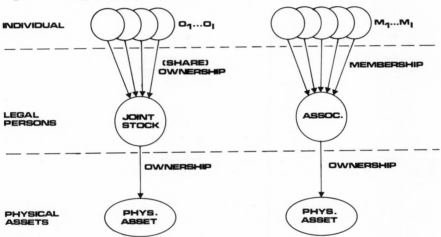

The two models differ in essence only in the modes of affiliation employed, ownership and membership, respectively. The theoretical questions that the use of this concept entails are reviewed in the next section. The main formal distinctions between ownership and membership are shown schematically in table 2.2.

### Table 2.2  Membership and Ownership

| MEMBERSHIP | OWNERSHIP (of stock) |
| --- | --- |
| Content defined by the organization | Content defined by company law |
| Degree of influence is a matter of members' decision | Inbuilt formal limit on influence |
| Imposes obligations towards the organization | No obligations vs. company or co-owners |
| Imposes mutual obligations | No obligations vs. co-owners |
| May be revoked/forfeit | Irrevocable. |
| Entry granted by organization or by other members | Free entry |
| Transfer regulated or prohibited | Free transfer |
| May not be accumulated | free accumulation |
| (potentially) refundable | no refund (save for liquidation) |
| Preferred treatment in deals with the organization | no preferred treatment |

The sharp distinctions outlined in table 2.2 tend to become blurred in practice. Members' certificates, for instance, may be freely tradeable both in theory (Sertel, 1980; Mygind, 1983) and in practice (Russell, 1984a; Berman 1982); obligations imposed by membership, as well as the rights it entails may be allowed to dwindle to purely ceremonial forms (theatrical democracy; see Trevena, 1980); and so on. On the other hand, a joint stock arrangement may be complemented by agreements that virtually convert ownership to membership. "starting with a stock business corporation /. . / and then reworking the articles of incorporation and bylaws to internally restructure the company" (Ellerman, 1984:268).

Arrangements of this type, mentioned by E. F. Schumacher (1974), David Ellerman (1984, 1986), and Joyce Rothschild-Whitt (1979:523) and systematically classified for the American case by S. E. Perry and H. C. Davis (1985), are common in the Swedish population of labour-owned firms (Stryjan and Hellmark, 1985; Jansson, 1983): An agreement between shareholders (*konsortieavtal*, eventually supplemented by an *aktieägarförenig*, a shareholder association) is superimposed on the joint-stock construction. The corporation now has a single owner that is de facto constituted by members (figure 2.2).

**Figure 2.2  From Ownership to Membership**

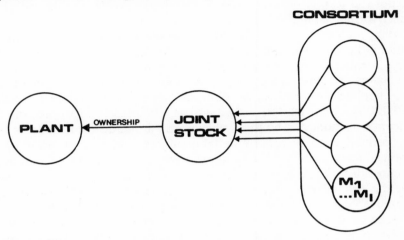

The transfer from ownership to membership is often tangibly marked by the fact that stock is physically removed from its owners' possession and locked in the association's bank safe (Jansson, 1983; Bucht et al. 1976). The shares are voted *en bloc* at the shareholder convention to ratify formally decisions that were made by the consortium.

The importance of such arrangements goes far beyond formal structure. The consortium is not bound (unless it so decides) by the limitations imposed by company law on shareholder discretion. The joint-stock form is thus, at least potentially, turned into a convenience flag for a member-based organization.

### 2.7 A NOTE ON THE CONCEPT OF MEMBERSHIP

The concept of membership evoked above is a typical example of a primitive concept, often resorted to but seldom, if ever, defined in the literature[51].

Within one group of organizations — societies, associations, and co-operatives — the term has, however, a strict formal content. Most commonly, the affiliation is formalized by possession of a member's certificate or registration in a roll of membership, this step, in turn, being conditional on certain criteria being met[52]. In the case of Swedish worker owned enterprises in the EDLA sample, the criteria generally in use were *employment* by the company and *ownership* of a share post. The formal content of membership would often be accompanied by less well-clarified normative expectations.

A major source of confusion, as regards the membership concept, is that an additional usage, which may be labeled as "traditional", exists besides the formal one. Traditional membership is ascriptive and, thus, unlike formal membership, non-voluntary. Broader organizational and sociological literature often meanders between the two usages (with the ethnomethodological approach strongly leaning toward the traditional one): Formal criteria of membership are generally laxed, while normative claims are maintained and, in the absence of a clearly defined subject, applied to arbitrarily defined populations (compare Scott, 1981:180ff). This has led Abrahamsson (1986:108-9) to question the concept's usefulness. The three objections Abrahamsson raises are: loosely defined content, loosely defined subject, and lack of attention to conflicts and tensions. "The broad category [paraplytermen] "members" obscures differences between various groups, and implies that all actors give the organization a support that is grounded in their values. The "member" concept directs attention away from differences in power between various groups in the organization, as well as [from] differences in the way they perceive the organization's goals" (Abrahamsson, 1986:108-109, translation mine).

The case strongly reminds one of an earlier debate concerning a similiar assault on the concept of bureaucracy. Abrahamsson's eloquent argument in defense of this concept (1977:19-23) could in fact be applied nearly verbatim to the case of membership[53]. The undoubtedly loose way in which this concept is often applied is seized upon by Abrahamsson as "an alibi for making a totally empty house" (ibid:20). Although Abrahamsson's critique of the usage that the membership concept is being put to is largely justified, his conclusions need not follow. Problems and ambiguities notwithstanding, the concept of membership may still be worth salvaging. It is possible to outline a content that is shared by most current approaches to membership, as we shall see below.

The major source of confusion around the concept of membership probably lies in the sweeping definition of the subject (who are members), equaling, in fact, a loose definition of organizational boundaries (Aldrich, 1979). It may well be that some organizations' membership cannot be defined in a meaningful way. How far and over what types of organizations the concept of membership can be applied is a matter that clearly extends the scope of the discussion here. It is touched upon in chapter 7. Instead, I restrict myself here to arguing a weaker claim, namely, that the membership concept is applicable to organizations with an unequivocally determinable member roll, a claim that, in the case of

SM merely amounts to a statement that a democratic body ought to have a definite constituency.

An unfortunate tendency to draw sweeping membership boundaries, often including antagonists in the environment as "members", may result in conflicts that are impossible to resolve, being incorporated by theoretical fiat into the organizations. Again, it is worth noting that such proceedings are only possible in organizations that lack a well-defined membership roll. However, nothing in the member concept precludes dissent. On the contrary, membership struggles may occur, precisely as do ownership struggles. The difficulties encountered in theoretically dealing with dissent and conflict have more to do with the organizational models used, a problem that is well evident also in the mandator approach than with the fact that they are populated by members.

Implicit in all usages of the term, from research to public relations, are the following elements:

a. A degree of permanence. Membership is not a matter of an isolated transaction but is perceived to stretch over time (in this sense, "membership in a market transaction" is a contradiction in terms, whereas membership in a market may, at least on certain markets, be a highly concrete issue).

b. A "community of fate". Members are in some way dependent on a future outcome that is relevant to them all (though not necessarily to an equal degree).

c. An (assumed) intrinsic worth. Members are normally assumed to view their organization as somehow worthy of their membership by being better, or different from comparable alternatives.

An additional element that, in the case of "members' organizations proper" is built into the organizational structure is members' input to maintenance of "the whole". The ethnomethodological school's heavy and somewhat misleading reliance on the term *member* is closely connected to this dimension[54]. It is generally understood that such inputs are continuous rather than historical (as founders and so on) in their character.

This brief discussion of membership has, apart from issues of boundary definition, abstracted from the question of organization. Organizational membership presupposes organizations. However, the organizational models available, especially where work and production organizations are concerned, seem hardly compatible with membership. Consequently, such models' suitability to deal with member-based organizations ought to be questioned. A contribution towards a membership-based organizational model of self-management is presented in the following chapters.

## 2.8 SUMMARY

The issue of ownership has occupied a central role in SM research. This preoccupation has all but relegated other, no less central elements of self-management to a residual role. An attempt to construct an organizational theory of self-management requires that ownership's "net contribution" is first assessed.

A brief examination of two groups of cases in which worker ownership was grafted upon an existing organizational structure was undertaken in this chapter; a Swedish sample of worker-owned firms and American ESOP schemes. In the Swedish group of cases, the process of takeover is shown to have led to some organizational changes, though their persistence and connection to ownership are somewhat inconclusive. The tendency apparent in the ESOP cases is of strengthened management control. These findings, butressed by a review of relevant theoretical work, undertaken in this chapter, suggest that a transfer of ownership does not inequivocally lead to self-management. A transfer of ownership merely eliminates external ownership as a source of control. It does not, in itself, constitute a strategy of control, least of all workers' control. Given a conventional firm structure, worker ownership tends, instead, to strengthen the position of management versus owners, who just happen, in this case, also to be workers.

The model of the SM enterprise as a "firm owned by workers", seems thus as both theoretically inconsistent and, where followed in practice, highly unsatisfactory. It merges, as it were, the shortcomings of the classical firm concept with those of the ownership concept into a doubly handicapped construct. Examining possible solutions to this problem, the chapter turns to a theoretical consideration of the concept of ownership, its relevance to organizational theory, and the way that property rights approaches may be applied in the case of complex, indivisible assets, such as industrial plant. Different ownership constructions are discussed, and the concept of ownership is contrasted with that of membership. It is argued that ownership constructions current among worker-owned enterprises do, in fact, represent attempts to convert ownership to membership.

The step of takeover constitutes a starting point for a variety of different and even contradictory scenarios. Self-management is only one of them but perhaps the only one in which the organization and its new ownership structure are preserved in the long run. The discussion of SM starts one step beyond ownership, the real issue being not "turning workers into owners", but one of turning workers (or worker-owners)

into members — but members of what? An examination of the issue
would require a model for a member-based organization, set in a theoretical framework capable of dealing with both members and organizations. A tentative outline of such a model is developed in the following
chapters.

# 3

# ON REPRODUCTION

## 3.1 INTRODUCTION

The aim of this chapter is to present a preliminary model of an organization steered and *reproduced* by its members. In earlier self-management research, the theme of reproduction was commonly presented from its obverse side, namely, as a problematic of degeneration. This concept of progressive and irrevocable adverse change in self-managed organizations (see section 1.2.1) was first explored by Beatrice Webb (1891). The basic notion it confers is of a process gone wrong or of a reproduction breakdown. The notion pursued here is, instead, that the study of reproduction of self-managed organizations should precede the study of such reproduction's flaws.

A basic problem that the construction of a model of an organization being reproduced through its members' actions is liable to encounter is the sparsity of available theoretical tools that can link together individuals and the organizations they are in. Theoretical frameworks in organization research tend to focus, alternatively, either on organizations or on individuals that populate them. The choice of one of these areas as a point of departure seems to have a nearly Heisenbergian effect, inasmuch as the import of the other is obscured. Peter Blau (1964:14), dealing with a limited aspect of the problem, namely, of research into interaction and structure, proposed elevating this handicap to a research canon: "sociological inquiry /. . / seeking to encompass both is unlikely to produce a systematical empirical or theoretical inquiry of either".

Although it is obvious that strong links between the two concepts (or, rather, the phenomena they designate) exist, conceptual frameworks and even single concepts that span both organizational and human "organization components" are fairly sparse. When seen from an organization perspective, individuals generally dwindle to the position of one of the organization's components or "resources" (see Scott, 1981:136). In individual-focused approaches, on the other hand, organizations are reduced to a backdrop against which to study individual or group attitudes and actions. Attempts to construct organization theories from individuals and up, or vice-versa, commonly falter on the difficulties and paradoxes aggregation entails (Abrahamsson, 1986).

Some concepts that span the gap between the two domains, and can therefore be of use in our attempt at theory construction, are reviewed below. The review is not complete; the concepts and approaches examined were picked for their relevance to self-management, the specific topic under examination here. Three clusters of concepts were singled out, dealing with affiliation, stability and inputs, respectively.

*Affiliation*: On pure commonsense grounds, we may suggest that organizations are, at some specific time (or in a lengthier process) constituted by individuals and, what is more important, are populated by individuals[55]. Individuals joining "their" organization at different times, would be *affiliated* to it in some mode, and their inputs would in some way be aggregated into the organization. Two modes of affiliation, those of ownership and membership, have been discussed in the previous chapter. It is suggested that different modes of affiliation may give rise to different organizations. Our concern here is with organizations that are membership based, though the suggested conclusions may also be of some relevance to other organization forms (see chapter 7).

*Stability*: In a limited way, affiliation addresses the problem of structure. It does not, however, address the problem of stability, that is, structure's continued existence over time. An obligation entered is not necessarily an obligation kept. The problem of maintaining participants' affiliations has generally been addressed in the study of organizations by the concept of *commitment* (Becker, 1960; Gouldner, 1960; Kanter, 1972)[56]. The term, the way it is employed in the literature, is somewhat of an omnibus concept, bundling together attitudes, actions, and organizational consequences. Its shortcomings notwithstanding, the concept of commitment can be useful as a provisional tool, linking organizational processes and structures with members' organization-oriented inputs[57]. A discussion of the concept of commitment in conventional organization research provides, therefore, a handy introduction to our topic. The models suggested in commitment research, of how commitment is generated and its effect on individual behaviour can be seen as one link in a reproduction loop. it is used in this manner in the simplified reproduction model presented in this chapter.

*Inputs*: Called into being, and reasonably stable, organizations still have to be redesigned and steered and their performance monitored. In the self-managed organization, these functions would, by definition, be carried out by the organizations' members. Steering, decision-making, and corrective adjustments to monitoring inputs amount, when considered as a continuous process, to a continuing organizational redesign. Together, the notion of members redesigning their organizations and the notion of organizations shaping their members' perceptions and modes of action, that is suggested by commitment research, would yield a rudimentary model of an organizational reproduction loop that is presented in this chapter. To simplify the presentation, this chapter primarily concentrates on inputs connected with formal decision-making. A more thorough discussion of members' inputs that takes into account daily interaction between the members and their organization will follow in chapter 4.

### 3.1.1    PROCESS, STRUCTURES, AND REPRODUCTION

The question of structure (conceptualized in terms of ownership structures or organizational blueprints) has traditionally enjoyed a privileged position in earlier self-management research and cooperative thought: "Since the time of Owen co-operators have been obsessed with formal structures, assuming naively that if the structure is right cooperation will necessarily flourish" (Fletcher 1976:181)[58].

Structure, in this tradition of thought, enjoys a clear primacy over processes and, thus, over members' actions. It emerges out of the blue, to dictate and steer developments, seemingly without being influenced by them. Rather than take structure as a constant, the reproduction perspective that is outlined below aims at presenting an organizational model that reinterprets organizational structure in a process-oriented framework. Stating that decisions concerning an organization's fate and way of functioning are taken primarily (and, ideally, exclusively) by its members implies that an organization's structure is open to continuous design and redesign by its members. This occurs in response to changing needs, goal formulations, changing environmental conditions, or all of these things together. In this way, the focus of study is turned from pre-programmed constraints to the opportunities for action and thus, to opportunities for modification or transcendence of structure, that structures themselves provide. Organizational blueprints, in this view, represent structure only to a limited degree. They are seen as momentary snapshots, taken in a continuous process of organizational change. The persistence of concrete elements in organizational structures (blueprint boxes and arrows) cannot be taken for granted (Baumgartner et al.,

1981, Burns et al., 1985). It would last as long as these elements are being reproduced (Weick, 1979).

Structures are, however, more than mere epiphenomena. While extant, a given structure would to some degree affect the reproduction process, as it is being carried out by the organization's members. Anthony Giddens' concept of "the duality of structure" is particularly useful in this context[59]: "The constitution of agents and structures are not two independently given sets of phenomena, a dualism, but represent a duality. According to the notion of the duality of structure, the structural properties of social systems are both medium and outcome of the practices they recursively organize" (1984:25).

Changeable as it may be over time, a structure does, at any given time, present a set medium for action, defining available alternatives and resources and setting action in a definite causal pattern. As such, it is both enabling and constraining[60] (Giddens, 1984:25). Structural modification and redesign are, in this limited sense, an outcome of the structure that is being modified (ibid, p. 26). Structure, thus, sets some of the basic conditions for the process of its reproduction by agents. It does not reproduce itself.

### 3.1.2 MODELS OF REPRODUCTION

Two theoretical models are drawn upon in the construction of the reproduction model in this work; Giddens' (1984) and Gudmund Hernes' (1977). Giddens' structuration theory sees systems as "the patterning of social relations, across time-space, understood as reproduced practices" (1984:377). Giddens' major emphasis is on individual, daily practices. Reproduction is seen as being borne by the actions of individual actors: "It is always the case that day-to-day activity of social actors draws upon and reproduces structural features of broader social systems" (Giddens, 1984:24; see also Hernes, 1977:514).

Repetitive practices are thus both medium and subject of system reproduction. The reproduction of a self-managed organization, if we follow this way of thought, would be carried primarily by its members, through recoursive daily organizational practices, and in the course of members' interactions: "Analysing the structuration of social systems means studying the modes, in which such systems, grounded in the knowledgeable activities of situated actors who draw upon rules and resources in the diversity of action contexts, are produced and reproduced in interaction" (Giddens, 1984:25).

The persistence of the self-managed organization as a deviant element within a larger system can be seen as a unique example of micro reproduction. Its existence would be made possible through imaginative utilization of macro-system faults and maintained through the reproduction of distinct practices and selective appropriation of societal practices (see chapterss 5-6). Thus, to take a simple example, it would be the surrounding world's language that would be spoken within an organization, but it would generally contain some organization-unique idiomatic usages or words. This chapter would be devoted, in the same vein, to some particularities of SM's organizational idiom of action and the way it is employed by members in structuring their organization.

The macro-societal scope of structuration theory gives it certain closed-system attributes; resources are generally internal to the system. The position of the isolated organization, tending to its own reproduction, raises questions of material preconditions and environmental exchanges in a much more immediate way. Hernes' (1977) reproduction model, dealing predominantly with the reproduction of material preconditions for systems' existence, will be drawn upon in pointing out some of these requirements. A broader discussion of environments and resources is presented in chapters 5-6.

### 3.2 THE ISSUE OF COMMITMENT

Stability of personal affiliations with organizations has usually been dealt with by organization research under the heading of "commitment". Like the concept of membership discussed above, the concept of commitment has long remained primitive and largely unexplored (Becker, 1960). H. P. Gouldner (1960), regarded commitment as "an issue of basic sociological interest concerned, as it is, with the diverse ways individuals attach themselves to groups" (p471).

Howard S. Becker (1960) regarded commitment as an explanatory variable behind engagement in a consistent line of action, for example, keeping to a professional career or to a workplace or maintaining membership in the Communist party. Commitment, according to Becker, results from a series of side bets entered by an individual in the course of his or her career. Side bets would be constructed in such a way that change of one's previously set line of action would imply hidden costs that are realized by the individual[61]. Becker's approach is applied to cases of worker-owned firms by R. J. Long (1978b). Mary Sheldon (1971) pointed out that side bets may also be placed on social relations with other employees. Thus, for example, a kibbutz plant manager considering a move to an attractive post in private industry would have to consider, beside the pros and cons of the respective jobs and, independently from ideological objections, also those costs, material as well as social, that leaving the kibbutz would imply[62].

For industrial sociologists, the concept of commitment is of considerable interest as a potential predictor of worker turnover (Hrebiniak and Alutto 1972; Steers, 1977:47). It is generally treated either as an attitude with high correlation to behaviour or as a directly observable behaviour (Mowday et al, 1979). Later research has developed more sophisticated and less instrumental interpretations of the concept than the one originally explored by Becker. The notion that the concept actually addresses "several distinct forms of commitment" was first raised by Helen Gouldner (1960:470). L. W. Porter and associates (1974) identified three possible components (see also Steers, 1977:46; Mowday et al., 1979:226):

1. A strong belief and acceptance of the organization's goals and values
2. A willingness to exert considerable effort on behalf of the organization
3. A strong desire to maintain membership in the organization.

The decision to leave or to stay is generally perceived in commitment research as purely individual. Individual decisions can be aggregated as turnover (see Bluedorn, 1978). The ambition is, at most, to find ways of reducing costs within an organization whose existence is taken for granted.

Rosabeth Moss Kanter's work (1968, 1972) applies the concept in the more extreme context of organizations whose existence is *not given*, namely, American nineteenth century utopian communes. The research of communes can provide us with a wider perspective that goes beyond narrowly perceived smooth functioning or turnover, and ties commitment to the problematics of survival. In serious crises, the choice between winding up and going on or reorganizing is generally decided by factors other than these two, important as they may be[63].

Collective endeavours, especially if both voluntary and long lived, require for their survival that some stable linkage be established between "self-interest and social requirements" (Kanter, 1972:66). This linkage stands at the focal point of Kanter's definition of commitment: "Commitment thus refers to the willingness of people to do what will maintain the group because it [the group] provides what they need".

Rather than subsume the issue with abstract ideas of harmony or brotherhood, the central lesson of Kanter's work is that commitment is built and maintained through mechanisms built into the group's mode of organization: "Commitment mechanisms are specific ways of ordering and defining the existence of a group. Every aspect of group life has implications for commitment" (1972:75).

Commitment, then, is not an organizational property that can be "postulated into an organization" by virtue of, say, formal ownership structure[64]. It is rather a set of orientations in need of constant reproduction. The process occurs at the individual level. Individuals each encounter their own "tangible manifestation" of the organization (Buchanan, 1974), represented by particular assignments, daily work contacts, and experiences of participation in communal living or in decision-making. It is these work experiences that would, if right, result in enticing and reproducing the individual's commitment (Steers, 1977). Concrete organizational practices and rules of daily action compose the mechanisms that tend to this reproduction (Kanter, 1972).

To recapitulate, the conclusions that commitment research suggests are as follows:

a.  That considerably more complex qualities than mere persistence are required of the organizations' members if the organization is to weather crises and environmental strains (Gouldner, 1960; Kanter, 1968, 1972).

b.  That these qualities are generated (or reproduced) by a continuing (re)socialization (Steers, 1977; Buchanan, 1974) tended to by "commitment mechanisms" that organize and operate through daily routines. (Kanter, 1972).

c.  That such (re)socialization would occur at the *individual* level and, as such, is the product of the concrete (and highly individualized) daily organizational reality each member is confronted with (Steers, 1977; Buchanan, 1974).

Kanter's work concentrates on organizational consequences. Those communes that survived are shown to have used some specific organizational mechanisms. Those mechanisms, in turn, are postulated to have elicited and reproduced organization's members' commitment. Both the mechanisms and the fact of survival are directly observable. Commitment, however, is not. The question is whether the concept of commitment, arbitrarily chosen, correctly labels whatever these mechanisms actually reproduce. The difficulties in tying commitment to organizational consequences encountered in later work (most notably, Steers, 1977 and Marsh and Mannari, 1977) seem also to strengthen these misgivings[65]. In referring to the concept of commitment in this chapter, we use it as a theoretical tool, rather than as an element of the reproduction model proper. It stands, in Kanter's spirit, as a shorthand notation for a complex of attitudes and competencies that are required to ensure an organization's perpetuation over time.

## 3.3 TOWARDS A MODEL OF ORGANIZATIONAL REPRODUCTION

The models that commitment research suggests are *linear* dealing with commitment's antecedents, components, and organizational consequences (Steers, 1977). They are viewed in the context of a given organization that is standing, as it were, *above* its members, rather than being in itself subject to reproduction. Commitment models address the issue of reproduction of attitudes and indirectly suggest that organizations may be "designed for commitment". They decline, however, to take up the key question of who is to do the designing.

Commitment research's linear model provides us with a vital understanding of one half of the reproduction loop, namely, of the way organizations "redesign" their members. Of self-managed organizations we know, on the other hand, that they are designed *by* their members. Combined together, the models of (a) an organization designed by its members and (b) of members being moulded, where their experience, attitudes, and ways of action are concerned, by their organization yield a tentative outline of a reproduction loop. A self-managed organization, then, is being subject to change and redesign by members whose perceptions have to a significant degree been informed by the organization they now set to redesign.

SM constitutes a special, and in some respects simplified case of organizational reproduction. The following assumptions, that are specific to this case, can be made:

a. *All participants are members.* The definition of membership is uniform and unambiguous.

b. *All members take part*, actually or potentially, in decision-making and implementation. The two categories of decision-makers and subordinate implementators, merge in this case. For the purpose of the discussion here, members are treated as wholly interchangeable with one another. This simplifying assumption will be relaxed in chapter 4.

c. *SM is a self-designing organization.* The locus for all decisions as to its internal organization and its strategy is situated within the organization.

d. *It is a decisional organization*, in that its continued existence is conditional on the members' active and, in principle, withdrawable consent.

The absence of different classes of members (superiors and subordinates) and of different locii of decision-making (external and internal, respectively) permits the application of a single generalized model of member *cum* decision maker *cum* "culture bearer". Accepting the thesis that the organizational core being reproduced ought to contain *at least* the prerequisites for the organization's continued existence (see Hernes, 1977:524), we can claim, at least for the case of SM organization, that the core the organization reproduces consists of its own *active membership* (Stryjan 1987)[66]. A concept of active membership that fulfils these specifications should encompass three basic aspects, all of which would need to be reproduced (Stryjan, 1987):

a.  Physical bearer (a corpus of members)

b.  A shared frame of reference, whereby definitions of situation can be generated

c.  A repertoire of options for action or members' inputs

A simplified model of such a reproduction process, with practical illustrations, is presented in the remainder of this chapter. It will provide some rudimentary answers to the concrete questions (e.g., What are repertoires of action? What frame of reference would be appropriate for perpetuating the SM organization?) that the application of this abstract model to real life organizations is liable to raise.

### 3.4 A SIMPLIFIED REPRODUCTION MODEL

In presenting economic models, economists often start with an application to a simplified version of reality. Complications are introduced into the model in a later stage by gradually removing the initial simplifying assumptions. In a similiar manner, the reproduction model will be demonstrated first using a simplified organization, residing in a docile environment. These simplifying assumptions will be relaxed in the following chapters.

Our simplified organization will have the following characteristics[67]: membership is stable (no significant recruitment or demise), and steering is done by formal decision-making. Formal participation in decision-making is the only input channel and, consequently, the only item on the members' repertoire[68]. It is assumed that decisions are frictionlessly carried into practice, so this repertoire is sufficient, and the eventuality of mistaken decisions is not dealt with. Unrealistic as they are, the assumptions above do actually underlie a great deal of SM and organization research.

Applying this model to the components of membership outlined above would yield the following specifications:

a. *Physical bearer*: since neither recruitment nor demise are significant, the only problem to be coped with in our model is that of maintaining present members' attachment to the organization or (which amounts, in our case, to the same thing) to their previous course of action. This issue has been already reviewed above (section 3.2) under the heading of "commitment". The discussion of commitment will therefore be used as an expedient introduction into our topic.

b. *Perspectives for action:* The ongoing process of organizational (re)design that is carried on by members can be presented as a succession of steps, each step yielding an organization to be redesigned again at the next step. The context of decision-making, that is, the organization itself, would change from step to step. What should be sought, then, are *premises* that guide decision-making — supplying a definition of problems and choice of outcomes in this process of organization design. These things can be perceived in terms of basic assumptions, values, "weltanschaung" and so on. Given a suitable set of premises, we should expect each successive step, if based on suitable premises, to yield an organization that (a) is self-managed and (b) provides its members with the competence necessary for undertaking the next step of design.

c. *options:* Decisions, in this simplified model, are taken in relatively formalized procedures of discourse or voting, depending on the particular decision-making mode the organization subscribes to. Members' options of action are, accordingly, restricted to participation and non-participation or, anticipating the discussion in the next chapter, voice and "non-voice", respectively. Maintaining participation in decision-making as a viable input presupposes that organizational procedures that permit participatory decision-making are maintained and that their credibility is reproduced so that members do not consistently choose the non-voice option.

Undergoing reproduction, in this simplified model, an organization would be continuously "redesigned for commitment and self-management" by its members, participating in decision-making and drawing upon their knowledgeability in their actions[69]. An obvious boundary condition, spelled out in specification *c.* (*options*), is that members participate in decision-making at all. This condition is dealt with, under the heading of organizational democracy, in section 3.6.

### 3.5 COMMITMENT REVISITED

A set of design specifications for an organization that is "designed for commitment" is outlined by Rosabeth Moss Kanter (1968, 1972). Kanter's specifications are, however, derived from *systemic* needs: continuance, cohesion, and control. The product is a somewhat reified structure[70]. Addressing, as it were, an omnipotent organization designer, the specifications do not provide members with any rules of thumb for democratic design of their organization, something that is basic for a reproduction model[71].

Two insights that may be useful in binding members' orientations with their contributions to organization design have, separately, served as focal points for two respective research approaches. The impact of "organizational cultures" on members and their decision making has been the central object of study of the "organizational culture" approach (primarily within business management research; see, for example, Sproull, 1981). Members' role in upholding organizational cultures and structures constitutes the core of the ethnomethodological approach. Both approaches, not unlike Kanter's, focus on *maintenance* rather than change; key elements of the respective models are treated as if given: Members neither design their myths, other than in a historical sense, nor, respectively, the structures they are called upon to enact.

The extent to which self-managed organizations can be predesigned at all is questionable (Baumgartner et al., 1981). Both successful communes, major cooperative movements, the Mondragon federation, and the kibbutz movement have, in fact, evolved gradually, nearly accidentally, in a succession of organizational choices and changes and not as a realization of a preconceived plan[72]. "They developed their communities by stages /. . / Members often made choices at each step of the way /. . / The full organization grew out of a series of smaller steps and built on existing commitment as the base for generating more commitment" (Kanter 1972:133).

What would have appeared to an outside observer at any time as an imposing organizational edifice to be analyzed is viewed by the member-participant as a *link in a process*. Whereas the analyst would be looking for mechanisms, the participant may (often but vaguely) perceive a dynamic, bound by tacit rules of "proper" development and conduct. These perceptions will, in turn, guide daily practice and the decision-making choices that constitute organizational design. Their principal import lies in ordering input data (thus shaping a definition of the situation and, less directly, the range of available options; see Beyer, 1981; Hedberg and Jönsson, 1978) rather than in directly shaping outcomes. It would, perhaps be too presumptuous to speak, in this context, about "cooperative logic" or a "cooperative paradigm"[73]. There is definitely room to speak of a "cooperative common sense" or a set of *assumptions* guiding daily decision-making[74].

Examining Kanter's work (as well as the history of the kibbutz movement) from the "members' oriented" angle suggested above (Stryjan, 1984b), yields a set of assumptions that are, in fact, the basic assumptions of membership: an assumption of permanence, of mutual dependence, and of the collective endeavour's intrinsic worth. Such assumptions' relation to reality as it would be seen by an external observer is somewhat problematic. They could, in fact be regarded as *meta-factual assumptions* that are simultaneously held to be true here and now (factual inputs), to be in need of proof or demonstration, and, ultimately, to be in need of protection, even to the extent of being removed from an all-too-harsh reality. One might state that we are dealing here with the dynamics of a *self-fulfilling prophecy*. To take a concrete example: increased propensity for long-range investment would both follow logically from an assumption that the enterprise is going to last (permanence), and, by stimulating investment, would help this assumption come true, committing, in the process, individual members' resources to the task. A simplified loop model of the the way such assumptions are reproduced and, in turn, guide the reproduction of the organization can be graphically presented as follows (figure 3.1).

**Figure 3.1  A Simplified Reproduction Loop**

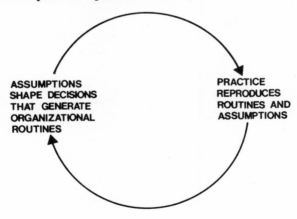

ASSUMPTIONS
SHAPE DECISIONS
THAT GENERATE
ORGANIZATIONAL
ROUTINES

PRACTICE
REPRODUCES
ROUTINES AND
ASSUMPTIONS

Schematically stated, assumptions guide decisions, decisions shape rules and institutions, and they, in turn, shape daily routine and serve as "manifestations" and, where exceptional decisions are involved, as an origin of "myths" and reinforcement of the basic logic.

Applied to concrete cases, in real-life organizations, such abstract assumptions would assume more concrete forms. Organization-specific applications would reflect the problems and routines of the organization dealt with. Such an application to the case of the kibbutz is presented in figure 3.2 (Source: Stryjan, 1984b). The somewhat abstract assumptions are replaced, in this diagram, by concrete, time- and organization-specific assumptions. A brief outline of the assumptions' organization-specific applications in different SM organizations is presented in the following three subsections (3.5.1-3.5.3).

## Figure 3.2 Time and Organization-Specific Assumptions

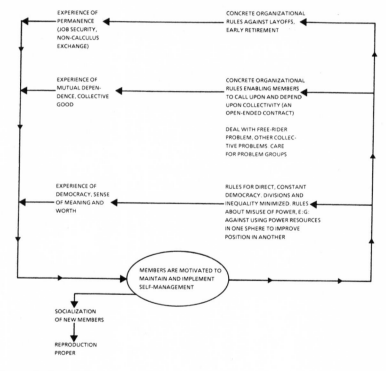

Source: Stryjan, 1984b

### 3.5.1 AN ASSUMPTION OF PERMANENCE

The belief that both the individual and the organization will be there tomorrow, seems trivial. The necessity of discussing it here stems primarily from the fact that it is all too often forgotten in both economic and organizational models. An assumption of permanence is an essential precondition of stability. Routines, and other forms of repetitive action such as rituals, can be established only under an assumption of permanence. At the same time, they also are an important means of establishing an air of permanence. The same thing applies to relations between members: Inasmuch as communities build on mutual exchanges of favours over long periods and, even more, on accumulation of open obligations and debts outstanding, an underlying assumption of permanence is a basic prerequisite for their existence and stability. At the same time, the entering new obligations that would, presumably, have to be discharged at some later time acts to strenghten the sysem even further. William G. Ouchi (1980) applied this principle to organizations and proposed an "clan"-organization model that is based on long-range obligations between individuals and their organization[75]. A mode of organization, where members have grounds to believe "that in the long run they will be dealt with equitably" (Wilkins and Ouchi, 1983), opens a third organizational alternative, beside markets and hierarchies, for the resolution of transaction-costs problems (see also Miyazaki, 1982:926; Grusky, 1960), and of control in organizations.

Both models constructed to deal with self-management and organization models that deal with problems of control and equitability of rewards often tend to abstract from both individual and organizational long-range considerations. The tendency to focus on short-range considerations is well exemplified by Mancur Olson's model of collective action and, within economic model construction, by Benjamin Ward's model of the "Illyrian firm" (1958; see also critique in Horvat, 1979b). Ward's model predicts that the worker-owned firm will be liable to underinvest, driven by the preference to maximize immediate income. Such a behaviour would amount to a tendency of the members to milk their enterprise, giving up future potential for immediate gain). Ward's prediction is incorporated into Jaroslav Vanek's work (1970, 1975a, see also Lichtenstein 1986) as an inimical "self extinction force" operating on such firms.

An investment behaviour of this sort would be rational for individuals that assume that their affiliation to "their" organization may be terminated at any moment. Indeed, the practice of shedding workers as a key method for short-run adjustment to market and cost conditions is postulated by the Ward-Vanek-Meade model (Berman, 1982; Stephen, 1982)[76]. Niels Mygind (1986) demonstrated that such a behaviour simply makes no sense, once permanence (and thus considerations that have to do with future performance[77]) is instead assumed. This case, discussed in the previous section, also demonstrates the assumption's circular character.

An assumption of permanence may enhance control and investment behaviour in an organization. Yet neither stability of control nor appropriate investment behaviour alone would suffice to uphold the assumption's credibility for the organizations' members. It is important to realize that stability of membership is required for the assumption to be held credible at individual members' level. In the case of SM, and not the least in job-saving cooperatives, the assumption of permanence can be expected to be related closely to notions of job security. Conversely, both ordinary departures and forced ones — through layoffs, expulsion, or firing — would undermine its tenability. Thus "cooperatives are unwilling to lay off or terminate their workers during slow periods" (Jackall and Levin, 1984a:11)[78].

Richard Fletcher (1976) ascribed such reluctance to normative considerations, related to the perception of membership. Members' "tenure" may also be formally codified as a contractual obligation (i.e., a duty to provide a member with work; see Berman and Berman, 1978; Berman, 1982; Bellas, 1975; Miyazaki, 1984). Whether contractual, normative, or merely emotional, such a clause would imply that solutions of job sharing are preferred to layoff in cases of crisis[79]. This, as Katrina V. Berman (1982:77) remared, clearly contrasts with the tendency to shed labour under crisis, predicted by accepted economic models of self-management[80].

For the individual member, the interest in "holding on to members" would to no small extent be guided by one's own need for security. It enhances consideration of individual problems and needs, an issue dealt with in the discussion of the mutual dependence assumption in the next section. It may also have some interesting corollaries where the problem of "administrative discipline" (see Webb, 1891) is concerned. Hajime Miyazaki suggested that "the organizational basis for enforcing contracts may ultimately be the factor that distinguishes the LMF [labour-managed firm] from the PMF [privately managed firms]" (1984:926).

What Webb in her time bewailed as "absence of administrative discipline" may simply mean that reliability of performance is ensured by other means. As the case of the kibbutz shows, permanence of membership may raise high thresholds to employment of institutional sanctions (especially expulsion) and dictate instead reliance on informal, "horizontal" control (Bradley and Gelb, 1981) and consensus-seeking[81]. Thus, although formal ways usually exist in membership-based organizations to expel a member (as opposed to a share owner, who cannot be disowned by his peers), the tendency would normally be to refrain from employing them.

The way the features discussed above interconnect can be graphically presented (figure 3.3). The schematic description of the dynamics involved may certainly be improved upon. The important point, at this stage, is that this model clearly clashes with practices, such as layoffs, workforce reductions, and managerial prerogatives to sack a worker, accepted as part of "the natural order of things" in conventional enterprises[82]. As we shall see in chapter 5, it also dictates recruitment and investment policies substantially deviating from those of conventional firms.

**Figure 3.3  Dynamics in an Assumption of Permanence**

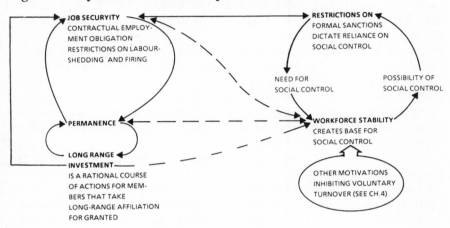

Source: Stryjan and Hellmark, 1985.

### 3.5.2 MUTUAL DEPENDENCE

The notion of interaction with and mutual obligations between fellow members, is built in the concept of membership. Only a minor part of a member's work-day will normally be spent in interaction with "the organization" at large. Naturally, most interactions will be with fellow-members, and a considerable portion of an organization's everyday routines will arise from these interactions. Mutual dependence, inbuilt in the fabric of this interaction would extend the permanence-web of obligations between members.

Martial Menconi (1982), reviewing Evsey Domar's (1966) "producer cooperative" model, demonstrates that an economic model of self-management cannot make sense, unless an "assumption of solidarity" is introduced[83]: "Everyone's work is [at] optimum if he bestows the same weight upon others' satisfaction as he does upon his own" (p. 341). Menconi's conclusions would still hold even in a less moral state of affairs where all participants merely share the understanding that their satisfactions are interdependent and, thus, attach a weight both to others' welfare and to the others' goodwill, that is, their concern to one's own welfare, a motivational input that Amartya K. Sen (1966) designed as "sympathy" or "social consciousness". Finally, Miyazaki (1982) proposed to see the labour-managed firm as a system of mutual contracts *between* members, attaching a strong weight to solidarity.

An assumption of mutual dependence would imply that resources needed to cope with problems — both individual and organizational — ought to be sought primarily (and, ideally, exclusively) within the collective. This imposes a clear obligation on members to respond to such needs if and when they arise. The list of potential needs is heterogeneous and probably inexhaustible. It may include arranging an unscheduled leave or flexible schedule for a member with an urgent personal problem, leaving one's own job, temporarily closing down a production line to help with a peak load elsewhere, redesign of a job for an aging member and so on. It may also, under certain circumstances, for instance in countries or regions with weakly developed welfare services, imply an offensive involvement on the organization's part in social insurance and services for members, such as health and day-care services (see Stryjan, 1984b)[84].

Looking for solutions *within* implies a certain limitation of perspective. It is possible to argue that a certain loss of efficiency is involved, as the solutions available within a small organization would, in many cases, not be the cheapest obtainable on the market. Maintaining the assumption does, however, make an important contribution to organizational functioning: (a) as an important complement to the assumption of permanence, not the least in designing ways to deal with the organization's "demographical fringe", composed on one side of the youngest, most mobile, and least integrated members and, on the other side, of those at the eve of retirement; (b) as an important motivator for organizational flexibility and lateral mobility and, thus, a means of increasing network density (see Wippler, 1986).

It takes a perception of the enterprise as a comprehensible, interdependent unity for such "natural and spontaneous cooperation" (Greenberg, 1984:191) to develop and be accepted by workers and staff of any organization. Openness to meet members' needs often entails exposure to breaks in routine and extra effort. Willingness to accept such inconvenience would be related to a clear notion of a beneficiary, whose needs the effort and the inconvenience incurred are meant to meet. To take a concrete example, an abrupt change in a worker's schedule redirecting him to another task or an unexpected request for overtime would, in this case, be legitimated by individual or common *need* rather than by a manager's or foreman's *authority*[85].

Mutual help is commonsensically connected with notions of desert and reciprocity. In other words, the assumption is most directly dependent on an unambiguous definition of membership. Conversely, when boundaries get blurred, through introduction of non-members (most typically, paid workers) into the organization (Cohen, 1972; Barkai, 1977), or when differentiation of competing subgroups occurs, mutual dependence would collapse[86]. Simply stated, one is no longer sure, under such circumstances, who it is one helps and whether the beneficiary is worthy of the extra effort. In an important sense, then, boundary conditions of mutual dependence would be set by the organization's demography.

SM organizations are often started by a relatively homogenous founder group[87]. Two conceivable demographic fault lines can often be observed in somewhat older SM organizations: between founders and new members (Meister, 1984) and between managers and managed. Situations in which the two fault lines coincide (e.g., with the founder group occupying the management posts and lacking contact with other members) can be particularly dangerous for a SM organization. A shared ideology and a high degree of interaction among the workforce, to be expected in such an organization, would, in fact, present a set of nearly ideal conditions for the emergence of a defensive "worker collective" (of the sort described by Sverre Lysgaard, 1976), *once and if* a managerial or a founder group comes to be regarded as a distinct and alien stratum by the remainder of the membership. The norms of equality, rotation and *lateral* mobility, generally recommended and often practiced in self-managed organizations, have a powerful preventive effect, through blurring potential intra-organizational boundaries and fault lines (see Kaufman 1960).

Finally, a perception of the organization as a unity may prove anything but easy to defend against "rational" organization modes and piecemeal redesign practices imported from the environment[88]: "a relentless pursuit of productive efficiency may induce a disintegration of labor-managed (sub) economies as social institutions" (Miyazaki, 1982:929).

Rationalization drives may, in fact, result in seeming organizational improvements — especially where efficiency is concerned. Such improvement may be but temporary: A hierarchical reorganization of resources may, for a short while, enjoy the best of both worlds, exploiting both potential advantages of "rational management" and residues of motivation and flexibility that it does not reproduce. Once these reserves flag, the obvious solution would be to substitute them with a yet stricter measure of rationality.

### 3.5.3 AN ASSUMPTION OF WORTH

An assumption of worth is possibly the most elusive of the three assumptions to be dealt with here. Bruce Buchanan (1974; in his discussion of commitment), discusses "a partisan, affective attachment to the goals and values of an organization, to one's role /. . / and to the organization for its own sake" (Buchanan, 1974:533).

Such an attachment may range in its character and intensity from a sense of ideological mission or being "chosen" (Niv, 1976, 1980; Kanter, 1972) through a self-perception of constituting an "alternative institution" (Rothschild-Whitt 1979) to "company spirit". Communes and "alternative" movement organizations could probably be placed near the top of this scale. The weaker end of the scale would appear more applicable to normal cases of worker-managed enterprises, where ideological overtones are often absent or intentionally played down.

The precise content of such an assumption, be it political, counter-ideological (see Herskin, n.d.) or otherwise, would vary from one organization to another. Generalizable over the varying contexts and of direct relevance to our discussion is the assumption's character as "a shared claim of uniqueness" (Wilkins and Ouchi, 1983:473). Organizations within our sphere of interest would also generally share a commitment to democracy, an issue that will be dealt with in section 3.6[89].

As a shared claim of uniqueness, the assumption's prime import is in legitimating the organization's "right" to conduct its affairs in its own way, regardless of elsewhere accepted rules of proper organizational conduct. It sets the frame, as it were, for the organization's routines, thus lifting the burden of constant accounting that the practice of (by societal standards) deviant routines would otherwise have implied (Goffman, 1974; Garfinkel, 1967). In a very basic sense, it thus makes such routines very "routineness" possible.

Alhough basically unreflexive, routine may often be infused with a sense of meaning, not the least when an organization or its members encounter environmental hostility[90]. As Max Weber observed in his typology of action: "Attachment to habitual forms can be upheld with varying degrees of self-consciousness and in a variety of senses. *In this case the type may shade over into value rationality*" (1978:25; italics mine).

The brief discussion of rationalization measures and their impact in the closing of the previous section illustrates the import of undramatic (as opposed to occasions of persecution) organizational choices[91]. At the least, an assumption of (own) worth may serve in such cases as a well-needed threshold against uncritical adoption of externally generated practices[92]. At best, as organizations cannot subsist on rejection alone, it would provide a point of departure for innovation or for creative adaptation (Katz and Golomb, 1974).

An important issue in this context is that of *internal legitimacy*. The legitimacy of deviant organizations would most often be questioned by their environment: "Organizations that omit environmentally legitimated elements of structure or create unique structures lack acceptable legitimate accounts of their activities. Such organizations are more vulnerable to claims that they are negligent, irrational or unnecessary" (Meyer and Rowan, 1977:349). What legitimacy such organizations would possess would be internally generated and, thus, directly dependent on the members' conviction that the task they engage in has some meaning. Once this assumption of worth falters, an organization is no longer perceived as legitimate by its own members, and a tendency to copy other organizations, perceived as more successful or legitimate, is likely to develop (DiMaggio and Powell, 1982; see also section 6.4 in this book).

Legitimation claims would, as John W. Meyer and Brian Rowan (1977) suggested, often come couched in efficiency terms. The measures of efficiency employed are, though, often ceremonial and may, in fact, be quite detached from the reality they claim to evaluate (ibid.). In a sense, then, the concepts of efficiency and legitimacy may, at least in certain contexts, be substitutable for each other.

A study of such an "efficiency quest" in the kibbutz movement was presented in "Self-Manangement: the Case of the Kibbutz" (Stryjan 1983b). It is argued that the strengthening of profit orientations (with profit measured in formal accounting terms) in a competitive quest between production branches "is the result of consensus-seeking, motivated by erosion of the original goals (Talmon, 1972), and tending towards the lowest common denominator" (Stryjan, 1983b:278).

Uri Leviatan's studies of managerial rotation in kibbutz industrial plants (1978) can illustrate this process[93]. Leviatan convincingly demonstrated, on the base of empirical evidence, that managerial rotation is indeed beneficial for organizational performance. He also noted that, empirical evidence notwithstanding, the "public opinion" in plants of two out of (then) three kibbutz movements had dramatically shifted *against* such rotation practices in the period between 1960 and 1969 (roughly from 20 to 60 percent; no recent trends given). Interestingly, the respondents motivated their opposition by considerations of efficiency.

The case is obviously one of decoupling between efficiency's two usages, as a measurable index of performance and as legitimation agent. Leviatan, obviously unaware of the problem, attempted to resolve the evident paradox by an empirical test. It is, however, public opinion, rather than research findings that guides the development of a democratic community. Accepting Leviatan's empirical conclusions, we are still left with the paradox of a community endorsing, for efficiency's sake, a less effective way of management. Where the kibbutz is concerned we also are left with an outline of a future problem.

### 3.6 A DEMOCRATIC ORGANIZATION

The organization's democratic character is a normative focal point at which SM research's normative dimension, formal definitions of co-operation, and, not the least, SM members' expectations converge. To claim that democratic organization automatically makes an enterprise worth it would be oversimplifying matters. But a perception that democratic procedures are important is, on some level, often evident in study cases[94]. Thus a principle of one person, one vote is often followed in worker-owned enterprises that are incorporated under the company act, independently of the way stock is distributed[95]. Both non-voting workers and non-working voters are considered a problem to be avoi-ded by scholars (who often decline to give this stand any explanation that would be consistent with their theoretical models) and members alike.

A principle of one person, one vote guarantees a formal equality of individual steering inputs. It does not define these inputs' character. Helge Tetzschner, 1982 suggested a triple classification of democratic forms. Democracy may thus be *discoursive*, that is, collective will-forma-tion in Jürgen Habermas' spirit, *plebiscitarian*, with plenum majority vote on every issue, or *elective-indirect*[96]. These three ideal types are rarely fully separate in reality. As suggested by Stryjan, (1984b), the dis-coursive approach may be the most suitable for the SM organization (see Rothschild-Whitt, 1979). However, technical constraints and considerations of expediency (Abrahamsson, 1980, 1982, 1983; Dahl, 1970) seem to weight the existing blends in favour of indirect democracy. The ever-increasing volume of decision-making with which a complex organization has to cope precludes the possibility of ever having every single decision dealt with in plenum[97]. One practical pro-blem any SM organization must thus cope with is to devise expedient shortcuts for decision making in a way that would not empty direct democracy of its meaning. The delegation of tasks that expediency requires creates, however, two problems: one of *compliance* with explicitly stated directives and one of *anticipation*, when reality necessitates taking a stand on an issue that is not yet covered by any decision. To the extent that individual decision-makers are indeed guided by the same assumptions as their "constituents", there is a fair probability that these requirements will be met. Plenary democratic organs would be primarily monitoring this performance. Monitoring is commonly effected by presence, rather than by deed (Stryjan, 1983b).

The key notion is that any decision taken within the organization *could* be contested in the assembly and should, in such a case, be either discoursively redeemed or reversed, if it fails the test. The credibility of such monitoring (and, indirectly, of the whole democratic system of governance) is determined by democratic organs' demonstrated ability to challenge administrative decisions and their readiness to test this ability whenever dissent arises.

The kibbutz democracy, in itself a blend of elements from the three democracy types enumerated above, can be taken as a case in point. All elements are, as in Joyce Rothschild-Whitt's model (1979) clearly subordinated to the principle of direct discoursive decision formation. Thus officials are being elected and power delegated as in a representative system. Elected officials are, however, held responsible to the collective and to the *weekly* general assembly *constantly*, rather than on rare reelection occasions. Formal voting is resorted to, as in a plebiscitarian system, but under the clear assumption that this is but a technical shortcut to a decision that could be discoursively redeemed (Rosner and Cohen, 1980)[98]. To yield substance to such an assumption, a discourse, actual or potential, must be clearly possible. From a discourse perspective (Habermas, 1976), this should be seen as a question of eliminating systematical distortions and blocks, and from a power perspective (Lukes, 1976; Conforth and Paton, 1981; Conforth, 1982), as a question of equal distribution (or neutralization) of power resources.

A question of major interest in our discussion is, how can the continuous reproduction of democratic practices be ensured. Carole Pateman's stand on the issue may be of interest here:

> The major function of participation in the theory of participative democracy is therefore an educative one, educative in the very widest sense, including both the psychological aspect and the gaining of practice in democratic skills and procedures. Thus there is no special problem about the stability of a participatory system; it is self-sustaining through the educative impact of the participatory process. (1970:42)

Possibly sound in the eschatological sense, the application of Pateman's prediction to concrete organizations raises a number of problems. The most pertinent is the question of the system's vulnerability to deviant (as judged by participative norms) behaviour. Although to a considerable degree self-propagating for its followers, the system is not self-enforcing. An effort to remedy this problem through design of elaborate governance systems (see, for example Saglio and Hackman, 1982) is likely to miss the point. As efficient functioning does require delegation of power, a risk is ever present that those presently in power positions would use them to secure further power resources, typically through control of information and agenda (Lukes, 1976; Conforth and

Paton, 1981) and monopolization of expertise, or of the right to crown experts, (see Stryjan, 1983b). The relevant issue, in this case is, not the amount of power *delegated* but the amount of power *left* at the disposal of rank and file members.

The more diverse channels of influence and sources of power there are, the more remote the possibility of their monopolisation by a hypothetical oligarchy. The kibbutz may be taken as a case in point. The multiplicity of areas to be coordinated in this case, as a result of the far-reaching inclusion of activities into the communally managed sphere, gives rise to a complex structure of interlocking committees and quasi hierarchies, none of which is allowed lasting precedence over the others. On the individual level, this complexity is reflected by a societal ideal of intentionally unbalanced status[99]. Efforts to homogenize one's status, employing power resources under one's control in one sphere to improve one's position in another sphere, are usually met with strong censure (Rosner and Shur, 1982).

The characteristics and boundary conditions of such a system may be summed up as follows:

1. The dynamism of the system is maintained by continual shift in participation/subgroup membership and in occupation of management positions.

2. The balance is maintained, i.e. no sphere of activity is allowed lasting precedence over the others.

Unfulfilment of the first condition may lead to establishment of a corporative elite. Unfulfilment of the second one- to the establishment of a unilinear (strong) hierarchy[100]. (Stryjan, 1983:270)

### 3.6.1 THE CASE OF ROTATION: AN ILLUSTRATION

It is, in reality, very easy to kill a dragon, but it is impossible to keep it dead.

-Ernest Bramah, *Kai Lung's Golden Hours*

The persistence of democratic forms of governance is a matter of constant maintenance rather than of successful organizational design. Democratic norms and practices, in other words, have to be constantly *reproduced*.

Delegation of power gives, by its nature, rise to momentary inequalities within an organization, at any given time. "Vertical" rotation can be seen as a way of equalizing the organizational distributions of skills (Leviatan, 1978) and power over time, thus preventing temporary differentials from becoming permanent and cumulative[101]. Rotation is a fairly common and widespread organizational measure in organizations

with democratic ambitions. The examination of rotation and its preconditions, undertaken in a simplified form below, could shed some light on
the boundary conditions of democratic governance and on the way that
formal structures and procedures may be maintained or reshaped
through a flow of individual members' actions.

It is easy to see that in a formal governance system with a fixed
number of authority positions, recruitment and retirement would be
tied to each other. As in a game of musical chairs, no seats are available,
unless those occupying them get up.

Now, let us assume that incumbent officeholders have a decisive say
as to staying on or leaving their post. It is reasonable to expect that the
majority of officeholders in a democratically spirited organization would
be perfectly willing to step back once they have served their turn. Some,
however, would not. If no precautions are taken, this would, in time,
lead to the whole governance structure being clogged by
"irremovables"[102]. The dynamics is one of a flow process with sedimen-
tation at the top. Permanent hierarchic structures grow in a way that
somewhat resembles processes of stalactite formation.

Processes of this sort can readily be observed in most democratic
organizations. However, they seldom proceed as thoroughly and unidi-
rectionally as the simplified description above would suggest. The description's seductive simplicity rests on the following assumptions:

a. There is a considerable proportion of actual or potential "office
   clingers".
b. Officeholders have decisive say as to their incumbency.
c. The authority structure is fixed. No new posts are added to the
   structure.

These conditions are in no way predetermined. The logic of the oligarchization process outlined above may, then, be taken as a starting point
for examination of the checks that operate, albeit imperfectly, in most
organizations.

*Selecting and motivating incumbents to step down:* A strong stress on
the desirability of rotation and the institutionalization of rotation as an
unquestionable organizational routine considerably facilitate smooth
rotation. Like many other norms, the norm of rotation is  most directly
reinforced by its practice. Normative orientations that endorse rotation
are often complemented and buttressed by mechanisms acting to reduce
the attractivity of offic, or aimed at weeding out prospective office
clingers[103]. An organizational culture encompassing such elements, has
to provide for a redefinition of "conventional" concepts of career and
office (Leviatan, 1978).

A strong stress on equal pay and working conditions, often evident in collectives and worker cooperatives may result in a "negative balance of rewards" (Talmon, 1972; Greenberg 1986:54) for officeholders. Official tasks are carried for little or no remuneration, often on the officeholder's free time. "I had that one year, and I really didn't like it too well. You get involved in all the business of the company. You have to make all the decisions. There's no extra pay for it. There's not even extra thanks for it, hardly" (Greenberg, 1984:204).

At the same time, the official is easily accessible during the workday and thus exposed to pressure from his workmates, as the following quotation (dealing with board members in an American plywood cooperative) illustrates: "We've had quite a few guys who couldn't take it and had to resign. For years I was the only member of the board to eat in the lunchroom.. Yeah, the rest of them would hide out in their car or have a nook and corner where they'd be all by themselves, cuz they didn't want to take the guff" (Greenberg, 1986:55).

*Forcing incumbents out:* Elected, and not discouraged by the scanty rewards the post offers, an official may still either refuse to vacate his or her post or, in more formalized setups, would see to it that he or she is renominated. Whether an official's will would determine the organizational outcome in such a case is largely a matter of organizational culture. Incumbents of office may, however, control the resources it takes to modify an organizational culture or to intimidate its adherents. The maintenance of a culture of rotation may thus be a question of power as well. Crucial, in our case, is the degree to which rank and file members can keep "their" officers in check. Although not expressly designed for this end, complex non-linear structures and the practice of unbalanced status discussed in the previous section can both minimize the rewards of incumbency and limit a recalcitrant incumbent's leverage. At the same time, they also increase the person's exposure to pressures from sources he or she cannot control. Consequently, such organizational features may supply important check and balance mechanisms in cases of executive deviance.

*Bypassing:* The fixity of an authority structure varies from one organization to another. Clearly, the more fixed  the structure (in terms of well-defined posts and rigid blueprints), the easier it is for it to become clogged. Conventional bureaucratic lore can teach us that office clingers can be bypassed through creation of a parallel chain of authority or sidetracked by creation of additional administrative posts. Practices of this sort may also be used in a prophylactic manner: the more openness there exists in an organization to create new domains of responsibility, with new authority posts to match, whenever the need and interest arises, the less sway old "irremovables" would have over the organization. Indeed, the more changeable the organization, the less reason there is for such irremovables to cling to their post.

This last suggestion opens about as many new questions as it resolves. Structures of the type recommended above would encounter problems of checking administrative costs (an issue neatly resolved in those organizations where governance is an after-hours issue) and of guarding against total formlessness and the risks of manipulation it carries (see Abrahamsson 1986). Furthermore, periods of growth, during which sidetracking officials may be a much easier solution than inducing them to rotate, may result in an amassment of unresolved organizational and personal problems that would weight the organization down once it entered a crisis. A discussion of such problems exceeds, however, the scope of this chapter, intended to deal with a simplified model and general design. Questions of spot interference and problem resolution are discussed in the next chapter.

### 3.7 THE REPRODUCTION MODEL: A RESTATEMENT

The reproduction model presented in this chapter envisages an organization that is being continuously designed and redesigned by its members. Members, in turn, are moulded by the organization through its daily routines. Today's organization is thus shaping tomorrow's members, who, in turn, will shape the organization's future.

Since members and, thus, also their organizations keep changing, the description above does not resolve the questions of identity and continuity, or in the concrete case we are dealing with, the question of how an organization can both change, something organizations most evidently do, and yet remain self-managed.

An organization's identity ought to be defined by that which it actually reproduces. Since most elements in any organization may (retrospectively) be ascribed a degree of functionality, it would be tempting to claim that all of a given organization's features ought to be reproduced. This would, in fact, amount to repetition *in perpetuo*. In systems of this sort, it would also prove impossible to establish any order of precedence between those acting and those acted upon. In other words, the celebrated stone axe would be as important to reproduction as the aborigine wielding it[104]. The relevance of such a model (which may be termed *simple reproduction*; see Hernes, 1977) to organizations in unstable environments and competitive situations is questionable[105]. A reproduction perspective adapted to organizations in changing environments ought to provide (a) an analytic distinction between core element(s) that are to be reproduced and ancillary ones, open, in principle, to modification and redesign without altering the organization's identity; and

(b) specifications as to who is engaged in the process and what forms this engagement would take.

Broadly speaking, the issue of reproduction is one of balance between stability and change. Core elements are being reproduced and, in this sense, they are stable, as long as the reproduction process is carried on, that is, "as long as their repetitiveness is continuously accomplished"[106]. Change, in this model, is constrained to ancillary characteristics[107]. Core characteristics do not determine ancillary ones (an organization cannot be analytically "derived" from its core). They do, however, impose constraints on the degree of freedom in choice and modification of ancillary characteristics, so that solutions that may impend on the core's reproduction are selected against. Thus we cannot predict which legal form of incorporation a cooperative may choose. We can, nonetheless, expect it not to register as a private firm owned by one dominant member. Redesign of ancillary characteristics can be seen as a way of coping with environmental pressures and instability (see Thompson, 1967), a proposition that is developed further in chapters 5-6.

The organizational core that is being reproduced ought to contain the prerequisites for the organization's continued existence. In our case, the core being reproduced is the organization's active membership. Its reproduction is primarily anchored in the organization's daily functioning (Giddens, 1984). Schematically, it may be presented as a loop, whereby organizational routines shape participants' perceptions and the participants' inputs, guided by these perceptions, contribute, in turn, to uphold or modify these routines. The discussion in the next chapter introduces an additional important and often overlooked element, namely, a corpus of participants to enact routines share perceptions and act upon them.

To recapitulate, the reproduction of membership involves membership's three aspects: These aspects also define the ways in which an organization is shaped and modified by its members:

a.  Physical bearer (a corpus of members)
b.  A shared frame of reference, whereby definitions of situation can be generated
c.  A repertoire of options for action or members inputs

Starting with flesh and blood individuals and ending with options for action which are by their nature collectively or even formally determined, this order of presentation may be interpreted as a continuum stretching from individual to structure. Such an ordering is more apparent than real; none of these aspects is in any way more "structural" than others. This may be illustrated by table 3.1.

**Table 3.1  Individual and Structural Antecedents of Membership**

| individual actions (re)shaping membership | membership | structural features shaping membership |
| --- | --- | --- |
| Joining/exit | bearer (demographic composition) | recruitment |
| discourse | frame of reference | 'organizational culture' |
| precedents, personal example | repertoire | rules, procedures |

Just as any of the three aspects may be traced to the outcomes of individual actors' actions (joining an organization, spreading a novel approach, setting procedural precedents, respectively), it may as well be derived from structural features (recruitment policies, organizational "culture", formal regulations). That some of these features appear more structural than others is due to the fact that the time scales for their impact are inverted, as it were, relatively to one another. An individual's exit or entry decision would have an immediate (however limited) impact on an organization's demography, whereas the effect of changes in recruitment policies would become manifest after a longer time. Conversely, the changing of rules would have a manifest short-range effect, while the impact of precedent setting and personal example would be gradual and harder to trace.

## 3.8 CONCLUSION, AND AN AGENDA FOR THE FOLLOWING CHAPTERS

A model of organizational reproduction of self-managed organizations was outlined in this chapter. Self-management's core process, in this model, is the reproduction of the organization's active membership. Reproduction of membership involves (selective) replenishment of the organization's *corpus of members*, the upholding of a shared *frame of reference* that guides members' actions, and the maintenance and updating of an established *repertoire of action* that members may resort to. The organization's everyday reality, shaped to a great degree by structural features and routines, plays an important role in this reproduction process. These features and routines are formed by members' decisions and inputs and through members' actions.

To facilitate presentation, the model was applied to a simplified version of organizational reality: an organization untroubled by its environment, with a stable corpus of members endowed with a fairly truncated repertoire of action. Holding the environment constant and sim- plifying two of the aspects of membership (corpus of members and repertoire) helps to set in relief the remaining one, that of a common frame of reference. A set of three meta-assumptions was proposed, which if adopted by members engaged in a democratic process of designing their own organization is likely to yield a self-managed orga- nization at every successive step of design and to counteract eventual degenerative changes.

The simplified model's chief strength lies in setting into relief the basic mechanics of organizational reproduction and underscoring the importance of members' perceptions. To set the agenda for the follow- ing chapters, we should critically examine the outlined model's weak- nesses as well to establish the directions in which it ought to be augmen- ted and developed.

One of the considerations guiding the presentation in this chapter has been to stress the differences between the proposed reproduction perspective and the dominant "degeneration-theoretical" one. Conse- quently, features that are positive, self-reinforcing, and at the systems, rather than individual level, were stressed, partly at the expense of other, no less important ones. The resulting picture has some charac- teristics of a "social perpetuum mobile", with all of the problems this involves. The one-sided stress on harmony and on organizational rou- tines as a means to reproduce values functional to that harmony has a deal of Barnardian overtones. As such, it is vulnerable to criticisms originally aimed at the Barnardian "Company Town"[108]. Is the replace- ment of conventional management by SM merely a replacement of manipulation by self-manipulation or manipulation by those in leading positions?

Although the SM organization is presented as a process running within fairly narrow tolerance margins, no account was thus far given as to its source of energy or eventual steering mechanisms and longstops that would keep it from derailment. True to the basic approach, ground- ing reproduction on individual members' attitudes and actions, answers to these questions should be sought at the individual level. But, al- though expressly focusing on members' perception of the organization, our model has thus far left the link between individual member's inputs and the system in the dark. Thus far we have only suggested what the organization should look like to make a member feel $X$ about it. Hardly anything has been said on how this member's sentiments reflect in turn on the organization and nothing at all as to what the member should do about the organization if (or once) he or she feels otherwise about it.

The somewhat exaggerated piece of devil's advocacy above points to some critical weaknesses and lacunae in the proposed perspective:

a.  A rosy view of the organization as a harmonious mechanism must be complemented with a view of its underside — the problems, conflicts, and shortcomings that are an inseparable part of an organization's daily functioning.

b.  The role of individual members as active, rather than passively conditioned, bearers of the SM organization should be clarified.

A more realistic view of the problems an organization is exposed to calls for a more realistic view of members' inputs. A basic point to be kept in mind is that an organization's everyday reality consists of much more than merely explicit decision-making. In fact, only few decisions permit of wholly unambiguous implementation, and only seldom can implementation be carried out wholly error free. The enormous complexity of the reproduction mechanisms outlined above entails a high degree of vulnerability to error and shortcomings. It is in this context of managing daily problems and repeatedly setting the organization right again that we should view the full import of members' participation. Coping with the organization as it really is, and on a day-to day basis, calls for a considerably broader repertoire of action than the one outlined in this chapter for the "decision-steered" organization of the simplified model. An outline of such a repertoire, set in the context of a more realistic organization model, of "the fallible organization" is proposed in the next chapter.

One more issue, conveniently kept constant in the discussion thus far, is that of the reproduction of a corpus of members. One part of this issue – changes in the composition of the body of members – is taken up in the later part of chapter 4. Another, dealing with recruitment of new members, is discussed first in chapter 5, as one part in the review of the SM organization's relations with its environment.

Finally, the simplified model also abstracts from the problems inherent in the SM organization's relationships with its environment. Far from being docile, as the model supposes, the environment can, in fact, be seen as a major source of problems and a threat – direct or indirect — to the organization's identity and existence. These problems, and the organization's way of managing them, are discussed in chapters 5 and 6.

# 4

# ORGANIZATIONS AND
# THEIR MEMBERS, MEMBERS
# AND THEIR ORGANIZATIONS

## 4.1 INTRODUCTION

The aim of this chapter is to extend the reproduction model outlined in the previous chapter, exploring the role of members in organizations and under conditions more complex than the ones the simplified model was based upon. One central notion in this chapter is that of *organizational fallibility*. All of the approaches applied in this work thus far have dealt either with organizations that, *ex definitio*, function as they should or (implicitly) with design specifications for yet better ones. However, a considerable part of the recorded cases in which members inputs have had an impact on their organization, and, certainly, most of the dramatically observable ones, are cases of dissent and dissatisfaction in organizations that evidently failed to function as they should. A fruitful application of the concept of membership would thus presuppose an organizational model capable of dealing with the incidence of failure on one side and of accommodating conflict and member's protest on the other side. Furthermore, since both conflict and protest (and, presumably, their preemption and avoidance) are actions that members engage in, this would also require a considerable broadening of our perspective on members' action repertoires, beyond that outlined in the previous chapter. An attempt to extend the theoretical framework along these lines, primarily based on the work of Alfred O. Hirschman, is presented in this chapter.

### 4.1.1 THE FALLIBLE ORGANIZATION

That organizations do often perform badly, or fail outright, is in itself hardly news (Starbuck and Nystrom, 1986). Traditionally, however, such occurrences were treated somewhat moralistically as a penalty for organizational wrongdoing of some sort, a consequence of deviating from theory rather than a phenomenon that ought to be included in it[109].

The notion of fallibility as a property basic for organizations was introduced into organization theory by proponents of open-natural approaches[110]. William H. Starbuck and associates (1978:114) argued that crises do not indicate abnormality. Organizations that encounter crises are in no ways different from those organizations that do not. Bo L. T. Hedberg and associates found failures and problems to be inevitable "since an organization always misunderstands itself or its environment to some degree, processes inevitably spawn unanticipated effects" (Hedberg et al., 1976). Karl Weick (1979) took the issue still further, stating that "The image of organizations that we prefer is one which argues that organizations keep falling apart and that they require chronic rebuilding" (1979:44).

Hirschman's approach, discussed in this chapter, offers a particular perspective on the question of organizational failure. Organizations, as such, are taken for granted and as understandable in rational terms. Not questioning aims ("products") that organizations are called into being to meet nor even the rational assumption that they are in principle capable of delivering their intended product, Hirschman nonetheless found that organizations' most basic attribute is that of *fallibility*. Organizations are stumblingly rational, as it were, permanently hovering on the brink of decay. This claim is, in a spirit remindful of Weick's, coupled with an essentially optimistic view: decaying organizations *can* and *ought* to be straightened out. It is just that they cannot be straightened out once and for all. "Optimal mixes" and solutions are never true in more than a transient sense, that is, until the new and improved form finds its own modes of decay. Since decay is going on continuously, correction should also best be carried through a continuous flow of inputs.

### 4.1.2 MEMBER REPERTOIRES

Change of course and correction of errors presupposes an agent (or a combination of agent and monitor) to prompt and effect the desired change. Hirschman's (1970) most radical departure from conventional approaches occurs at this point. Setting a decaying organization right is generally assumed to be the task of its management[111]. In variance with this tradition, Hirschman proposed to search for regenerative inputs on "the organizational floor", be it constituted by clients or rank and file participants. This suggestion is of central importance to our discussion.

For a member of an organization, deterioration or deviance from the course normatively judged right would manifest itself as a decline in quality[112]. In responding to such an adverse change, he or she would exercise a monitor function. The dissatisfied member's response may take the form of either of the following two courses of action: *Exit*, whereby a member leaves the organization or a customer stops buying a company's products, and *voice*, or protest, formulating complaints and/or concrete demands for change and redress (Hirschman, 1970). The choice between responses is mediated by *loyalty* (ibid.) and *involvement* (Hirschman, 1982).

The four concepts in Hirschman's armamentarium will, after some modification, be used below, in constructing a basic typology of member inputs. If properly registered or amplified by an aggregation of numerous member's inputs, such responses constitute steering (corrective) inputs of prime importance. If we perceive an organization's history as being a continuous tale of deviations and corrections, generation of such inputs is also membership's most important role. Seen from the member's angle, we may perhaps venture stating that it is the occurrence of problems, coupled with the ability to straighten them out, that ultimately gives membership its meaning.

### 4.1.3 AGGREGATING MEMBERS

A discussion of members' repertoires should not abstract from the fact that such repertoires are bound to actual human beings. Variations in the use of potentially available modes of behaviour are inevitable and would manifest themselves as personal variation, or differences between groups. Reproduction of a body of members is clearly more than merely a question of numbers or names; discussing an organization in terms of what specific (different) members do opens a complementary, demographical perspective on the question of aggregation. Proficiency in, and inclination for, different modes of "organizational behaviour" on the members' repertoire may be differentially distributed through the organization, and the overall composition of the corpus of members, seen in those terms, may vary over time. Some organizations may attract and retain involved members, whereas others would drive them out. A critical attitude may be considered a merit in nomination and election for office in one organization, a liability in another. Beyond their obvious role as resocialization tools, such preferences may function, if consistent over time, as a set of selection mechanisms, yielding discrete demographical patterns (a phenomenon best known from studies of race and gender discrimination). The discussion of exit and its consequences in section 4.3.4 sets the scene for a tentative discussion of the problem of demographic structure (section 4.4). An examination of shifting demographical patterns, with a particular focus on the prevalence and the positioning within the organization of members employing the modes of involvement and protest, and such members' recruitment and retainment may provide an additional insight on processes of "degeneration" and "regeneration" dealt with in self-management research.

## 4.2 THE HIRSCHMANIAN FRAMEWORK: A BRIEF REVIEW

Hirschman's work introduces into the study of organizations a unique combination of three important elements: a view of organizations as inherently fallible and, therefore, in a constant need of monitoring; a qualitative criterion by which to evaluate performance; and, finally, a concept of corrective monitoring inputs, triggered by negative evaluations that originate at the bottom of the organization rather than at its top[113]. A basic repertoire of two modes of member input and of two mediating attitudes is provided: Exit and voice, loyalty and involvement (the latter added considerably later), respectively.

Both exit and voice are, if without these general labels, fairly well known phenomena. *Exit* is traditionally accepted as the dominant mode of expressing customer sentiments within economic theory. *Voice* has been traditionally assigned to the political arena. Hirschman's major innovation has been in pointing out that both voice and exit may be applicable in one and the same organization. The claim that both options belong to one repertoire raises a new question, namely, what guides a member's, or client's, choice to prefer one over the other.

Individual considerations of cost provide one part of the answer: exit will be preferred as long as it is the easier alternative. Voice, generally a more costly alternative, will be resorted to first *after* exit is excluded as inconceivable, impracticable, or ineffective. Thresholds to exit may then be posed by external constraints: technical, organizational, or demographical. But it is intuitively clear that constraints may also be internally lodged (Hirschman, 1970:98). *Loyalty*, a third concept suggested by Hirschman, is precisely that: an internalized threshold to exit, shifting preferences to voice in cases in which exit would have appeared the easier way to the external observer[114].

"Exit, voice and loyalty" (Hirschman, 1970), as the title implies, explores the field of possibilities these three concepts open. The repertoire assigned to the individual in this framework, however, appears too narrow. Given the high threshold of uncertainty as to both costs and outcomes built into the voice option (Wippler 1986), the original model offers no convincing explanation as to why would people ever act at all. After all "there is always an option of silent non-exit" (Barry, 1974:97). A lack of choice may as well have led to passivity and silent frustration instead for voice, especially if the organization can intimidate critical members (Birch, 1975). On the other hand, people sometimes *apparently want* to exercise voice (Barry, 1974), without any clearly identifiable calculation. As Howard Aldrich (1979:238) stated: "the issue cannot be treated solely in instrumental, individualistic terms. Voice appears to be a result of expressive or solidary-purposive incentives /. . /, rather than of individual calculations regarding costs and benefits.

These reservations led Hirschman (1982) to supplement his armamentarium with a fourth concept, namely, that of *involvement*[115]. When present, involvement would effect a complex transformation of costs to benefits. Activity, hereby voice, becomes in such a case more than merely an exchange of present costs for (uncertain) future benefits. It may as well be its own reward, here and now. This is a situation or mood the devout member, follower, or activist may experience. While keeping within the individualistic framework economic theory sets, the concept does not define away solidarity and social contexts. Instead, it centres on the way an individual subjectively perceives and acts upon such contexts.

The Hirschmanian perspective's chief contribution to our quest lies in supplying us with a conceptual framework capable of dealing with both members and organizations (Aldrich, 1979:232) and an action-oriented approach to the role of members in organizations. Important as these things are, they do not, as originally formulated by Hirschman, add up to a view that is directly applicable to self-managed organizations.

The chief difficulty lies in Hirschman's exclusive emphasis on negative input or feedback modes: exit and protest[116]. This emphasis gives necessarily rise to a one-sided organizational view. An organization is, if we follow this view, steered by its members or clients exclusively through rectification of mistakes and of deviations from a previously agreed-upon course, made explicit by a certain product label, a political program, and so on. But how would such a course be set? Still more important, by what standard should the membership decide that deviations or mistakes are being made? Indirectly, this omission also introduces a distinction between the steering and the steered: the latter should interfere only in cases of either clear incompetence or an attempted coup d'état by the leaders. Other than as watchdogs, the members are not really considered a *resource*. This makes direct application to our model of self-management problematic[117].

Hirschman tends to take "the organization" for granted. The problem simply may be that the organization taken for granted just happens to be a wrong one for our purposes. An adaptation of Hirschman's perspective to organizations in which members have a broader discretion in the role of "quality-makers" Hirschman assigns them (1970:99) will be attempted in the following sections.

## 4.3 EXTENDING THE FRAMEWORK

One basic feature underlying the Hirschmanian analysis is that Hirschman's "members" are outsiders to their own organization. The organization-client exchanges dealt with are sporadic, after-hours, intentional ones, be it occasions of buying a product, of applying to an authority, using a service, or participating in a demonstration. Only a narrow and highly directional segment of an individual's activities is involved.

In the case of the self-managed organization, the member's degree of inclusion in the organization (see Allport, 1962; Weick, 1979:96) is considerably higher than in the organizations Hirschman generally deals with[118]. This means that a considerably broader and less directional segment of a member's activities ought to be considered an input. In plain speech, dealing with a worker-owned enterprise, we may claim that nearly all a member does during working time, and perhaps a great deal of what he does after hours *is* in principle to be considered an input, as far as the organization is concerned[119].

It is clear that the resulting multitude of inputs cannot be uniformly classed as negative/corrective. A broadening of the range of inputs to include contributions as well would necessitate a corresponding extension of the original Hirschmanian categories:

a.  The prevailing majority of inputs consists primarily of upholding routines. Such inputs could, at least in normal times, be classed as "loyal", a category not quite developed by Hirschman (Laver, 1975:477)[120].

b.  Involvement appears, in Hirschman's writings as exclusively associated with protest actions[121]. That this is the case has more to do with Hirschman's observations being fetched primarily from American protest movements than with any theoretical or principal considerations. However transient protest movements and "alternative" organizations may have proven to be, they are, or were, organizations in their own right, and as such, they convincingly demonstrate that involvement cannot escape being a creative input, contributing to creation or constructive modification of structure rather than merely a corrective, negative one. An exclusive channeling of involvement to protest modes, in keeping with the Hirschmanian description, may instead be a specific feature of organizations in which positive paths of expression are non-existent or blocked.

c.  The same line of reasoning may be applied to the case of voice. It would be as easy to see voice, in keeping with the democratic tradition the concept is derived from, as a potential bearer of positive or constructive messages and innovative suggestions for improvement rather than merely a denouncement of present arrangements. The context of voice need not be exclusively conflictual one. In some situations "voice in the form of participation in the affairs of some collectivity is simply a part of the form of life /../ as a member of that community" (Barry, 1974:93)

Both voice and involvement, as presented in Hirschman's work, are innovative and creative inputs in the sense of transcending the organization's routine. Loading voice and involvement with both positive and negative signs may be justified but would cause a confusing duplication of concepts. To avoid this, we shall from this point on use voice or protest to denote negative/corrective inputs. Involvement, whose sign is not explicitly set in Hirschman's work, will be used in this work to denote positive inputs. Voice and involvement will be denoted here as negative-creative and positive-creative, respectively. A mapping that reshuffles, as it were, Hirschman's key concepts may then be suggested, as shown in figure 4.1.

### Figure 4.1  Exit, Voice, Loyalty and Involvement

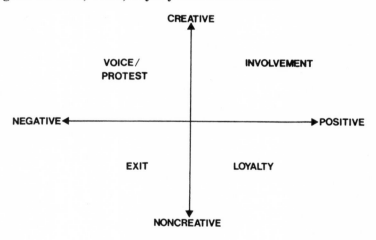

The locus of our analysis is situated *between* the individual and the system planes. We must, therefore, keep in mind that any classification of activities would have a dual meaning: regarding the individual, we may speak of *modes of behaviour* versus the organization; from an organizational angle, it would instead be possible to speak of *steering inputs*. The four main modes suggested above, some of the possible paths of transition between them, and, finally, the potential effect that the practice of these four modes would have on the organization are reviewed in the four subsections that follow[122].

### 4.3.1 LOYALTY

Loyal membership can be, in certain organizations, an utterly passive behaviour (for example, membership in a trade union in which membership dues are automatically withheld from wages. Loyalty is then expressed by a member by *abstention* from activity). For the SM member, nearly at the opposite end of the continuum, loyalty would at least presuppose a satisfactory carrying out of work functions under the workday.

It is important to distinguish in this context between loyalty and compliance. As noted by Hirschman (1970:83), only the potential feasibility of disloyality, there directly understood as exit, makes a concept of loyalty meaningful[123]. In other words, loyalty is the residual left after power has been subtracted from structure, a residual that is definitely less than the Barnardian "cooperative" consent (Barnard, 1938), but, nonetheless, far from negligible. Although loyalty's importance can legitimately be questioned in purely coercive organizations (see Etzioni, 1961; Giddens, 1984:157[124]), it rises directly with the degree of openness and voluntariness.

The fact that loyalty is, but for exceptional situations, a "non-happening" tends to obscure the vital importance of loyal behaviour to organizational reproduction. Rules and rule systems are reproduced by being repetitiously followed (Giddens, 1984), which is, after all, the essence of loyal behaviour[125]. Although the modes of behaviour that will be dealt with in the following sections are considerably more spectacular, it is important to keep in mind that other modes' import notwithstanding, it is loyalty that sets the stage on which these modes are acted out. Between phases of activity, it is also the state that involved activists, protesters, and, at times, even would-be leavers return to.

More often than not, loyalty would be unreflexive. We can state, somewhat paradoxically, that loyalty, at its best, consists of a deep-rooted reluctance to consider or conceptualize, let alone problematize, alternatives that, at the same time, are very tangibly within reach[126]. A preserving rather than innovative force, it can most closely be linked where decision-making and individual cognitive makeup are concerned, with the assumption of permanence, outlined in the previous chapter.

The loyal member need not be particularly motivated or, rather, not at all times. At the same time, loyalty alone is not enough to keep an organization going. Breaks in routine, unexpected crises, and exigencies usually require more than mere loyalty to be handled successfully. Conventionally, this is the point where the much eulogised qualities of "creative leadership" are brought on stage. Although it is clear that creative innovation is called upon on numerous occasions during the course of an organization's operation, there is no convincing ground to the claim that this resource is hierarchically distributed[127]. Once we start from the premise that creative inputs may originate anywhere in the organization, we discover a whole new category of behaviour, that would best fit under the Hirschmanian category of "involvement", discussed in the next section. The distinction between the modes of loyalty and involvement is not between passive and active but between *innovative* and *non-innovative* modes of behaviour, loyalty standing, in our case, for the degree to which routines are followed, actively or passively, of own volition; involvement for the readiness to transcend creatively such routines when the need arises.

### 4.3.2 INVOLVEMENT

Involvement, as seen by Hirschman, implies that initiative is taken by a member of the organization, in pursuing goals that would advance his organization or the organization's goals or remove obstacles that hamper it. Such action can, in a narrow and literal sense be considered "altruistic", inasmuch as no personal reward commensurate with the degree of effort has been set beforehand. This label is somewhat misleading; as pointed out by Hirschman, in an observation that makes immediate intuitive sense, involvement means precisely that activities, grounded in "a partisan, affective attachment", become intrinsically rewarding[128]. We advance here, as it were, one step beyond Kanter's definition of commitment[129]. A paraphrase of Hirschman's concept in Kanter's terms could be formed as follows: "Involvement thus refers to the willingness of people to do what will maintain the group because *the act of doing it* provides what they need"; the involved member does not invariably strive to maintain an organization just in order to have it supply his needs, as Mancur Olson would probably have it. He may as well be exerting himself on behalf of his organization, because he finds the *exertion itself*, for what he considers a worthy case, intrinsically rewarding.

Involvement is not uncritical enthusiasm, if only for the simple reason that no organization can sustain uncritical enthusiasm for too long. The functioning of any organization is well spiked with minor disappointments and breakdowns (see Stryjan, 1985a, 1986). These may either be coped with and overcome or, if left unattended, serve as a starting point for protest. "Because small irritants, like grains of sand in an eye or even in a shoe, may arouse discomfort out of all proportion to the source, they merit attention on strategic grounds as well" (Kaufman, 1973:69[130])

Involvement's most crucial input is precisely in resolving such difficulties, be it by direct action or through a monitor function. This implies, and nearly presupposes, that members exceed their formally defined positions and functions. Such a tendency has often been observed in worker cooperatives: "the job boundaries, while existent, are less rigid and more permeable when, in the opinion of the people actually involved in production, the situation demands it" (Greenberg, 1984:191).

Transcending job boundaries often involves two parts: the one butting in and the one(s) into whose domain of responsibility he ventures. It may have a friendly character of mutual help, of a sort that tends to dominate idealized descriptions of cooperation but need not do so (Paton, 1978). The following interview responses (Greenberg, 1986) afford a practical illustration of both aspects: "I see somebody needs help, whey you just go and help them.. I also tend to look around and make sure things are working right a little more than if I didn't have anything invested in the company" (p. 42). And, on the more conflict-oriented side: "If the people grading off the end of the dryer do not use reasonable prudence and they start mixing the grades too much, I get hold of somebody and say, now look [here follows some technical discussion of the problem], What the hell is goin' on here?" (p. 41)

Openness to a broad, non-routine range of demands presupposes and presumably also shapes a different style of work, and places on the workers a different set of requirements than routinized organization forms would. In other words, it requires "a capacity for being involved". Rothschild-Whitt found that alternative organizations require "multitalented individuals" (1979:514) and that the worker-ideal in such organizations is the "amateur-factotum" (1979:517) rather than the specialist. Not the least among these requirements is also tolerance for stress and conflict (Paton, 1978). Jackall and Levin stated: "In order to survive and flourish, cooperatives have to put a premium on certain kinds of workers — namely, those who can live with the ambiguity of structural tension, but who also can find creative ways of meeting contradictory demands" (1984a:11)

The demands that such requirements place are taxing and cannot be shouldered indefinitely. To some extent, the small daily triumphs that involved action may score serve to refuel a member's involvement. At the same time, it is the invariably more numerous small daily defeats, miscalculations, and pinpricks that eventually cause involvement to fade out. Involvement is thus a phase, often triggered into being by concrete, limited issues (Paton, 1978) rather than a steady expression for "personal traits" of one or other sort.

In the organizations Hirschman dealt with (1982): primarily informal, loosely knitted protest movements, fading out of involvement is about identical to fading out of membership. This would hardly be the case in a workplace, let alone a cooperatively owned one. Fading out, if such occurs, would rather be toward loyalty, that is, toward becoming an "ordinary" worker-member. As the quotation below dealing with environmental activists illustrates, this shift is, in principle, reversible: "Many of these activists retire after some years, back to the ranks of less active members, since the pressure of activism cannot be borne indefinitely /. . / By the movement's own definition, most of these are a reserve troop that will come forwards once the need arises" (Herskin, n.d.:91; translation mine).

A member may thus "retire" temporarily to return to active ranks later in his organizational career. In other words, the presence of loyalty makes phenomena known from other types of organizations as "burnout" *potentially* reversible in the long run. The mobility between the involved and the loyal camps may be a matter of an organization's structure and character, rather than merely of personal predispositions. Seen in this context, rotation can can be considered as an attempt to shape formal structure so as to approximate actual fluctuations in involvement[131]. Although it would be naive to expect elected officials to maintain their involvement all the time they are in office, one may at least assume that every recurring election may offer an occasion for mobilizing those just then involved into the governance of the organization, the more so on occasions when new posts are shaped in response to members' emergent needs and demands.

### 4.3.3 INVOLVEMENT AND PROTEST

Loyalty, involvement, and protest, though not possible transitions from one to the other, are presented in an interesting way in the following quotation, taken from kibbutz research: "A young factory operator: There are two sorts [of kibbutz members], the active and the passive. The active [member] is a rebel, and looks for new ways. He seeks for solutions and perceives problems. The passive [is] understanding and attentive, but somewhat too satisfied with the way things are. I myself am a bohemian, I hope that I can be counted in the rebel category" (Sørensen, 1970:103; translation mine).

Apart from the somewhat derogative description of loyalty, the quotation above illustrates an additional important point, that of the thin and fluid borderline between involvement and protest, both bundled here in a "rebel" category. In this fairly uncommon organizational context, innovative inputs are given a predominantly positive connotation. In other words, the lattitude and degree of legitimation given in this case to individual inputs is such that involvement would but rarely be forced into protest channels. It is easy to conceptualize organizations where such an ambiguity would instead be used to brand any uncalled for innovative input as "troublemaking".

Drawing a clear demarcation line between involvement and protest may then be a fairly complex matter, for theoretical as well as practical reasons:

a. The theoretical framework supplied by Hirschman seems most fragmentary just on this issue. Voice, including presumably both involvement and protest, and involvement were taken up in two separate works (1970 and 1982, respectively) and were moreover related to different types of organizations: formal and "informal" or alternative, respectively.

b. The vagueness may be an intended feature of the organizational settings and may reflect a dégree of internal dissent between different interest groups as to what is to be considered "constructive critique or intrapreneurship" or "mess-hall advocacy" and unruliness, respectively.

c. Unlike exit and loyalty, which may be directly deduced from observable behaviour, the issue here is of content and intent, self-assumed or imputed. We deal with a complex interplay of organizational context, cultural norm, personal intent, and, at times, with interests of an organizational elite.

The distinction between the two modes may then be fairly vague, and in many organizations intentionally so. The actual input would be classified by an interplay of organizational context and the actors' intentions at least to the same degree as by its information content. To the extent an objective distinction is at all possible, it would seem that involvement would tend to have organization-specific norms as its frame of reference, whereas protest generally departs from universal norms or an ideal model of the organization as it *ought* to be. The protester would generally be oblivious to the personal consequences of his or her stance. In an important sense the protester does not any longer take the organization, or his or her place in it, for granted. From an organization-bound perspective the protester's position would often appear unrealistic and impractical[132].

Such "impracticality", or praxis-uncoupling, could, in principle, be considered an organizational asset, both within decision-making processes and in extra-parliamentary contexts. The incidence of non-standard views within decision-making processes increases an organization's degree of variety (Robinson, 1981b) and thus responsivity to change and facilitates double-loop learning processes (see Argyris and Schön, 1978; Morgan, 1986:87ff). Major revaluations and changes of the organization's course presuppose a capacity for reframing and thus availability of innovative views (Hedberg, 1974). Where a serious structural strain exists, a single protest *may* have an "extra-parliamentary" impact, through a snowball effect (see Smelser, 1962) that triggers collective action: "The effect of voice of one person (who noticed the decline earlier than others) 'feeds back' into the system, causing dissatisfaction among the others" (Laver, 1976:465).

However, challenging the collective consensus, as represented by organization-specific norms, by the policies criticized, or even by self-complacency, that the protest is set to puncture may often prove risky, the more so as members tend to become personally bound up in the outcome of disagreements (Paton, 1978:49). Even when wholly justified (in terms of truth-value; it is important to realize that protesters can, at times, simply be wrong), the protest stance would all too often prove self-defeating. In a well integrated and consensus-based organization, protest's main effect would often be that of isolating the protester.

Is there "life after protest"? The chances are slim. "Bearers of bad news are rarely made welcome and are often fired" (Morgan, 1986:90). Given the way organizations are, it is seldom that protest would be given the chance to turn again into involvement. This is most likely in the rare cases that protest is wholeheartedly adopted either by the organization as a whole or by a considerable fraction within it and in those fairly exceptional organizations in which a broad legitimation for dissent exists. Elsewhere, the unwritten rule would require a protester to recant first. Individual choice would then stand between passive loyalty and exit. The alternative chosen would to a great degree depend on whether the member, in his protest, has passed a point of no return in his or in the collective's eyes (see Stryjan, 1985a). Whichever the choice, both the organization and the member are likely to emerge as losers

### 4.3.4 EXIT AND BEYOND

Exit is the disaffected member's ultimate response. It may be preceded by a stage of deliberations (Stryjan, 1985a; Hirschman, 1970), not once accompanied by bouts of activity[133]. Situations of implicit or explicit bargaining, in which a threat of exit is employed are also possible

(Hirschman, 1970). They lie, however, outside the domain of exit proper. Once leaving, the ex-member nearly *ex definitio* gives up ambitions of influencing his or her organization's future course, leaving, as it were the framework of our discussion. Nonetheless, exit itself remains an important steering input, generating some impact on fellow members, and, especially in smaller organizations, perhaps requiring a deal of accommodation and reorganization.

A discussion of the three other modes of behaviour could be put under a common heading of "the member and *his* organization". Where exit is concerned, this common denominator no longer exists. Exploration may then proceed along any of the two diverging paths: that of studying personal impact *or* organizational impact, respectively.

A brief study of the process leading to — and the personal aspects of exit — can be found in Stryjan, 1985. It is, however the organizational impacts and, eventually, ways of managing them that are of relevance to our discussion. The most immediate of these, is the impact a member's exit has on an organization's demographic composition. This direction of approach would eventually lead us toward a demographic perspective on the practice of loyalty, involvement, and protest.

A customer-based organization must, if aggregated exit signals gain strength, either regain its clientele, find a new one, or perish. Not unsimilarily, a public, openly traded corporation would normally respond to price fluctuations in the value of its stock, reflecting aggregate entry and exit flows, with an attempt to regain its present, past, and prospective shareholders' confidence. A member-based organization in the same situation would but seldom exert itself to regain "renegade" members. This unwillingness would often be accompanied by a tendency to deny that the quality of the organization has played any part in their exit decision (see Stryjan, 1985a), ascribing the blame for "defection" on the leaver alone. "Most of the blame has been usually put on the individual's inability to acclimate to the kibbutz environment. A member of Har indicates that those who leave are the weak /. . /: 'Those who wear out prematurely, throw up their arms and leave.. should be considered with pity and nothing more, for we cannot blame the weak'" (Rayman, 1981:139).

Rather than learning, the demographic shift that exit implies, would primarily trigger *unlearning* (Hedberg et al., 1976; Hedberg 1979). The organization would move in a direction opposite to that for which the departing member(s) strove. A second loop unlearning process may also be envisaged. If giving vent to his dissatisfaction *after* leaving (Aldrich, 1979:233; Birch, 1975), the exiting member may also affect the organization's recruiting base. The organization would not merely get rid of a proponent of a given view or mode of behaviour. It may also , for better or worse, reduce the possibility of his or her likes ever again applying for membership in the future.

Unlearning in itself is not an undividedly negative phenomenon. As pointed out by Starbuck and associates (1978) and Hedberg (1979), unlearning is a potentially vital ingredient of organizational development. But precisely as in the case of learning, the pertinent question in this case would be: is the organization unlearning the right things? When unlearning is precipitated by exit, the question can also be rephrased into less abstract terms, namely,: are the members that leave the organization the right ones? This question, coupling member attributes to physical persons, introduces a new dimension into the discussion, namely, that of organizational demography.

## 4.4 ORGANIZATIONAL DEMOGRAPHY: A TENTATIVE OUTLINE

Assuming an organization whose members are not wholly substitutable for each other and that is affected by its members' actions, the issue of these members' properties and attitudes is not devoid of interest. Specifically, the way that qualities are distributed across the population and the way that this distribution varies over time, that is, questions of *organizational demography* (Pfeffer, 1982) would have an impact on an organization's performance and its reproduction. Tying together the twin questions of what do members do (repertoire) and who the members are opens a limited perspective on the last aspect of reproduction, namely, that of reproducing a corpus of members.

An organization's demographic composition is a composite product of two flows, namely, recruitment and initial retainment on one hand and exit on the other hand (Robinson, 1981a). An organization's demographic *structure*, in the sense of how individuals or groups bearing certain characteristics are positioned vis à vis each other within the organization, is a more complex product of the incoming and outgoing flows' interplay with internal dynamics.

Descriptions of demographic processes in the literature on self-management are rare and fairly fragmentary. Mike Robinson (1981), in his simulation model for self-managed organizations, provided some interesting insights into the mechanics of growth and exit. Keith Bradley and Alan Gelb (1982a) reviewed demographic factors underlying the success of the Mondragon group. Raymond Russell's (1984b) is perhaps the only work providing an explicit description of a demographical change process in a cooperative organization. The scarcity of research is probably due to the topic's extreme complexity, caused by the labyrinthine causality chains and the long time horizons involved. In this sense, demographic structure may offer the purest examples of unintended consequences of action (see Giddens, 1984) within the study of organizations. It is, indeed "a result of human action, and not of human design", as will be illustrated by the relatively simple example below[134]:

> Kibbutz B's expansion of the apple orchard branch coincided with the absorption of a large French group. Consequently, the branch came to be manned by French immigrants, then in their early 30s. With time, the majority of Frenchmen left the kibbutz. For a variety of reasons (not the least among them, the failure in absorbing the "pilot" group), and the repercussions this has had both in the kibbutz and in the French movement, no further French groups were ever absorbed. The orchard remained, for some 15 years hence, a distinctive, progressively aging francophonic isle in the population.

This example, trivial in itself, illustrates some of the major forces operating in shaping a demographical structure:

a. Organizational development, partly facilitated by external opportunities and constraints, shapes *vacancies* to be filled by available members.
b. This coincides with a *recruitment drive* focused on a definite *target population*/recruiting base.
c. Recruitment fails to lead to retention. Most group members choose exit.
d. The *recruiting base* is changed.

All of these processes and decisions combined have yielded one insignificant fleck on the organization's demographical chart, in a way not unlike that whereby flotsam is deposed on a shore. It is easy to see that the diversity of thinkable interferences and of the alternative combinations that their operation could have produced is enormous. Only a small fraction of them can be explored below and merely in a schematic fashion. As mentioned above, the major flows shaping the organization's demography are exit and recruitment. The stress here is primarily laid on exit, since it is to a higher degree traceable to mechanisms that are internal to the organization. Recruitment, occurring at the interface between the organization and its environment, is guided by yet more complicated dynamics[135]. Given the diversity of environments and organizations, the results would also be highly idiosyncratic. Issues of growth and recruitment are presented, mostly in section 4.8, in a highly schematic manner, largely abstracting from environmental constraints and dependencies, which lay beyond what our framework at his point can handle.

## 4.5 EXIT AND THE QUESTION OF SELECTIVITY

The impact of a member's exit on a small, closely knit organization's composition is self-evident. In bigger organizations, and once the discussion is carried in terms of member categories, rather of than individuals, one of two models may apply:

a. Occurrence of exit is distributed randomly over the organization. In such a case (and assuming a possibility of equivalent replacement through recruitment), the demographic composition remains unaffected.

b. Some groups are more exit prone than others. Exit would, in such a case, be selective. This situation is examined below.

In our discussion thus far, the member was presented as an independent, normatively motivated agent and his or her deliberation between staying and leaving as a normative problem[136]. It is clear that additional restraints and considerations exist. Material or personal thresholds may impose a prohibitive transfer cost on exit (Laver, 1975:479); the organization's boundaries may prove impossible to cross[137]. A member may, in other words, **will** to choose exit but may be unable to put this choice into practice. The member may even avoid the option of protest, if perceived as inescapably leading to exit or as leading to exposure to repressive measures in the absence of viable exit options (see Birch, 1975). The actual outcomes would to a high degree be dictated by the way an organization's boundaries are set and managed and depend on opportunities available for leavers on "the other side" and on the alternatives to exit offered within the organizational setting[138]. That these thresholds operate differentially on different parts of an organizational population means, in plain speech, that some people are a priori in a position to quit a given organization, and others are considerably less so or not at all. This distinction can be drawn regardless of whether the people in question ever explicitly considered leaving or not. It should accordingly be possible to outline a demography of exit.

The population groups shown to be exit prone are not necessarily doomed to disappearance but attrition, operating in principle on all groups, may, if left uncountered, be quicker and more thorough in such groups than in the remaining population. Although the characteristics of "risk groups" may vary from one organization to another, one characteristic is nearly self-evident: when members are in some way *materially* dependent on their organization, as is the case in self-managed enterprises and communes, but also in any ordinary workplace, young and single members will be more exit prone than others (Price, 1977; Bluedorn, 1982:84). The same would apply to members with highly marketable skills. We would also expect higher propensity for risk taking and higher tolerance for uncertainty, which are both involved in an exit decision, from young and motivated members[139]. Following Hirschman's initial line of reasoning (1970:vi), we may also expect attrition in the group where quality consciousness and exit proneness coincide. Thus, "In 'a sequence of population transforming operations' (Garfinkel, 1967:236), only one category would be subject to attrition. Ironically, the category affected is precisely the one both normatively and functionally considered a sine qua non of a decisional community: the involved, ideologically bent young member" (Stryjan 1985a).

An essentially similar model of an unlearning and negative selection process, though applied to organizations with a somewhat different normative content, was suggested by Aaron Wildavsky[140]: "As the true believers depart, personnel who are least motivated by the evaluative ethic will move into higher position. Revitalization of the organization via the promotion and recruitment of professing evaluators will become impossible" (1972:516).

The process of reproduction can easily be turned, in such a case, into a one of essentially dysfunctional selection. A possible scenario for such a development will be presented in the next section.

### 4.6 DEGENERATION RECONSIDERED

Degeneration has been treated in this work primarily as a manifestation of a failure of reproduction. This section deals with a complementary perspective, namely, that of degeneration as a failure in input management, primarily where handling involvement is concerned, and this failure's eventual demographic effects.

A tendency evident in a great deal of organization research is to equate between officeholding and involvement. Life would be simpler indeed if we could assume that those who really feel involvement for the organization's fates would, given reasonable endowment of talent, also be the ones in positions of authority. Conventional research can resolve the issue by fiat, by assuming "leadership qualities" in those who lead. Conventional administrative praxis resolves it, instead, by banning involvement by those who do not. The actual issues for the democratic organization should instead have been those of facilitating and using non-incumbents' involvement and of co-phasing involvement and incumbency. However clear in principle, this path is hardly a simple one to follow.

Involvement is, obviously, an enormous source of energy, but at the same time it gives rise to a considerable steering and coordination problem. Too high levels of involvement are likely to cause overload and incapacitate the organization rather than envigorate it. An additional feature of involvement that complicates its integration into large, bureaucratized and/or universalistic organizations is its unpredictable and unstable character. Involvement is a cyclical or sporadic phenomenon rather than a constant quality that could occupy a neat space in an organizational chart. Finally, when the organization is clearly split between different fractions or interest groups, involvement at one quarter will invariably be perceived as threat from other quarters.

Ideally, one would expect that these problems would stimulate the development of effective ways of managing and responding to involvement. The traditional tendency would often be that of restricting it instead, sacrificing effectivity for expediency's sake. Large, formally democratic organizations would often tend to impose limits on legitimate involvement. The democratic principle of "one person, one vote" is reinterpreted so as to mark not a mere baseline for participation but its ceiling as well (Hirschman, 1970, Pateman, 1970).

What is initially accepted as an organizational expedience can easily become an institutionalized organizational canon[141]. Involvement implicitly becomes a leadership prerogative and is frowned upon if originating "lower down", all in the name of expediency (see Abrahamsson, 1986). R. Wippler, in his model of an oligarchization process, argued that such a state of affairs would be self-reinforcing: "If it is assumed that organizational members acquire organizational skills by carrying voice into effect (because voice requires the gathering and processing of information about organizational policies, opportunities etc.), then the outcome /. . / leads to new alterations /. . /, namely, an increase of the difference in the average cognitive and social skills of members, and the same average of leaders" (1986:7).

It has to be kept in mind, when considering such a development, that free exercise of involvement would require a degree of decentralization of control over the organization's agenda. However, the right to decide which issues are important, and what problems are worth the trouble to solve, is to a large extent an issue of power distribution[142]. At the same time: "The short-run interest of management in organizations is to increase its own freedom of movement; management will therefore try to strip the members- customers of the weapons which they can wield /../, and to convert, as it were, what should be a feedback into a safety valve" (Hirschman, 1970:124)[143].

With time, and in the absence of appropriate checks, the distinction between an organization's smooth functioning and its leaders' convenience would get increasingly blurred. Silently staying on thus gradually becomes the standard against which authorities judge responses by discontented members (Aldrich, 1979:235).

When no innovative ideas coming from the bottom are welcome, *any* such idea is per definitio negative. A member would generally be aware of the predominant norm. His or her intentions would to a great degree be shaped by the options and channels that are available. Stepping forward under such circumstances, a member would usually know beforehand that he or she risks sanctions and censure. One uncalculated effect of policies designed to curb involvement maybe that involvement, to the extent it is not altogether thwarted, will be diverted into channels of protest/voice. When tolerance for protest is low, as generally would be the case for organizations that do not tolerate involvement, involved members are likely to be led to exit.

Degeneration can thus be seen as a combined product of two processes; the one, a gradual restriction and, eventually, elimination of all steering inputs, save for loyalty; a restriction commonly legitimated by reasons of expedience; and the other, a successive deterioration in the quality of membership, through selective exit of involved members.

Organizations thus tend to curb involvement, often inadverently channeling it to protest forms instead. But they also put a high price on protest and immunize themselves against protest's eventual impact, thus blocking the way for eventual regenerative change. The only safe option left open is loyalty. The result, in terms of permissible inputs, is mapped in figure 4.2[144].

**Figure 4.2  The Disciplined Organization**

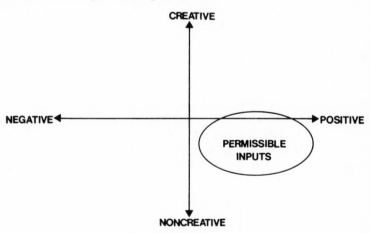

Those still unsatisfied may then freely choose between resignation and burnout. Their choice would be guided partly by degree of motivation and "quality consciousness" (Hirschman, 1970:140ff) but to a significant extent also by demographical factors. When, as outlined before, this leads to a weeding out of the youngest and most involved, we may conclude that an organization pursuing this course disposes with its human capital in order to maintain smooth operation or merely to keep its leadership cosy.

### 4.7 DEGENERATION AND REGENERATION

Degeneration was described in the previous section as a process whereby a change in organizational practices interlocks in a mutually reinforcing circle with a change in the organization's demography. The description of the process' ætiology above, suggests that its onset is caused by mismanagement of involvement. Such a development, though not uncommon, is by no way deterministic. Furthermore, even when set in, the process may yet be checked or outright reversed by steering inputs from below. A reversal of the sort may be possible at least as long as potential channels to convey such inputs have not been obliterated; that is, in the case of self-managed organizations, as long as a formal democratic structure still exists, however atrophied.

When the depletion of human resources has not proceeded too far or has been offset by a demographical change (see below and Stryjan, 1983b:268), the structural strain that diffuse dissatisfaction generates, may under the right circumstances, evolve into collective action (see Smelser, 1962). As one of Helge Tezschner (1981) respondents has stated, in an account of a "members' mutiny" in a worker cooperative, neatly tying up the issues of exit, demography, and collective protest: "that what we rebelled against was [first and foremost] that it felt like it was the right folk that left, and the wrong ones that were kept. We simply felt it did not go the way it should" (1981:14).

Cooperative forms and traditions may if sufficiently strong, constitute a mould that can channel such action and a set of qualitative criteria to formulate alternatives by[145]: "The rhetoric and the formal cooperative structure of the enterprise indicate the direction for change" (Batstone, 1983:151). Provided that new members can be recruited into the cooperative and that at least a portion of the veterans would become involved, an apparently degenerative process would be turned into a cyclical, regenerative one.

Eric Batstone's analysis of a survey population of French worker cooperatives provides an interesting illustration of such a process. Batstone found that the percentage of members in the cooperatives' workforce plotted against the cooperatives' age follows a U-shaped path; with increasing organization age, the percentage of members in the workforce first drops and then rises again. Derek Jones and Saul Estrin (1987) confirm these findings and, using a panel sample, preclude cohort effects (i.e., the pattern cannot be accounted for by new cooperatives being in some way different from the old ones). This pattern of membership is also shown to correlate with the degree of prominence of other cooperative traits such as democratic forms of governance and a particular financing behaviour, although no causal mechanisms can be established from the survey material.

The explanation that Batstone offered is a "life-cycle" model. This model takes on flesh once we realize that the mechanism underlying the "democratic revival" described for the cooperatives in question may have been generated primarily by a generation shift. With the founder generation away, a structural strain develops: "The gap between formal structure of the co-operative and actual experience may grow deeper and, without the charisma of the founders, becomes increasingly more difficult to justify" (Batstone, 1983:151). This provides the preconditions for a member revolt of the sort described by Tetzschner. An interesting and fairly unique feature in the French case is the role of non-member employees in the process. Employees in French producer cooperatives have a statutory right to apply for membership and, since membership per se does not entail direct material benefits, would refrain from using it, as long as membership is not perceived meaningful[146]. Such cooperative employees, which declined to join during a degenerative phase, can be considered a "reserve army" of prospective members that *may* step in once membership acquires a meaning. A democratic revival, which in the described cases seems to have been effected by activation of trade-union channels, can start a self-stoking process, whereby an influx of members would improve the quality of organizational democracy, and this improvement would motivate additional workers to join.

Inflows of new members, an issue that has not previously been dealt with in this work, play a central role in the regenerative processes described in this section. A limited review of the issues of recruitment and growth is presented below.

### 4.8 PATTERNS OF GROWTH AND RECRUITMENT: AN OUTLINE

An organization's growth rate, be it positive, negative, or null, is an important factor in determining organizational demography (Pfeffer, 1982), with differential rates contributing to differential demographic structures. The case is most obvious when dealing with rapid growth: a simple arithmetic computation (ibid.) can show that, in an organization growing at a rate of 20 percent a year, the founders would find themselves in minority within four years, even if none of the original group leaves. For organizations striving to maintain and reproduce a distinct set of values and orientations and a high network density, high rates of growth would be highly disruptive (Wippler, 1986). As a matter of common sense, "the more newcomers, the greater the effort that must be devoted to the socialization of newcomers" (Bluedorn, 1982; see also Price, 1977). Given the rather complex content of resocialization in SM organizations, too rapid growth is likely to lead to a breakdown of reproduction mechanisms. Oligarchization and introduction of authoritarian control in rapidly growing organizations and movements, may be interpreted in this context as a response, no matter how counterproductive, of the founders to such a breakdown threat.

Sustained moderate growth tends to create a continuous, even distribution of tenure within the organization (Pfeffer, 1982), although a large and stable founder group may skew the distribution upwards. However, having no control over its environment, as regards economic opportunities or flows of aspirants, such an objective can seldom be kept. A succession of leaps and bounds in growth may produce discontinuities and bumps in the distribution and thus a segmentation of the corpus of members into distinct cohorts, a situation that may easily lead to conflict (see section 3.5.2). To compound the picture's complexity, members joining at different times may be coming from fairly different backgrounds. Founders of the French Communities of Labour (Meister, 1984) were recruited from amongst resistance veterans. This background could hardly be shared by any members recruited later than the 1950s. Organizations that encounter mounting difficulties in finding suitable members may be easily tempted to stop recruiting altogether.

Zero or negative growth may be caused by economical straits, overdriven caution, recruitment difficulties, proliferation of exit, or any combination of the above. It would produce (except for the rare cases in which it is the founder group that leaves) a progressively aging group that will find it increasingly hard to fill vacancies in its ranks. As one of the respondents in Tetzschner's study described the period before his cooperative's "1977 revolution": "It was hard to start here, there were all the old ones, everybody was old. It felt like no new ones were wanted. They'd stare one down, like, and check on whatever you did" (1981:34-35).

A generation gap between the dominant member group and the prospective entrants would make retention difficult. The resulting pattern would be of a stagnating nucleus and rapid turnover at the periphery. Since recruiting a member is in many respects more expensive than taking on an employee, such repeated failures in recruitment may lead to an increasing reliance on non-member employees[147].

Such processes of demographical deterioration are not irreversible. Whether their outcome would reflect Michel's "Iron Law of Oligarchy", or Alvin Gouldner's (1961) "iron rule of democracy" is predominantly a question of timing or, more specifically, as suggested in the previous section, of whether a group of younger members can crystallize before the stagnating veteran group runs the organization down or finds itself forced to sell it[148]. A demographical turnaround in such cases would at times bear coup-like characteristics (see section 4.6). However, such sharp and risky demographic fluctuations, as described above and in sections 4.5 — 4.6, mark boundary states, or even pathologies, rather than describe normal reproduction processes.

A more typical pattern of growth for self-managed organizations would open with a fairly turbulent formation stage, followed by stabilization. Growth, henceforth, would be slow and cautious. Such a policy would, to some degree, be caused by external constraints such as institutional or legal hinders for expansion of membership (Berman 1982:84), economic limitations, and recruitment problems. To as great an extent, however, prudence would be a natural corollary of the fact that adding a member implies a more serious obligation than would taking on one more employee (Jackall and Levin, 1984a; Fletcher, 1976:183 – 184).

Recruitment would often proceed through personal affilliation and friendship networks (Meister, 1984; Rothschild-Whitt, 1979:514). Paradoxically, such a mode of recruitment, though slow and prudent, would hardly be controllable. In other words, an organization would be at least as prone to recruit new members when appropriate candidates materialize or good friends cannot be turned down, as in a response to economic imperatives, the way an economic model would presuppose. The resulting picture may then be of continuous adjustments of organizational structure or production profile to demographic changes and opportunities, rather than the other way round (see section 5.4.1).

The last proposition is less preposterous than it may seem to the economically minded. Organizational adjustments to workforce characteristics are, in fact, a self-evident practice in small firms. Adjustments to personal characteristics of management is also known to occur (see Geeraerts, 1984, for the case of family business). Procedures of internal recruitment, common in clan-like organizations (see Wilkins and Ouchi, 1983) can also be seen as a way of decoupling organizational or market demands from recruitment policies. The questions such organizational behaviour raises centre around the degree of freedom organizations would enjoy and their strategies of reconciling environmental demands with internal ones, issues that are discussed in the following two chapters.

## 4.9 SUMMARY

The aim of this chapter was to extend the simplified model, outlined in chapter 3, and to apply it to a somewhat more realistic set of conditions. Two of the simplifying assumptions employed in chapter 3 were relaxed to some degree:

1. The (implicit) assumption of organizational infallibility was replaced with a notion of built in fallibility.

2. Membership is no longer held constant. Both outflows (exit) and inflows (recruitment) are considered and incorporated in the model.

In this chapter, decisions are no longer seen as guaranteeing implementation; implementation no longer guarantees success. The proliferation of defects means, metaphorically, that the member, as seen in this chapter, shifts countenance and role. Instead of seated behind the wheel, the member is now portrayed, in a manner inspired by the work of A. O. Hirschman, with a tool kit laying under the vehicle.

The member's tool kit of modes to relate and respond to his organization, together with a rough sketch of their potential contribution to and eventual negative effects on the organization is outlined in table 4.1.

**Table 4.1  Members' Inputs and Their Organizational Consequences**

| input | effect/contribution | problems |
|-------|---------------------|----------|
| Loyalty | ensuring baseline performance | passivity, oligarchic tendencies |
| Involvement | problem-solving, mobilization, learning | Overload, chaos |
| Protest | Double loop learning warning signal | overload and/or increased exit |
| Exit | Warning signal, org. unlearning | attrition, negative selection |

All four modes are, in principle available, though not necessarily held in high esteem in any but the most repressive organizations. The actual propensity to employ any of them would, however, be a product of a complex interplay between demographic characteristics, ideological premises, and elements of organizational structure. Structure can, to a great degree, determine the payoff matrix in terms of cost and outcome expectancies (see Wippler, 1986). Different organizational structures thus may give rise to differing paths of organizational change, affecting the probability of different modes of input being chosen by members. However, the constraints they pose are real only in a probabilistic, not in an absolute sense (Giddens, 1978, 1984). They may be transcended, modified, or replaced by agent-members, acting to change their organization.

The organization of the extended model both loses members and recruits new ones. This calls attention to the quality of members being added or lost, and to the way different combinations of selective flow processes may affect an organization's composition and the positioning of different categories of members versus each other within the organization. The assumption of stability of membership was, however, only relaxed rather than removed. The focus of the discussion in this chapter has primarily been on exit and its consequences and on internal reshufflings of the composition of the member group it would entail. The issue of entry is touched upon relatively briefly, in sections 4.6 and 4.7, and the organization is generally assumed to be able to recruit and select all the replacements it may require.

Even under such a simplifying assumption, an organization's attempt to reproduce its corpus of members, which is what the balancing of entry and exit amounts to, seems a fairly complex affair. It involves reconciliation of conflicting demands, of maintaining a stable rate of recruitment and long-range perspectives in an often unstable economic environment, of recruiting members for compatibility (Guion, 1981), as social considerations would suggest, or for competence, as rules of economic conduct would. These questions introduce an additional dimension that has been left outside our framework thus far, namely, the relationship between the deviant organization and its environment.

With the completion of this chapter, the discussion crosses the organization boundaries, as it were, to occupy itself with the organization's relationship with its environment. The model we have now, is considerably less idealized than the first sketch was. Even in this form it is only a simplification of reality, not its simulation. The organization-environment relationship would, for reasons of expediency, be discussed in terms of organizations' rather than members' actions and strategies. It is important to keep in mind that these formulations would be used as a shorthand notation of the complex processes of decision-making, monitoring, and correction that were outlined in this and the previous chapter.

# 5

# INTRODUCING THE ENVIRONMENT

## 5.1 INTRODUCTION

A process of organizational reproduction necessarily evolves within the context of a given environment. The discussion of the reproduction model thus far has largely abstracted from this fact, focusing exclusively on issues of organization and *internal* dynamics. Environmental contexts were only referred to in passing as sources of disturbance and change. A perspective that integrates such seemingly random disturbances into a broader view of the organization-environment relationship is introduced in this chapter and developed further in chapter 6. The first part of the discussion, presented in this chapter, deals with one limited aspect of the organization-environment interaction, namely, with procurement and processing of resources.

Organizations are not self-sufficient. This means that an organization would be maintaining a constant exchange with the environment, exploiting, bartering, or competing for environmental resources (Pfeffer and Salancik, 1978) and utilizing thus won resources in a continuous construction and replenishment of itself. Most of this chapter is devoted to a description of such a quest for resources. The somewhat arbitrary division of resource categories employed here as a presentation aid roughly approximates Wilkins' and Ouchi's (1983; see also section 5.3) and includes[149]:

    a. Recruitment of new members

    b. Material resources (capital, capital equipment, access to markets)

    c. Professional competence and skills.

For simplicity's sake, the different resource categories are dealt with separately, as if an organization were dealing with only one resource at a time. Some insight into the complexity of trade-offs involved in real-life situations of simultaneously securing multiple resources and of coping with isomorphic pressures under organizational change in a changing environment is provided in section 5.7 and illustrated by the case of industrialization of the kibbutz movements.

Dependence on environmental resources is, presumably, general to all organizations. The self-managed organization's specific resource requirements, as well as its way of meeting such dependences may, however, differ substantially from those of conventional organizations. The quality requirements such an organization would set on required resources would often be non-standard. Being different, its needs would be different from those that society at large is geared to supply (see section 5.2). For instance, it would require would-be members to come equipped with a set of orientations that are uncommon or even deviant in the society at large, and would seek technologies that are compatible with its deviant mode of organization. Those requirements are determined by the demands that the organization's reproduction sets.

Resources that satisfy these quality requirements may be hard to obtain, and their supply is prone to be erratic. Consequently, a considerable portion of the organization's effort will be directed to ensuring itself against uncertainties of supply of suitable resources and, if those resources cannot be had, to digesting less suitable replacements or localizing their disruptive effect on the organization. The organization described in this chapter leads a sort of "hunting and gathering" existence (Stryjan, 1989), its major tools being knowledge of the environment and internal accommodation.

Organizations can also try to resolve their resource problems through modification of the environment, a notion that is developed in chapter 6. The focus of this chapter, however, is on the way environmental challenges are met through internal accommodation. Not willing, for the time being, to complicate the issue with a discussion of SM organizations' offensive involvement in the environment, the view of the environment presented in this chapter is somewhat simplified. The environment, as seen here, is treated as *given* and as inaccessible to purposeful modification (from the SM organization's side). Although incompatible with the SM organization, it is merely passively inhospitable rather than intentiously hostile. In an important sense our organization is seen as living off, not in the environment. These last simplifying assumptions are lifted in the discussion of coping, in chapter 6, that presents a model of an active organization coping with a hostile environment.

## 5.2 THE ENVIRONMENT AS A PROBLEM

When discussing an organization's quest for resources in the environment, it is useful to keep in mind that resources are not objective, physical phenomena: "their 'materiality' does not affect the fact that such phenomena become resources /.. / only when incorporated within processes of structuration" (Giddens, 1984:33).

An organization's environment consists, predominantly, of other organizations (Meyer and Rowan, 1977). These organizations would be conforming to norms of organizational and economic conduct that the self-managed organization deviates from. Obtainable resources would be processed, coded, and shaped by other organizations and, generally, shaped on these other organizations' premises to suit their quality requirements[150]. They would, in an important sense, be "system-bearing": "One of the main propositions of structuration theory is that the rules and resources drawn upon in the production and reproduction of social action are, at the same time the means of system reproduction" (ibid.:19).

A thinkable provisional definition of a deviant organization in this context might be "an organization that reproduces some elements that do not fit in the process of societal reproduction". Dealing with the key resource in our discussion here, namely, that of membership, we may, following Sven-Erik Sjöstrand (1985), present the situation as shown in figure 5.1[151].

**Figure 5.1  Organizations, Members and Environments**

|    |                               |                |                                           |
|----|-------------------------------|----------------|-------------------------------------------|
| A) | Organizations  Environments   | shape/reproduce | Organizations  Environments  Individuals* |
| B) | Individuals                   | shape/reproduce | Organizations                             |

* Actual or potential organization members.

The self-managed organization would, in other words, be reproducing a membership equipped with a set of orientations and trained in organizational repertoires that differ substantially from those the environment at large produces and reproduces as a lead (and carrier) in its own reproduction. Conversely, orientations and repertoires that are reproduced outside the organization's boundaries may not be smoothly absorbable by it. The same would apply to externally generated professional knowledge, routines, and equipment, all designed with conventional users in mind. A constant influx of such incompatible elements and building blocks may partly account for the proliferation of problems, shortcomings, and mistakes that the organization's members (as described in chapter 4) are called upon to handle.

A tendency to revert to more conventional practices, that is, to become *isomorphic* with their environment, has often been observed by students of deviant organizations. Rosabeth Moss Kanter explained this tendency by the pressure to adapt the organization's form to the resources and the sources of supply that are available.

> social systems that attempt to conduct relations with one another, should generally share language, symbols and media of exchange, which isomorphism implies. /. . / labour and experts imported from the outside are more easily deployable in organizations that are isomorphic in respect to the environment /. . /; roles in such a system are familiar and can be adopted by new members with less elaborate preparation /. . /. Similarly, resources and information can be imported without having to transmute them. (Kanter, 1972:153).

The twin concerns of an organization with non-standard requirements would be those of securing the "right" resources and of digesting the "wrong" ones, inserted into the organization either of necessity or as a result of oversight. Both involve exposure to isomorphic pressures. Such pressures can, in various ways be coped with and accommodated to. Roughly, we could distinguish between *internal* accommodation, taking the environment for granted, and offensive action, aimed to modify the environment. This chapter predominantly deals with the first of the two, the ways such pressures are met through internal accommodation. Seen from this angle, concerns with the compatibility of resources can be defined in terms of *quality*.

## 5.3 DEALING WITH RESOURCE DEPENDENCIES

Access to, and the ability to use the environment's resources were identified early in the history of self-management research as crucial problems of self-managed organizations. Beatrice Webb's analysis (1891) names among the reasons for producer cooperatives' failures the deficiencies in access to capital, markets, and organizational competence. Henk Thomas and Chris Logan (1982) marked the importance of trade skills. Branko Horvat (1974), focuses on difficulties of access to capital and managerial competence. He also noted that self-managed organizations tend, as they age, to experience recruitment problems[152]. Daniel Katz and Naftali Golomb, in their model of the kibbutz (1974/1975), were the first to introduce explicitly an additional element, that of attracting and retaining new members. Dealing with a related problem, that of preconditions for the establishment of clan-like organizational cultures, A. L. Wilkins and W. G. Ouchi (1983) identified three crucial categories of resources; (a) supply of capital, (b) technological competence, and (c) suitable members. In the initial, most vulnerable stage, the clan-organization would require a head start or some other means of buffering environmental turbulence in these three areas. Once established, it would, presumably, be required to see to a continued supply of these resources on its own.

Not all resources that are accessible in the environment would be compatible with the deviant organization's needs. This is self-evident where the search for appropriate "member material" is concerned. Questions of technology that is adapted to non-standard forms of work organization or of professionals capable of functioning in unconventional work settings, can prove as crucial. Such concerns with the compatibility of resources can be seen in terms of *quality*.

Quality requirements indirectly influence the reliability of supply. The problems encountered by organizations with non-staple resource requirements resemble the maintenance problems encountered by an owner of a rare car. Resources of a particular quality sought by self-managed organizations may be scarce and their supply erratic and uncertain not because of high demand but, as a result of demand being too feeble to support any steady supply. This is an anomalous situation that self-managed organizations would share with other deviant organization types. One of its most important implications is that a deviant organization, by setting its quality standards, indirectly determines the degree of turbulence to which it would be exposing itself. The more exacting the standards, the more erratic the supply of resources that pass the requirement test is likely to be.

Variation in supply and quality of available inputs would be a major source of environmental instability to be dealt with[153]. James D. Thompson (1967) noted that organizations generally strive to protect their organizational core from environmental uncertainty[154]. To this end, they avail themselves of *buffering techniques*, aimed at either limiting instability, or to minimizing its impact on the organization. A comprehensive list of such techniques is provided by W. R. Scott (1981). The following techniques would be most readily applicable for self-managed organizations:

1.  *Coding*: classification and preprocessing of inputs to ensure predictable and, preferably, even quality. Resources processed and shaped in the environment would often require a great deal of preprocessing and adaptation before they could be accommodated by a deviant organization. *Substitution*, inasmuch as it would require a great deal of preprocessing of the substitute resources, could be considered a particular case of coding.

2. *Stockpiling*: "organizations are likely to stockpile critical resources, resources whose supply is uncertain, or resources whose prices fluctuate greatly over time" (Scott:191). Internal generation of resources, a technique not mentioned by Scott, may be considered as a special case of stockpiling.

3. *leveling*: strategies reaching into the environment aimed at establishing some influence over actual or potential suppliers. Some implications of such strategies clearly exceed the scope of buffering techniques and should be considered as environment-shaping practices (see chapter 6).

Useful as these techniques may be, their application is certain to entail some problems. Most obviously, neither of them is cost or error free. Coding consumes resources and is always imperfect (Scott, 1981:191). The costs of stockpiling, be it in terms of storage space, interest, or wages, are self-evident, and besides, a great deal of resources, not the least, human ones, would deteriorate in long storage. Leveling may involve investments in goodwill and extensive transactions with the environment and thus increase exposure to isomorphic pressures.

Concrete ways of dealing with particular pressures that resource procurement and processing involve would vary from organization to organization, and from one situation to another. Optimizing in this quest for resources involves trade-offs, for instance, between alternatives that require bowing to external pressures and alternatives that provide resources that are cheap to obtain but are expensive, and potentially problematic to process. An organization may, for example, have to choose between cheap production equipment that presupposes, for its efficient operation, a work division of a sort that its members would not want to accept (Stryjan, 1983b) and obtaining a considerably more costly custom-tailored one at the price of increasing its dependence on external capital sources. Or it may choose between purchasing professional services on an expensive consultative basis and enticing an otherwise unattractive professional to join the organization as member. Furthermore, the organization may also choose between cultivating reliable sources of supply and a hunting and gathering pattern, whereby it accepts high instability while keeping exacting quality standards. The different approaches may, besides, be combined in endless ways.

From an analytical vantage point, the picture outlined above may appear impossibly complex. This complexity has to do with the difficulties inherent in systematic accounting for practical consciousness. Handled by knowledgeable agents, it would mostly be a matter of "understood complexity" (Hirschman, 1981:265). The prescriptions for action it would generate would be of no higher order of complexity than the statements "I'd never buy pastries at baker X's, but he has excellent buns on Saturdays" or "Strawberries are cheapest Saturday afternoon". Trade-offs are calculated on the ground of extensive practical knowledge. The examples of concrete strategies that are presented in the following three sections illustrate some of such calculations' basic ingredients, presenting a pursuit of one specific resource at a time, with the organization held constant. Real-life situations are considerably more complex. They often involve multiple trade-offs between resources (e.g., acceptance of a highly attractive offer of government support may tarnish an organization's "non-establishment" image and alienate potential members from joining). They also involve an organization that itself is changing, often as a consequence of previously adopted strategies. An attempt to approximate the complexity of real-life situations is made in the discussion of the kibbutz movements' industrialization in section 5.7.

### 5.4 RECRUITING NEW MEMBERS

An influx of new members is necessary for any self-managed organization's continuous existence over time[155]. Circumstances permitting, organizations would tend to be selective in their choice. Particular organizations would *recruit* particular members or, when relying on voluntary joining, would make themselves differentially accessible and attractive for potential aspirants for membership. Shopping, as it were, for the "right" attitudes, social compatibility (Guion, 1981), competences, or skills, an organization would normally restrict its recruitment to definite population groups where such qualities are likely to be found, a fact that is most evident when advertising for and hiring professional staff. Considered economically, this practice generates substantial savings in costs of schooling.

A self-managed organization would reasonably search for prospective members that would come equipped with a compatible set of values and with certain social competences besides professional ones. Social compatibility of new entrants would, ideally, both restrict the disruptive effect the introduction of new members is prone to have and keep down the costs of "social recoding", that is, organizational resocialization. The combinations of skills and orientations that self-managed organizations would require are often "non-standard" ones (section 4.3.2). The coupling between professional skills and a generalist competence (Rothschild-Whitt, 1979; Jackall and Levin, 1984a) is a typical example of the sort of combinations required by self-managed organizations and seldom provided by formal professional schooling. Furthermore, that a certain combination of qualities is non-standard means, in practice, that no well-defined groups harbouring such qualities can be identified and/or that no standard criteria of assessing the blend would be available.

Non-standard requirements, then, all but seal the SM organization off conventional labour-mobility channels, the more so since members with previous organizational experience would carry with them their former organization's culture and beliefs (Baty et al., 1971) that often prove incompatible with the self-managed organization's and yet are difficult and expensive to socialize away.

The practice of recruiting through friendship networks, already mentioned in section 4.8, is one (though rather imperfect and unreliable) way of coping with these difficulties. Friendship networks often follow age lines. Thus a single-cohort cooperative (established and run by members all belonging to the same age group) is liable to experience a drying up of recruiting sources as its members grow old and their friendship networks with them[156]. An important role in the recruiting growth of Mondragon was played by the Basque men's drinking clubs (Bradley and Gelb, 1982a), which seem to be of a less uniform age composition. The Mondragon Group also seems to have bridged potential generation gaps through the use of community and family networks. Thus "Mondragon emphasises the degree of integration into local communities- the 'morality' of workers in hiring decisions /. . / and by preferentially hiring children of cooperateurs" (Bradley and Gelb, 1982a).

Rather than waiting for Prince Valiant with all of the desired qualities, organizations may settle for more readily available trade-offs, instituting coding practices designed to upgrade available aspirants to the organization's level of expectation (see Thompson, 1967). Schooling members may be found, in this case, to be a cheaper solution than resocializing skilled workers or professionals, especially if the investment in schooling can be seen as a lifelong one. Members would be recruited while young, and (in principle) for a lifetime, and gain competence within the organization. Such a practice of recruiting young members at the bottom, combined with internal recruitment for vacancies, typical for kibbutzim, also constitutes a central characteristic of clan-type organizations (Ouchi, 1980). A policy of lifelong recruitment virtually dissolves the conventional close coupling between vacancies (and, thus, competence requirements) and recruitment, largely insulating the organization from inter-industry flows of personnel mobility. To yield satisfactory results, such a strategy would presuppose the existence of some "competence reserve" within the organization and a mode of organization that is capable of managing and localizing the ripple effects that internal recruiting practices are liable to cause[157]. Organizations that practice rotation, would experience least difficulty in fulfilling these specifications.

The ability to recruit members selectively is subject to the obvious boundary condition of being able to recruit any members at all. A population group where prospective joiners could reasonably be sought may, to the extent it can possibly be delimited, be considered as the organization's *recruitment base*. Recruitment bases are, predominantly, an (intended or unintended) product of the environment and not of the recruiting organization. This holds true even in the case of deviant organizations. The reproduction of deviant organizations is, at least at this point, irrevocably tied to societywide processes[158]. Thus the specific demographic features of the alternative health clinic, or the law firm, described in Joyce Rothschild-Whitt's classical article (1979) and by Rothschild and J. A. Whitt (1986), both endowed with professional, committed, and transient membership, may be traced to the existence of a specific academic subculture on the one hand, from which members can be recruited through friendship networks linking it to the organization (Aldrich, 1979), and to the organizations' clear (though unintended) integration in conventional career paths on the other hand. As long as these environmental features hold, the organization can count on a steady stream of interested aspirants that would invest maximally but for a limited time, eventually moving on to resume more conventional career paths.

A match of this sort, between organizational requirements and environmental configurations, would by its nature be tenuous and unstable. It may be broken by a change in the environment, eliminating the recruitment base, or by a change in the organization in question that makes retainment of new members difficult, a development described in section 4.6. It also may be terminated by a breakdown in communications between the organization and its potential members that causes it to lose its attractiveness in this group's eyes. Once the match is broken, an organization may experience either a dearth of aspirants or a situation in which it is unable to assimilate and/or retain the ones it still does attract. Difficulties of this sort were described (in chapter 4) in the case of French worker cooperatives and in the case of the Danish *Malerne* cooperative. A similar problem was also observed in the veteran British "cloth-cap" cooperatives (Oakeshott, 1978).

Clearly, the ability of organizations to influence the social structure of surrounding society so as to ensure the continuity of their recruitment base is highly limited. This is the case even for organizations acting in concert, through a federative organization, as is the case with the kibbutz movements and, to a somewhat lesser degree, Mondragon. Efforts would commonly be directed toward maintenance of contacts and, to some extent, also to exploration of possible ways of broadening and diversifying the current recruiting base. Once these objectives can no longer be met, the choice would be between establishing a new base (a tactic that, presupposes an environmental involvement, and would often require some modification of the organization's recruitment criteria) and gradual attrition[159].

The kibbutz movement's history presents a long and often dramatic illustration of recruitment strategies and their application to a changing social and, to some extent, global order: traditionally, the movement has depended on an inflow of groups that were recruited by, and ideologically and socially trained within, the respective youth movements. "The latter [the youth movement] is not just a large scale recruiting operation but an effective mean for improving and controlling the 'quality' of prospective members" (Niv, 1976:323).

This policy has remained fast for some 50 years. Geographically, however, the focus of recruitment has shifted, following historical developments and cataclysms. Beginning with Eastern Europe, the center of gravity has moved to Israel and the West[160]. Changes notwithstanding, the candidates the movement appealed to were of a fairly similar cast: gymnasium youth with radical sympathies and middle- to lower-middle class background (for Israel, see Shapira et al., 1977)[161]. However, although the recruiting demands of the kibbutzim increased with the growth of the movement, the contact with recruiting bases, both at home and abroad, gradually eroded. The number of youth groups (*Garinim*) available fell below demand, and the retention rates dropped[162]. In the 1970s, this precipitated a wave of "private" kibbutz recruiting initiatives, bypassing their respective youth movements. Such initiatives, though not altogether unsuccessful, often foundered on low retention rates.

The late 1970s and the 1980s have seen a rise in the prominence of two previously undervalued recruitment sources: absorption of families, essentially an attempt at recycling the leftovers of the former recruiting base, and natural growth: "Statistical facts expressing the attracting force of the kibbutz as a social organization /. . / show that in the last few years the potential sources for the increase of the kibbutz movement are mainly internal — its own offspring who have grown up to become members" (Leviatan, 1975:11).

In the Haartzi federation, the least "family oriented" of the federations (Maron, 1987), 50-55 percent of the increase in the number of members for the period 1960-1975 is accounted for by the kibbutz born (Leviatan et al., 1977). The percentage of kibbutz-born members for the movement as a whole, has risen in the years 1968-1973, from 20.0 to 32,3 percent (ibid.). This trend is likely to continue: Between 1980 and 1985 the total population of the kibbutz movement increased by 18.0 percent. Of these, nativity accounted for 11.8 percent (Maron, 1987). In 1986 the rate of natural reproduction in the kibbutz movements was higher than in the population at large. Net absorption for the same year was negative (Maron, 1988).

Besides acceptance of demographic facts, an increased interest in natural growth testifies also to a certain ideological reorientation inwards[163]. This development may mark the end of an imaginative path of adaptation, with the setting of a permanent tendency that will place the kibbutz nearer the closed-commune organization type and thus limit the kibbutz' relevance for the study of self-management. Alternatively, it may merely turn out to be a phase between different external bases. The final outcome will be determined by developments in the kibbutz' national and international environment but also by internal developments within the kibbutz.

### 5.4.1 MEMBERSHIP AND ECONOMY

A central place in the model of self-management suggested here is accorded to membership. This does not signify that the self-managed organization would be impervious to capital and competence requirements. However, its preferences as to level and timing of demand, as well as the *quality* of resources in demand, may be somewhat unconventional. A comparison to the firm of economic theory may be of use here: ideally engaged in the reproduction of capital, the classical firm, in order to pursue this objective, has to draw on additional resources (labour, raw materials, competence, and so on). The level of demand for these other resources would, however, be primarily set by considerations of capital gain. The classical firm would, for example, be taking on new employees as long as this pays, in terms of marginal costs and returns. Constraints set by the labour market would be considered along with other material constraints. The self-managed firm would, instead, be subordinating its resource intakes to its membership policies, within constraints set by its economy. It could, for instance, be expected to expand its economic activities, once and as long as it considers taking in additional members[164].

The reproduction of membership, as the discussion above indicates, does not equal stability; on the contrary, the uncertainties of supply where suitable prospective members are concerned and the risks of exit of present members induce instability and indicate growth and stockpiling. Growth may also be an objective set for the organization by its members for social or normative reasons (Cohen, 1972; Katz and Golomb 1974/1975, for the case of the kibbutz; Thomas and Logan, 1982, for Mondragon). An important corollary to these statements is that a conscious application of recruitment and retainment policies presupposes that the organization's economic carrying capacity would continuously have to be adjusted to its changing demography, present and projected, rather than the other way round, as the model of the firm would have suggested.

Simply stated, a decision to take on an additional member also entails that the organization's revenue be increased to a matching degree. Ideally, an organization would be extending operations before and as a preparation for planned recruitment, whenever the need to expand membership is perceived. In practice, the phasing of the two steps, of recruitment and expansion, respectively, is largely a question of actual supply of members. A small, new cooperative, embedded in a friendship or neighbourhood network, may have a waiting list of unemployed friends waiting to come in. In such cases, given a positive economic development, the pattern of growth would closely approximate that of a conventional enterprise, with employment phased in with expansion. Given a more erratic supply of prospective joiners, a scavenging pattern would develop: an organization bent on growth would alternate between hoarding members, that is, accepting candidates it would loath to lose, despite temporary lack of employment and hoarding jobs, so as to have a vacancy ready to be filled in, once a suitable candidate materializes. The first of these behaviours is expensive in economic terms and can only be sustained for relatively short periods until a way of increasing revenues is found. The other, in fact, a practice of constant undermanning and "self exploitation", is often typical of new cooperatives in their early stages of development[165]. Undermanning and the consequent work overload it places on members do not entail direct *economic* costs for the organization, as long as exhaustion d does not impair effective functioning. On the contrary, they may be considered a way for capital accumulation. They do, however, place a strain on members that cannot be borne indefinitely. Failure to resolve such strains, through adjustment either of the scope of economic activity and level of revenue or of population size, is liable to generate pressures for introducing hired labour into the organization.

### 5.5 MATERIAL RESOURCES

The relation to capital sources is often noted in cooperative and SM research as a major source of vulnerability for such organizations (Baumgartner and Burns, 1979). Such vulnerabilities are manifested in their most dramatic form in phases of maximum dependence on external resources and goodwill, namely, the phases of formation or of takeover or of crisis (Levin, 1984:249ff; Rothschild and Whitt, 1986:117). The following quotation, taken from an interview with a financial counsellor, in an account of the VAG takeover (Zwerdling, 1980), provides a blatant example:

'Something we *don't* want to see', investment counsellor Andrew Field said /. . / 'is an employee owned-corporation ending up with decisions being made on the floor of the stockholders' meetings. /. . / If any lender suspected that, you wouldn't get a dime. And I would not be a party to it,' Field said, 'if it would degenerate into a situation where all the employees got to elect the board of directors from within the plant.' (p58)

Banks and investment funds, besides being more reluctant as far as extending credit to deviant enterprises is concerned (Horvat, 1974), may also be considered a potential menace *after* having granted loans or credit. Being more sceptical from the outset as to such enterprises' "prospects", creditors may have a lower threshold in calling for bankrupcy or reconstruction once the enterprise gets into difficulties, however passing. The confidence gap, evident in such cases, would tend to be aggravated by the fact that self-managed organizations' standard responses to difficulties, as well as, one might suppose, their way of generating difficulties, may deviate from the established norm. Reconstruction is likely to be made conditional on change in the ownership structure[166]. In less extreme cases, interference is less obstrusive and is exercised mainly through influencing the composition of the board of directors (see Aldrich, 1979)[167].

A degree of wariness in the relations to banks may therefore be expected (Vanek, 1975a:445). Not being able to legitimate in accepted terms, neither its recruiting policies, which would often be seen as a proneness to employ the "wrong" people, at the "wrong" time, nor its investment policies, which would often lead it to try to mobilize capital at precisely the points when it's economic performance would appear the least prepossessing, the organization would have to be prepared for the eventuality of being denied credit precisely at those junctures where it is most necessary. Stated in economic terms, such preparedness would be expressed by lower debt ratios, higher propensity for saving, and, eventually, higher liquidity.

In his survey of French worker cooperatives, Eric Batstone (1982, 1983) found that, compared with conventional firms in their respective branches, cooperatives generally tend to rely to a lesser degree on external financing and maintain a higher proportion of liquid means. Internal savings and retained profits are used in this case so as to restrict and buffer dependence on credit lines. The tendency of the studied cooperatives to "isolate themselves from the capital market" (Batstone, 1983:47) varies in degree between cooperatives and is shown to be related to the percentage of members in the workforce, that is, to ideological rather than economic features of the organization[168]. A high propensity for saving has also been noted in the case of kibbutzim. Haim Barkai (1977:165) found that kibbutzim's saving ratios considerably exceed those of the Israeli population at large. Excessive rates of profit reinvestment, keyed to the same purpose, were also noted for the case of young kibbutzim (Stryjan, 1983; Darin-Drabkin, 1963)[169]. Since young kibbutzim's profitability at the period studied by Haim Darin-Drabkin was fairly low (Barkai, 1977), this reinvestment rate indicates a general attitude rather than an actual performance level. Keitha S. Fine (1973) suggested that an important motive behind the kibbutz industrialization thrust was the will to eliminate the dependence on (Jewish Agency controlled) agricultural development funding. In the same spirit, Amitai Niv (1976:8) suggested that the preference for agricultural settlement forms, evident in all early utopian and communal attempts, has had to do with the relatively low investment and short time span required for such communes to achieve economic independence, compared to industrial experiments in urban environments.

Besides undertaking the economically troublesome strategy of self-financing, an organization may also attempt to tap potentially sympathetic groups and favourable environmental configurations for financial resources, most notably at the local community level. Community resources may either be directly used by the organization or employed for leverage in obtaining better endowed actors' cooperation. In this manner, community savings and loans have had a central role in the establishment and subsequent development of the Mondragon group (Oakeshott, 1978). Local resources can also be put to other uses; political contacts at the local level may facilitate access to publicly controlled funds, where such exist (Lindmark, 1983), and community involvement may persuade commercial banks to get involved, with a gain of local goodwill in sight[170]. The aim, in all cases, is to achieve independence from potential sources of coercive pressure, either through self-chosen isolation and internal substitution (self-financing), or through tapping unrealized or otherwise inaccessible resources, or by opening new ways of access to resources through mobilization of power.

### 5.6 MOBILIZING PROFESSIONAL COMPETENCE

Like any other organization, self-managed organizations would be in need of professional services and competence. Such a need can be real or imposed. Competence of a given sort may be genuinely needed to carry out an activity the organization is engaged in or considers initiating. But an organization may also be compelled by existing licensing practices, safety regulations, and so on, to employ formally certified personnel in some functions, regardless of actual needs, since "the delegation of activities to the appropriate occupations is socially expected, and often legally obligatory" (Meyer and Rowan, 1977:344[171]).

Whatever its reason, the introduction of professionals and professional knowledge may be a problematic step for a self-managed organization. Professionalization is carried out through standardized professional education and professional organizations and networks: "Such mechanisms create a pool of almost interchangeable individuals who occupy similar positions across a range of organizations and possess a similarity of orientation and disposition that may override variations in tradition and control that may otherwise shape organizational behavior" (DiMaggio and Powell, 1983:152). Professionals would be prone both to perceive problems in highly standardized ways and to generate fairly standardized solutions, regardless of the organization they found themselves in. Organizations employing professionals in key positions would tend increasingly to resemble each other, a tendency Paul J. DiMaggio and Walter W. Powell have given the label of *normative iso-morphism*.

SM organizations often develop policies geared to control and limit the influx of professionals and professional knowledge into the organization or to localize their impact, once employed. At times, such policies would be quite conscious. At other times, they might simply be an offshot of a deep-seated suspiciousness of external expertise, sometimes grounded in some past experience, at other times motivated by plain avoidance of cash expenditure[172]. One self-evident way of restricting demand for external competence would be to restrict activities to those areas where competence already is at hand, within the organization. Clearly enough, such action is likely to lead to stagnation unless balanced by an imaginative recruiting strategy. When no licensing regulations exist, the necessary competence may also be generated or substituted for internally. This tendency is most pronounced in the case of managerial competence, discussed in subsection 5.6.1.

When the requirement is for formally certified competence or when some other circumstances necessitate having the skills in question imported, at least four alternatives exist:

a.  Recruiting a person with the desirable skills for membership. This practice seems to dominate Rothschild-Whitt's (1979) sample of "alternative" professional organizations. However, combinations of desirable qualities and attitudes with desirable skills may be fairly rare and hard to find, the more so since professional socialization is unlikely to fit membership requirements (DiMaggio and Powell, 1983). To the extent this is practically possible, organizations would tend to "hoard competence", not the least through staffing with overcompetent individuals or attracting members with many-sided competence (Rothschild-Whitt, 1979).

b.  If sufficiently endowed, organizations may start their own professional training. This path would normally be chosen by federations rather than by single organizations. The most prominent examples of such education systems are the Mondragon federation's managerial and technical training facilities and the kibbutz movements' managerial, agricultural, and teachers' training.

c.  An organization may send members "out", to conventional trade or academical schooling[173]. Common in the kibbutz, this procedure inverts the conventional order of schooling and nomination: people elected for a task would then be sent to acquire the necessary competence instead of people already possessing the skills in question being elected[174]. Coupled with rotation, such an approach leads to progressive accumulation of competence reserves within the organization (Leviatan, 1978).

d.  In the last resort, or as an interim measure until an internal solution is found, professional services can be bought. Such truly external expertise would have to be coded so as to limit its disruptive impact. A not uncommon pattern, in such cases, is that a boundary line is drawn between the service and its supplier. Thus kibbutzim that experience a shortage in, for example, teachers or nurses or are interested in having a resident physician would commonly proceed to hire such personnel rather than try to recruit it. Although such employees may, in due time, apply for membership, they are neither expected nor routinely encouraged to do so. The fact that applying for membership would commonly entail a certain lowering of income and standard of living also serves as an indirect disincentive for joining.

The practices described may be seen as particular applications of coding techniques (Thompson, 1967; Scott, 1981:191). Coding, in this case, would be geared to disentangling of competence from undesirable appendages, either through bringing in "pure" competence, through the agency of members entrusted to go and get it, or through an encapsulation of the imported professional.

### 5.6.1 MANAGERIAL SKILLS

Managerial skills represent a special and somewhat problematic case of external competence. External recruitment of managers, when practiced, would imply that individuals who are least predisposed to follow SM values are put in a position of top influence. Martin Carnoy and Derek Shearer state, on a related issue: "As long as French managers are trained in elitist engineering schools, it is highly unlikely that they will participate willingly in the development of non-hierarchical models of decision making for French public enterprises" (1980:44-45).

The issue of management also tends to be considerably more normatively and emotionally loaded than other forms of expertise. Since no accreditative or legislative constraints exist in this field, it is possible to act out such sentiments when setting up an organization. Robert Oakeshott's description of one of the British veteran "cloth-cap" cooperatives amply illustrates this point:

> "the shoe makers who set up the Equity enterprise insisted in their constitution that their 'committee of management' /. . / should include none but 'practical men'. Thus it was almost twenty years before that committee of management could bring itself to appoint someone with the title of Manager /. . / none of the first four holders of that post left on speaking terms with the committee" (1978:64).

It is useful to distinguish, at this point, between two components of managerial competence: internal coordination or monitoring and management of external contacts (Pfeffer, 1982). At least where management of an organization's internal affairs is concerned, the predominant pattern would be of internally substituting for professionalized managerial competence, most notably, with collective competence within suitably modified control systems and with "horizontal control" (Bradley and Gelb, 1982a:155). In other words, self-managed organizations often manage with a considerably smaller supervisory staff than comparable conventional ones (Greenberg, 1984, 1986; Lee, 1988). The reduced number of middle-management posts left to be manned would be filled through internal recruitment.

Administrators manage their environments as well as their organizations. An important component of a manager's role, besides internal coordination and monitoring, is the management of external contacts. For organizations active in the mainstream institutional environment, expertise in this field may be hard to stockpile or generate internally, and external recruitment often proves necessary[175].

The case of the American plywood cooperatives (Greenberg, 1986) exemplifies an interesting solution to the problem of managerial competence: Managers are, as a rule, externally recruited. They are given a fair degree of discretion in pursuing their task, which seems to be predominantly *externally* oriented. At the same time, they are kept at arm's length, so as to minimize their influence on internal affairs[176]. Foremen, in significantly reduced numbers, as compared to conventional plants, are recruited internally. A high turnover of managers, to which the arrangements described above probably contribute, is reported for the plywood cooperatives (ibid, Berman, 1982). It does not seem to affect the enterprises' economic performance adversely.

## 5.7 PREDESIGNED STRATEGIES AND CORRECTIVE MEASURES

The examples given in the preceding three sections have mostly dealt with piecemeal strategies, designed to deal with specific problems encountered in procurement or accommodation of one resource at a time in a stable environment. Relatively simple problem situations, like those discussed, can be dealt with through orderly application of predesigned strategies. However, a great deal of the situations organizations find themselves dealing with are considerably more complex. This is most evident in cases of change and innovation. Accommodating to environmental change and introducing internally or externally originated innovations entails, by definition, unknown qualities and thus, also, unforeseeable problems. The central challenge, in these cases, is quick localization and correction of unwanted consequences rather than prophylactic design.

Bjarne Herskin's (n.d.) model of the alternative organization deals with the management of unintended effects. According to Herskin, the actual interfaces between the organization and its environment are located *within* the organization. Internal changes, induced by changing environmental constraints, may, if incompatible with the organization, release compensatory mechanisms to offset change's disruptive effects and reconcile them with the organization, as it were. An entertaining illustration of the operation of such mechanisms in a deviant community can be found in the following account of a minor clash in the Hutterite community: "When the young men began to wear belts instead of suspenders a few years ago, there was no problem-until belts began to be embellished, made into many styles in worldly fashion. The /. . /assembly of preachers issued a ruling against the wearing of belts. Today no man is to be seen walking about the colony without suspenders" (Hostetler, 1977:301).

To recapitulate: an innovation (in Hutterite terms) has been introduced by the young members of the community and was accepted as long as it seemed to provide convenience without destabilizing the accepted style of clothing. However, once undesirable effects become evident, the licence was withdrawn. It is worth mentioning that the same role division between innovators (younger members) and conservatives also obtains, in the Hutterite case, in matters of modernization of the community's means of production (Hostetler, 1977:297). Control of change is institutionalized, and compliance is ensured by the fact that the population group given licence to experiment with innovation is the least powerful one and can, therefore, be checked if the need arises[177].

The merit of the anecdotal example above lies in its simplicity. The industrialization of the kibbutz movements provides a considerably more complex but also more relevant illustration of the way in which changing needs and resource configurations may prompt a more thoroughgoing organizational change and of the multiplicity of pressures and constraints that have to be dealt with in the course of such a change. Industrialization was to a great degree forced upon the kibbutzim by a combination of external pressures and internal needs. Some experiments in industrialization were begun already in the 1930s as a way to cope with underemployment and with seasonal labour fluctuations inherent in agriculture. "The early endeavours were considered adjuncts to agricultural way of life, not substitutes for it" (Fine, 1973:247). The first serious thrust toward industrialization, during the 1950s was, to a great degree, caused by strong government pressures coupled with advantageous credits for industrial investment (Peleg, 1982). All that in a period of otherwise scarce credits, agricultural surpluses (Rayman, 1981:106) and of financial straits for the kibbutz movements[178].

On the whole, industrialization was accomplished without a sizable influx of externally recruited professionals. The choice of a particular industry was often guided by the competence that some members of the kibbutz already had. Although accomplished largely by their own effort, industrialization has nonetheless exposed the kibbutzim to a considerable pressure for change. While developing their agricultural production, kibbutzim enjoyed an undisputed technological lead that allowed them to formulate their own organization principles[179]. Within industry they found themselves, instead, compelled to adapt to already established conventional patterns. Industrialization of the previously predominantly agricultural communities has required influx of professional knowledge, introduced organizational constraints built into purchased equipment (Stryjan, 1983b), and, finally, demanded bowing to external constraints and conditions bound with financing arrangements and often involving commitments to employ hired labour.

Although these pressures have been common to all kibbutzim, the patterns of handling them had varied between the movements. Menachem Rosner and Michal Palgi (1982) demonstrated in an inter-movement comparative survey of kibbutz movements' industrial plants that ideology varying between the three movements has had a clear impact on the respective paths of industrialization taken[180]. The movement with the strongest egalitarian and communal commitment (Haartzi) is shown to score highest on measures of internal plant democracy, integration of the plant into the overall kibbutz structure, and avoidance of hired labour, with the other two movements' ranking corresponding to the strength of their respective ideological pre-ferences. Haartzi movement's strategies were threefold:

a. A stronger coupling of the industrial plant to the kibbutz at large counters external "mimetic" influence (see chapter 6) on the organizational structure of the plant, by providing different pat-terns for emulation, and checks the diffusion of "conventional" organization patterns built into the physical equipment and inad-verently purchased together with it.

b. A consciously selective choice of industry: Haartzi plants are concentrated in capital- and (often) skills-intensive production (plastics, electronics). Industries with a high unqualified labour component and process industries (that involve rigid manning demands) are generally avoided (see Zamir, 1972). Such choice is commonly motivated by a quest "for such industries as members would be willing to work in".

c. Not the least due to ideological reluctance (Peleg, 1982), the industrialization of Haartzi movement started relatively late. This has allowed the movement to learn from the other two movements' mistakes.

To recapitulate: in industrializing, the Haartzi movement responded to a set of constraints, namely, population growth, the finiteness of agri-cultural resources, and, lately, also an agricultural crisis. Reconciling these constraints with ideological imperatives (commitment to growth, obligation to provide members with work, democratic principles), solu-tions were designed that stress "creative" innovation (Katz and Golomb, 1974/1975) and minimize environmental strain, mainly through location in "appropriate industrial branches". Proceeding in this mode, the movement found, at least temporarily, a way of applying kibbutz organizational principles to a novel area of operation.

The strategy of the Haartzi federation centres on vicarious learning and on the application of the lessons learnt to strategic design. As for the remaining two federations, it seems that the considerable drift that the early stages of industrialization obviously have caused has generated a deal of internal corrective inputs, resulting in a gradual change of course in a direction similar to the one taken by the Haartzi federation. "The growing number of hired workers was seen as by kibbutzim as a threat to the collective way of life, and the industrialization effort of the 1960s was therefore deliberately reoriented towards lines which could be run efficiently on a small scale. /. . / The new crop of industrial enterprises were accordingly devised as smaller units /. . / a change which meant moving away from the traditional /. . / and into science-based industries" (Barkai, 1977).

While bound to its initial course by heavy investments, kibbutz industry, regardless of movement affiliation, seems to have embarked on an incremental course of reorientation toward units that are, at least potentially, more compatible with the kibbutz community. This trend is well illustrated by the change over time in one important indicator: the percentage of hired workers in the kibbutz industry (Table 5.1).

**Table 5.1  Percentage of Hired Labour in Kibbutz Industrial Plants**

| year | Artzi | Meuchad | Ichud |
|------|-------|---------|-------|
| 1969 | 22 | 36 | 77 |
| 1972 | 20 | 31 | 73 |
| 1975 | 20 | 26 | 65 |
| 1978 | 16 | 21 | 59 |

Source: Leviatan (1982:68)

As the table shows, the trends in all three movements are virtually identical, despite the extreme differences in the respective point of origin. The overall trend is composed, in fact, of three distinct tendencies: (1) change in the character of new plants, (2) reorganization and modernization of existing plants (Rayman, 1981:222), and (3) in extreme cases of big plants with labour requirements that lie well beyond a kibbutz' manning capacity, divestment of plants, or production lines (ibid.). One important factor in the dynamics was the introduction, in all three movements, of a voluntary tax, payable to the respective movement's fund, on employment of hired workers (ibid.).

Adjusting to new resource configurations has, in the case of the kibbutz, led to an extensive organizational change. Vicarious learning, predesign, and strategic foresight are, as the comparison between the three movements shows, of definite advantage for those in a position to enjoy them when managing the process. The development described above also demonstrates the impact of corrective inputs and the possibilities for a turnabout in cases in which foresight, and the ability to resist pressures have initially failed. Members' corrective inputs; protest, creating pressure for change, and involvement, generating novel solutions, would be of major importance in such situations.

The art of swimming against the current, which is what continued reproduction of self-management in a conventional environment amounts to, requires, besides the ability to take right decisions, the propensity to spot and correct those that prove wrong. To secure its reproduction, an organization would have to manage the task of *self- evaluating* (Wildavsky, 1972) over a considerably broad front and for the lowest possible cost. The import of flexible structures that permit quick assessment and relatively simple and inexpensive correction and of members' individual corrective inputs that make such correction possible should be appreciated in this context. That the maintenance of an organization that relies on individual initiative in evaluation and correction presupposes "self-evaluating members" (Hedberg and Jönsson, 1978) or, in other words, a membership that knows what it is doing.

## 5.8 SUMMARY

Organizations are engaged in a continuous pursuit of environmental resources. Such resources would normally be secured and processed at a price. When dealing with a deviant organization, striving to preserve its deviance, the specific price tags that procurement of different resources would carry can also be conceptualized in terms of pressures for change and *isomorphic adaptation*, adaptation standing, in this case, for acquisition of conventional features. Such pressures may be open and coercive, in that access to a resource (and thus the possibility of ensuring its steady supply) is made conditional on the organization behaving in a certain way (e.g., being registered on the company- or on the mutual societies register, as the case may be, in order to be eligible as a transaction partner). They can also be indirect (e.g., having to adjust the work time to the timetables of public transportation or having to put up with a disagreeable professional the organization can ill afford to lose).

Some thinkable combinations of resources and pressures are summed up in the table 5.2 below.

**Table 5.2  Sources and Types of Environmental Pressures**

| Resource | pressures: coercive (direct) | Indirect |
|---|---|---|
| material (capital) | Banks' attitudes | "preprogrammed" production equipment |
| competence | licensing standards | professional socialization |
| members | labour and company legislation | influx of incompatible norms and practices |

Overt, coercive pressures, traceable to distinct features in the environment (powerful organizations, legislation nd so on; see DiMaggio and Powell, 1983) are often explicit and thus, possible to forecast and guard against. An organization may, in other words, choose policies and modify its structure in advance so as to limit or avoid expected pressures. Such preventive action often takes place *outside* the organization or at the organization's boundary. Indirect pressures operate through channels that are more diffuse and therefore harder to block. To a large extent, such pressures would be traced to unintended and therefore unforeseen consequences of previous action. They would often become manifest *after* having generated some undesirable internal effects. They would, to a considerable extent, be dealt with internally and in reactive/corrective ways.

The ability to correct errors and unintended consequences that are generated in a process of change or adaptation is of paramount importance since the occurrence of error in such processes is, as was also suggested in chapter 4, virtually unavoidable. Not all constraints are explicit and realized in time, and not all compromises are intended or, if intended, lead to intended consequences. Importing personnel and materiél across boundaries is often tantamount to importing problems. New production equipment calls for new task definitions and altered maintenance routines. Forms of budget reports, work planning and accounting, and so on, are changed to fit acquired office equipment and software. New members would bring with them new behaviours and habits. Some of these implants would fit and improve existing patterns. Others that do not may generate disruptive ripple effects through the organization. Which of them is which may often be hard to determine beforehand.

The notion of managing such problems by watertight, predesigned strategies and meticulously formulated quality standards has a certain rational appeal but appears unrealistic, given an unpredictable environment and the limited ability to predict all consequences of a given change. Preemption, through institutionalized vigilance, extended to cover all domains and subjecting all change to institutionalized scrutiny would have required an effort of superhuman proportions. The balance between preemptive and corrective measures is, thus, ultimately a question of economy, and the outcomes of the trade-off would vary, depending on changing circumstances and on the organization's members' discrimination and skills.

# 6

# PADDLING UPSTREAM:
# THE POLITICS OF COPING

> Little attention has been given to the role of ideology
> in discussion of the relationship between the environ-
> ment and the organization and discussions of the
> effects of contextual variables on organizational struc-
> ture. (Rosner and Palgi, 1982:17)

## 6.1 INTRODUCTION

The self-managed organization has been presented in the preceeding
chapter as a deviant organization within an environment patterned to
facilitate quite different organization forms. In its quest for environmental resources, such an organization would find itself exposed to recurring pressures to change and adapt to its environment so as to facilitate access to necessary resources and their smooth utilization, once
secured. The review of seemingly isolated problems encountered by the
self-managed organization in a basically indifferent environment, presented in the previous chapter, is integrated in this chapter into a model
of a hostile environment, consistently acting to impose subordination to
environmental demands and thus isomorphism with conventional organization forms.

### 6.1.1 SURVIVAL, REPRODUCTION, AND COPING

Constant adaptations to changing environmental demands naturally
raise the issues of the adapting organization's identity and continuity
over time[181]. An important distinction, namely, between the concepts of
*survival* and *reproduction* ought be drawn at this point. The concept of
survival, commonly employed in organizational and ecological theory,
deals primarily with point diagnostics of economic and physical perfor-

mance[182]. It abstracts, however, from the very issues of identity and continuity that are central to the reproduction concept.

Questions of identity are hardly relevant as long as we are dealing with the conventional organization or firm. Although particular organizations and firms may have a distinct identity at any distinct time, the abstract concepts do not. There are neither legal nor normative expectations that would bind any organization, least of all commercial ones, to a consistent (if any) identity over time[183]. "Corporations are legal entities but also collections of equipment, personnel, and expertise. The legal entity can disappear but not the operations of the business, or vice versa. How to count each of those eventualities is not immediately clear" (Pfeffer, 1982:189).

Bjørn Gustavsen (n.d.) commented that the company concept constitutes an abstraction "in the Marxian sense of the term, in that it gives a selective picture of the object rather than a simplified one". Selectivity, in this case, builds on a correspondence of "inside" with "outside" rules and modes of action, as organizations reflect socially constructed reality (Berger and Luckmann, 1967). The absence of deviation from rules that are reproduced in the society at large makes such an abstraction practicable and, automatically, obscures the issues of identity and reproduction[184]. The obverse of this proposition, namely, the claim that issues of identity would be central to the study of an organization embedded in an environment it strives not to reflect, is pursued here[185].

To sport an identity, one must keep oneself alive. The preservation of identity is conditional on the continued presence of an "organizational host". Successful reproduction thus presupposes survival and, as this work ventures to suggest, *contributes to* survival. The opposite does not hold. Indeed, various degeneration theorems (Webb, 1891; Clarke, 1983) rest on the claim that, where deviant organizations are concerned, the requirements of survival would, a priori, exclude reproduction. Denying this postulate, we come up with a proposition that at least two survival scenarios are available for such organizations, namely, *sheer survival* at the expense of the reproduction pattern; a development that amounts, in fact, to emergence of a new organization (see Hannan and Freeman, 1977) that would no longer be self-managed, and survival *through* successful reproduction.

Seen from this angle, the prominence of "degeneration theories" in the research of self-management has to do with the fact that, in these organizations, failures and shortcomings do lend themselves to generalization more easily than successes do (Stryjan, 1983b). It is possible to suggest that such regularities ought to be traced to regularities in the environment and in the organization-environment relation rather than to some fatal faults in the organization itself. Accepting the degeneration theorists' basic assumption about the existence of a fundamental opposition between the self-managed organization and the conventional environment, it may be useful to refer to the latter mode of survival, that involves negotiation of environmental hinders (at times even turning them to the organization's advantage) so as to maintain organizational reproduction, as to *coping* (see Stryjan, 1983).

### 6.1.2 THE SPECTRE OF ISOMORPHISM

Having chosen coping as our object of interest, it would be of clear relevance to us to conceptualize and chart those features of the environment that are to be coped with. The theoretical tools for the task will be provided by ecological research and the study of institutional isomorphism. Common to these theoretical approaches is the preoccupation with the general rules shaping standard populations, that is, what in our frame of reference is treated as "the environment". Accepting the existence of a norm, that the self-managed organization deviates from, implies that some leveling forces or processes operate on the organization's environment so as to eliminate or limit incidence of random or outright deviant outcomes such as the SM organization itself. Operating on populations and single organizations within the same environment, they yield a population that is uniform and, thus, by definition, convention bound. Within ecological research, this effect is commonly labeled as *isomorphism*. For the deviant organization, struggling to preserve or spread its identity, successful reproduction presupposes that isomorphic pressures that the environment generates are coped with.

The perspectives guiding research on isomorphism are thus, in an important sense, the inverse of the general perspective guiding the work at large. Throughout the work, the focus has been on reproduction processes, with disturbances and faults treated as accidental to the "logic of reproduction" explored. For the purposes of the discussion below the focus will, instead, be placed on systematic patterns of disturbances, expressed as processes of drift from an ideal course in an environmental force field rather than on the course itself. Reproduction will be temporarily relegated to the background[186]. A basically similar approach, akin to the "degeneration-research tradition" was employed by me previously in Self-Manangement: The Case of the Kibbutz (Stryjan, 1983b), and discussed in Stryjan, 1984a.

### 6.1.3 COPING STRATEGIES

Seen from the SM organization's horizon, the environment may indeed be viewed as a problem, as the environmental perspectives suggest, though not necessarily as an unsolvable one. A search for solutions would necessarily take us beyond the scope of environmental theory.

An important complement to the environmental perspective is provided by the resource dependence perspective (Pfeffer and Salancik, 1978; Pfeffer 1982), discussed in section 6.5. It presents a promising attempt of integrating an essentially environmental view with a more active perception of the organization as an active participant in the organization-environment relationship and provides us with a highly useful charting of the major strategies that organizations may employ in their pursuit of autonomy from the environmental demands that their dependence on external resources imposes.

Dealing with conventional organizations, Pfeffer and Salancik saw organizations' quest for autonomy primarily as an insurance policy for survival. However, the insight their work provides into the armamentarium at organizations' disposal is instrumental in integrating the piecemeal descriptions of resource-procurement tactics, presented in the previous chapter, into a more unified perception of coping strategies employed by deviant organizations whose objectives lie beyond sheer survival. Applied in this way, the theory may help to clarify the paradox, central to this work, of maintaining a distinct organizational identity in the context of a law-bound environment.

### 6.1.4 FEDERATIVE STRATEGIES

This work has focused on the *single*, self-managed organization. Located in an environment it deviates from, such an organization would try to make the best of a given world. Significant modification of the environment would presuppose access to power and meta-power, a task that lies beyond the reach of most SM organizations, not the least due to their deliberately small size.

The concept of power has been kept out of the discussion thus far for the simple reason that SM organizations generally lack power. The closing two sections of this chapter go beyond the limited scope of this work and proceed to outline some guidelines for a strategy of change. Federative strategies represent an alternative to growth and an effort at modifying an organization's power-position vis-à-vis the environment and, ultimately, a promise of modifying the environment itself. A brief outline of such strategies, based on case descriptions of existing federative organizations closes the chapter. It has no pretensions to sketch the foundations of a new order. Although it is clear that federative strategies may solve some of the member-organizations' problems, such structures, however well developed, would hardly be capable of resolving them all. Besides, many of the problems inherent in the organization-environment fit would merely be elevated to a higher level of aggregation. The problems that were described above as organization-specific would, in other words, manifest themselves, if in a somewhat different guise, at the federation-environment interface. While member-organizations may find the burden of reproducing their own organization somewhat lightened, they would, instead, face the task of reproducing the federative one and of protecting it from isomorphic pressures. The issue of environmental fit cannot thus be wholly "organized away". These issues lie, however, well beyond the scope of this work. The ambition here has been, at most, to point out a possible direction, not to chart a way or design a destination.

## 6.2 THE ENVIRONMENTAL IMPERATIVE: TWO APPROACHES

> Any attempt at implementation of self-management would necessarily involve the establishment of non-capitalistically owned and managed units within a capitalist economy. Even an ambitious effort of country-wide transition is bound to encounter this problem — in the context of a world economy gone international. (Stryjan 1983b:244).

The problem of SM's environmental (mis)fit was first tackled, if somewhat indirectly, by Beatrice Webb (1891). Tom Clarke's work (1981, 1983) is in many respects a development of Webb's basic themes. Branko Horvat (1974) provided a critique of the (economic) environment as the chief explanation of SM's lack of spectacular advances. The underlying dichotomic perception of organization versus environment, evident in these approaches, is a basic feature of the "degeneration-research" tradition. It is closely (if unknowingly) related to ecological models. The environment's leveling impact on organisms and populations, a central element in ecological approaches, is best subsummed in the concept of *isomorphism*. Introduced into social ecology by Amos E. Hawley, the operation of isomorphism on organizations was described as follows:

> Units subject to same environmental conditions, or to environmental conditions as mediated through a given key unit, acquire a similar form of organization. They must submit to standard terms of communication and to standard procedures in consequence of which they develop similar internal arrangements within limits imposed by their respective sizes. Each unit, then, tends to become a replica of every other unit and of the parent system in which it is a subsystem (1968:334).

Hawley's approach addresses itself to the individual organization. However, the total lack of friction and opposition, perhaps the model's oddest feature, blurs the distinction between individual and population levels. Although change is said to be accomplished solely through adaptation, that is, action on individual organizations' level, it is nonetheless expected to be universal, that is, pertaining to all organizations. The organization's supposed freedom of action is clearly limited to compliance. Environmental determinism is introduced through a failure to realize that organizations may do something as unreasonable as to resist change.

Subsequent research has devoted considerably more attention to the *mechanisms* of isomorphic change. It is possible to distinguish two lines of thought, each departing from a different perception of the environment. The ecological perspective sees the environment in terms of resource matrixes. Isomorphism is a product of natural selection among different competitors for scarce resources. The institutional approach, briefly touched upon in the previous chapter, stresses, instead, the fact that resources are *defined* by and *mediated* through institutional structures and organizations (see section 5.1.2). Resource scarcity is differentially distributed, rather than absolute (compare Sen, 1981). Isomorphism is induced or enforced primarily through transactions with mediators and gate keepers or carried in through cultural influence. The two approaches, and their implications for understanding the problems self-managed organizations would face in their relation with the environment, are briefly discussed in the following two sections.

### 6.3 THE ECOLOGICAL PERSPECTIVE

Michael T. Hannan and John Freeman (1977), and later, Howard Aldrich (1979) depart from Hawley's approach, though expanding and modifying it considerably. Realizing that some organizations may be unable or unwilling to change in the frictionless way assumed by Hawley, Hannan and Freeman (1977:930ff) suggested a population-oriented approach to the phenomenon of isomorphism, more in keeping with the general ecological perspective[187]. A specieswide adaptation occurs through the combined effect of individual adaptation and populationwide selection: "any observed isomorphism can arise from purposeful adaptation of organizations to the common constraints they face or because nonisomorphic organizations are selected against. Surely both processes are at work in most social systems" (ibid.:957; see also p. 937).

Some organizations would adapt; others would not. The latter would be weeded out as unable to maintain their competitiveness. Organizational fates, immaterial in themselves, would, when aggregated, yield a more uniform population, with a higher degree of fitness[188]. Hereby, organizational fitness may be defined as: "a composite measure of fitness that includes both selection (actual loss of organizations) and mobility among forms (extreme adaptation). Fitness would then be defined as the probability that a given form of organization would persist in a certain environment" (ibid.:937).

Considered in the context of self-management research, these statements offer an ecological reformulation of Webb's degeneration thesis (see section 1.2.1). Once we assume (as Webb clearly did) that the SM "species blueprint" is environmentally unfit, the environmental choice such organizations face is, inevitably, "go capitalist or perish" (Stryjan, 1983:250). Here, indeed: "From a population ecology perspective, it is the environment which optimizes. Whether or not individual organizations are consciously adapting, the environment selects out optimal combinations of organizations" (Hannan and Freeman, 1977:939-40).

The major mechanism attending to selection in this perspective is competition over distinct resources. In Webb's analysis, proceeding along essentially similar lines, the crucial resources are capital and market slice, and SM's inability to compete is a result of its postulated built-in inefficiency. In Branko Horvat's analysis (1974), the scarce resources in question are capital and managerial competence[189]. The difficulty to compete is, however, *externally* located. It is attributed to the politically hostile environment's, "the mould's", to use Jaroslav Vanek's words (1971:97), discrimination of this particular organizational form. Indirectly, this introduces a distinction, totally overlooked by Hannan and Freeman, between "internal" efficiency in processing those resources that are at the organization's disposal (that Bengt Abrahamsson would refer to as organization logic) and an external one, geared to ensure access to such resources[190].

The interest of Horvat's analysis lies in in its problem orientedness, as opposed to the ecological approach's determinism, and in the suggestion, implicit in his conclusion, that environments are, at least in principle, open to modification and intentional structuring. According to Horvat, such a restructuring ought to aim at a removal of a central environmental parameter, that of private ownership over means of production. Ownership, in Horvat's analysis, is to be considered a feature of the *environment*, rather than as a strategy for self-management, the way it is also presented in chapter 2 of this work. More important in the short run, that is, where survival of more limited "experiments" is concerned, is Horvat's suggestion to create means for state support for self-managed organizations. Restated in ecological terms, this would amount to engineering a special niche, where precisely such organizations could freely compete for resources[191]. Solutions of this sort require, however, access to power and meta-power, which the organizations dealt with here seldom possess. This issue is discussed in some detail in section 6.8.

Horvat did not attempt to formulate any recommendations for the single SM organization, assuming, obviously, that the environment must be modified first. Furthermore, his approach, as well as the other approaches summarized above, focuses primarily on the *economic* environment, most specifically on its representation as an abstract market. As indicated earlier in this work, this is but one, if the most visible, element of the problem complex. In fact, it would seem that "degenerative" changes and drift tendencies, albeit much slower, can be discerned even in organizations that seemingly have managed to compensate for, or insulate themselves against the particular environmental deficiencies that both Webb and Horvat identified (Stryjan, 1983b). Exchange with the environment, as the discussion in the previous chapter illustrates, cannot be treated as merely a matter of traffic with goods and payments. It involves traffic with ideas, routines, action algoritms, and, finally, people. Furthermore, exchange itself is often regulated by normative arrangements that the would-be participant must bow to. An insight into the potential leveling impact that such traffic exerts on organizations is offered by the institutional isomorphism approach, reviewed in the next section.

### 6.4 INSTITUTIONAL ISOMORPHISM:
### THE ENVIRONMENT AS MYTH AND CULTURE

Rosabeth Moss Kanter (1972) conceded with Hawley as to the universality of isomorphic pressures. Unlike Hawley, however, she saw such pressures as cultural rather than ecological. The reference in Kanter's work is to the single deviant organization, gravitating toward a "societally dominant" type or being subject to pressures to do so. Compelled to interact with their environment, organizations, according to Kanter, would be induced to remodel internal structures after patterns current in this environment so as to reduce their external transaction costs[192]. Such pressures, however, may be, and under certain conditions are, resisted by deviant organizations[193].

Her chief preoccupation being with the problems a single deviant organization would face, Kanter did not attempt to formulate any integrated perspective on the environment. P. J. DiMaggio and W. W. Powell (1983) proceeded beyond Kanter's somewhat diffuse problem formulation. The pressures that a single organization is exposed to are not an individual predicament, arising in the interaction between a deviant organization and its specific environment, but, instead, they reflect a basic feature of the environment at large, namely, an ongoing process of institutionalization (Meyer and Rowan, 1977). An organization's environment is more than an abstract resource configuration. It consists, predominantly, of other organizations. They engage, individually or in concert, in pursuit of uncertainty-reducing and buffering strategies (Thompson, 1967). Uniform norms of organizational conduct emerge as a negotiated, or an unintended, aggregate product of the strategies pursued by members of the organizational population (Meyer, 1983). Environmental constraints that come to shape the population are thus, to a considerable extent, *produced* by the population itself (Meyer and Rowan, 1977), yet remaining, at any given moment, beyond any single organization's scope of influence.

DiMaggio and Powell (1983) see the institutionalized environment as an "iron cage", that moulds organizations to its pattern[194]. Their work provides a highly useful charting of the mechanisms through which institutional isomorphic change can be induced in, or imposed on recalcitrant organizations. Three types of mechanisms are identified (ibid:150):

1. Coercive isomorphism that stems from political influence and the problem of legitimacy
2. Mimetic isomorphism resulting from standard responses to uncertainty
3. Normative isomorphism, associated with professionalization[195].

*Coercive isomorphism* "results from both formal and informal pressures exerted on organizations by other organizations upon which they are dependent and by cultural expectations in the society within which organizations function" (DiMaggio and Powell, 1983:150). Externally originated practices may be imposed on an organization by threat of sanctions. Central agents of isomorphic coercion are the state, primarily through legislation; other powerful organizations; and national or corporate monopoly services. The coercive role of the state is discussed in a separate subsection below. An organization may also be dominated by another organization, such as an important creditor (Stryjan, 1983b; Baumgartner and Burns, 1979; Aldrich, 1979), a major supplier or a major customer, that the organization is linked to through an exclusive subcontracting relation. The bluntest form of coercion, described in some length in the previous chapter, consists of denying a supply of resources (most typically capital) unless certain conditions are met. More subtly, coercive pressures would manifest themselves in the way normative considerations enter the judgment of an enterprise's "prospects" or credit worthiness and thus, its eligibility for credits.

"Peer" organizations do not normally have a legitimate right to interfere in each other's internal affairs (Pfeffer and Salancik, 1978:151)[196], and would be normatively expected to respect each other's sovereignty (Meyer, 1983). However, the extent to which "illegitimate" organizations are covered by such conventions is unclear. The anxiety "to pass" (Garfinkel, 1967) and maintain a respectable "front", is often experienced by self-managed organizations. Thus none of the worker-owned enterprises surveyed in the EDLA sample (Stryjan and

Hellmark, 1985; see also chapter 2) advertises openly that it is worker owned[197]. This anxiety seems to be related to a will to partake in the system of normative agreements regulating interorganizational conduct (Pfeffer and Salancik, 1978:151) and providing protection against "illegitimate" forms of influence.

*Mimetic isomorphism:* When faced by uncertainty, whether internally or externally generated, organizations may mimic other more successful ones. In the case of deviant organizations, expected to maintain consciously their uniqueness, such susceptibility to environmental models would require an explanation. Rather than a self-evident tendency, such a course of action should be interpreted as a symptom of reproduction breakdown, a phenomenon discussed in section 3.5.3. Such a breakdown may be precipitated by internal conflict or by the introduction of external, incompatible elements into the organization as an effect of coercive or normative pressures.

When internal standards of evaluation get blurred, as a result of introduction of "alien" norms and procedures, external standards and models are likely to be resorted to, with only a token reinforcement by external pressures, either as an element in a some partisan group's strategy or as a way to avoid conflict, (Stryjan, 1983b)[198]. In a manner of speaking, the problem of environmental fit is internalized. The internal tensions and disruptions this is likely to cause, may, in turn, lead to further internal adjustments, whereby routines and organizational blueprints would be adapted to the imported features (Stryjan, 1983b). The internal logic of the given organization thus risks being gradually supplanted. A search for new models and beliefs would be likely to ensue[199]. A classical example of such a development from a closely related organizational field, is the tendency of established consumer cooperative movements to pattern themselves after trends in the mythical "business community" (see Nilsson, 1986).

*Normative isomorphism*: Solutions that are isomorphic with the environment need not be *imported* into the organization. They may also be generated, seemingly independently, by the organization's own members. In this case, it is norms and general algorithms to derive solutions by that are being imported rather that specific solutions.

Professionalization and the lateral mobility of chief executive and professional personnel across organizational boundaries are an obvious vehicle for such a transfer of norms (Baty et al., 1971). A brief description of such problems and the ways in which they may be dealt with by self-managed organizations was supplied in the previous chapter. An organization that fails to code external competence that it imports so as to localize or eliminate its undesirable side effects, risks an inflow of incompatible normative inputs.

Given the importance of rank and file inputs in a self-managed organization, the import of normative isomorphism on this level deserves to be examined. Rank and file members' contacts with the business environment are, naturally, less intensive than those of senior staff. Normative influence would nonetheless be carried in, through members' contacts across the organization's boundary, through the mass media, and, to a certain extent (depending on the rate of recruitment) also by new entrants (see Pfeffer, 1982:280, and section 4.8 in this book). It may affect perceptions of efficiency, attitudes to authority, discipline, or licence for cutting corners in cumbersome democratic decision-making processes, or, indeed, the underlying tendency to see democratic procedures as cumbersome and inefficient[200].

### 6.4.1 COERCIVE ISOMORPHISM: THE ROLE OF THE STATE

Legislation would play a central role in the imposition of patterns isomorphic with the environment on deviant organizations (see Jones, 1983). Perhaps the most basic of them is the tripartite division into owners, employers, and employees imposed by legislation on most economic enterprises. This division is well evident in taxation laws and company regulations[201].

Company regulations often impose definite and, for the purpose of self-management, generally inappropriate governance structures. Withdrawal of liability limitations is, perhaps, the weightiest deterrent employed to keep organizations from choosing illegitimate forms of governance. Thus, S. E. Perry and H. C. Davis (1985:289) observed that direct worker control may jeopardize a company's limited liability unless a great deal of legal niceties are observed, which are "rather onerous and time consuming", especially when coming as an addition to the actual decision-making process. Such niceties may also prove quite expensive to design, since they require access to legal expertise. On a different level (the employer-employee interface), legal liability in cases of work accidents may set direct penalties on decentralisation of workfloor authority.

A tax system, by allocating different types of holdings and income to different categories and tax scales, depending on source, uses, and holder (personal income, personal dividend, personal and corporate property, retained corporate income, untaxed and taxed reserve funds, and so on), and by setting selective tax detraction criteria does, as a matter of fact, channel corporate behaviour and structure. In the case of Swedish worker-owned companies, tax regulations can impose considerable penalties on stock transfer from leaving members to new entrants and indirectly complicate the whole issue of member recruitment. Workers *cum* shareholders in a SM company have the freedom of choice between different ways of taking out surplus, such as higher wages, bonus stock (free or locked in investment fonds), perks, dividends, or appreciation in the values of stock. Their personal income-tax-optimizing considerations would also have an indirect and uncalculated long-run influence on capitalization, investment, and dividend distribution policies. No serious theoretical analysis of the problem's impact on SM has been done thus far (Stryjan, 1985a), and the discussion has restricted itself to pragmatical considerations[202]. As David Ellerman (1986:56) stated "The current debate about the most appropriate structure for workers' ownership is often conducted in terms of such matters as reducing taxes or gaining access to conventional capital markets. But this distorts and trivializes the basic issue".

Tax considerations do often prescribe, or considerably facilitate, certain ways of structuring a company. Of immediate interest is the way a tax system may be setting penalties on unorthodox forms of surplus allocation to the workforce, such as welfare services and family or cultural benefits (see Stryjan, 1984b), while often encouraging such practices in the case of senior staff, and the influence taxation has on structuring accounting procedures and internal information. An all-out pursuit of tax advantages would be likely to lead to an isomorphic development, with the organization increasingly coming to resemble other, conventional organizations in the environment. On the other hand, a refusal to follow suit would entail a penalty, in the form of foregone tax advantages, and might undermine the organization's competitiveness.

An additional, no less important but somewhat less direct, form of coercion can be exercised by the state in its capacity as a gate-keeper, controlling access to resources. Legislation often implies that an organization would have to fulfill certain requirements to be "accredited" as a transaction partner on resource markets, or a recipient of state benefits, tax breaks, or contracts. To qualify, an organization may have to fulfill the requirements for entry on the company register or mutual societies register, as the case may be, employ certified professionals in certain functions, regardless of actual competence requirements, and so on[203].

One way of coping with such coercive requirements would be to pretend to be somebody else. An example of such a strategy was presented in the discussion of ownership forms in chapter 2 of this work. Worker-owned enterprises, reluctant, for various reasons, to assume a cooperative form (credit-worthiness being an important one), may instead modify their incorporation form so as to present a corporate front, while maintaining a membership-based internal organization. Similarly, Israeli kibbutzim may maintain, besides their actual governance structure, a "village council", so as to meet the requirements of local government legislation[204]. Council posts are held, in this case, *ex officio* by actual kibbutz functionaries, so that the basic requirements are met without affecting in any way the kibbutz' actual governance. To take a more trivial example, some of the Swedish alternative grocery cooperatives have employed a considerable deal of ingenuity to avoid being classed in the hard-regulated category of grocery stores, whose premise and equipment standards are formulated to fit supermarket chains' scope of operation and financing possibilities.

Camouflage techniques of this sort maintain a loose coupling between the organization and the image it is required to project (see Meyer and Rowan, 1977). Although the maintenance of a double front doubtlessly requires a deal of resources and creativity on the part of the organization and its members, its cost and complexity need not be overestimated. Use of loopholes and legal leeway is, after all, a practice that is hardly restricted just to deviant organizations. It may even be argued that the fact that the self-managed organization integrates elements that are conventionally assigned to different juridical categories (labour, management, and capital; in the kibbutz case, also enterprise and municipal unit) makes such maneuvering potentially simpler to accomplish than the case would be in more conventional organizations.

However, versatility would also involve some risks, if carried too far. Accommodation to external demands, even when undertaken with purely tactical ends in sight, does introduce a deal of ambiguity into an organization and, thus, increases its vulnerability to mimetic pressures. An all-too-efficient camouflage may also alienate potential external supporters and groups in the organization's recruiting base[205]. The skills of balancing such long-range consequences against immediate gains and, even more important, of correcting unintended outcomes once developments have proven the once-drawn balance wrong would be crucial for a self-managed organization.

## 6.5 ISOMORPHISM AND RESOURCE DEPENDENCE THEORY

The research on isomorphism offers some valuable tools for understanding the problems a SM organization has to cope with. It does, however, offer little by way of solutions. One obvious consequence of a preoccupation with the norm is the difficulty in dealing with exceptions, as is the case of SM in this work. The way the environment operates on members of the population is so convincingly described that there is scarcely room left to account for the fact that some organizations do nonetheless manage to cope with environmental, presumably imperative, pressures with a fair degree of success and over considerable time[206].

The lucidity of theoretical formulation is achieved, in this case, at the price of systematical underestimation of the environment's complexity as well as of organizations' initiative and ingenuity in pursuing the opportunities that this complexity offers. One-sidedly stressing the environment's impact on organizations, these approaches either ignore organizations' attempts to assert their autonomy and exercise discretion versus their environment (Hawley, 1968; Aldrich, 1979) or view such tendencies as liabilities (Hannan and Freeman, 1977).

Stripped of their deterministic trappings, the conclusions the study of isomorphism suggests merely add up to the statement that organizations cannot avoid being influenced by their environment and that an attempt to resist environmental influence may entail costs that, in turn, would jeopardize their ability to compete with other organizations for available resources. The supposed "iron cage" is reduced to a set of pressures that, though considerable, may be coped with and overcome. Negotiating them would be a matter of determination and ingenuity, two qualities that a self-managed organization would seem to be endowed with.

"Environmentalist" assumptions, as to the purely reactive behaviour of organizations, are not universally shared. Manipulation of the environment by organizations was studied by Philip Selznick (1949), and other followers of the institutional approach (see Perrow, 1979). An explicit view of the organization as a purposive agent was forcefully argued by John Child (1972). Although the impact of environments on organizations should not be neglected, it would seem that the relationship is a two-way one: "Organizations are not simply constrained by the institutional environment. They often define their own position in it" (Zucker, 1981:12).

The perception of adaptation as an active process, whereby human beings "respond to and modify" their environments (Giddens, 1984:235; see also 1978), rather than as a reactive submission to constraints is given a concrete organizational application by the resource-dependence perspective (Pfeffer and Salancik, 1978; Pfeffer 1982). The perspective presents a promising attempt at integrating an essentially environmental view with a more active perception of the organization as an active participant in the organization-environment relationship. Rather than seeing organizations as being passively immersed (or incorporated) in an environment, it may be more useful to envisage them as actively relating to their environment. This formulation encompasses two closely connected notions: one, of the relation to the environment being, at least to some extent, a matter of the organization's own choosing, and two, of the environment itself as less of a uniform field than a considerable portion of organizational ecology research would have us believe.

Dependence on environmental resources, and the constraints such a dependence imposes are, according to Geofrey Pfeffer and G. R. Salancik (1978), major explanatory factors in accounting for the way organizations act. However, such dependencies only set the stage for organizational action but do not predict it, since action is not restricted to compliance. The environment, in other words, does not predict organizational outcomes any more than weather would predict a sailing ship's destination. Organizations are endowed with the capacity to maneuver, as it were, among environmental parameters, selectively assembling the parameter set they would rather be controlled by: "In one sense, organizations create the environments to which they adapt /. . / by excluding some elements of the environment and including others" (ibid.:103; see also p. 13).

In their environment-creation endeavours, organizations would consistently seek to minimize external control (Pfeffer and Salancik, 1978:271). Domains of discretion (in the sense of freedom of choice and action) are carved out of the environment, as it were, through an array of tactics. Their prime aim is to limit or dodge direct resource dependencies through stockpiling or spreading of sources and suppliers, avoiding demands, pitting pressure sources against each other, and adjusting resource intake and choice to circumstances. A considerable portion of Pfeffer and Salancik's (1978) and Pfeffer's (1982) work is, in fact, devoted to a survey of the armamentarium standing at organizations' disposal.

Having shown the considerable discretion organizations may be capable of, Pfeffer and Salancik failed to conceptualize any ends that it may be turned to. The central theme of their work remains that of environmental control *over* organizations. Discretion is seen as an insurance policy of sorts, a view strongly remindful of J. K. Galbraight's (1967)[207]. Organizations strive to expand their grade of freedom mainly due to the fact that they are unable to meet all of the demands there are simultaneously. That an organization may avail itself of the degree of freedom it can achieve, in order to pursue an objective or a course of action of its own, is hardly taken into account[208].

Two corollaries to this perspective are in place, in the case of self-managed organizations: First, the pursuit of broader discretion and freedom from constraints, general to all organizations, may, in our case, be subordinated to the organization's overall coping strategy. The self-managed organization would be employing the gained freedom of action in a more directional way, as it were, so as to facilitate its own reproduction. An organization employing maximum ingenuity to resolve problems that a refusal to compromise its identity may generate is not simply declining to choose a state that would have offered it more freedom, as Pfeffer and Salancik would probably have argued. It simply attaches differential weights to different constraints and, thus, to different freedoms[209]. Second, such organizations may, by virtue of their constitution, have access to resources that lie, as it were, beyond the reach of conventional organizations[210]. In this sense, their environment may be substantially different from that of any supposed "non-self-managed twins".

The complexity of the situations that these two corollaries generate may be more apparent than real. The "strategical" considerations involved are, as already argued in section 5.2, no more complex than those conventional organizations would be engaging in. They are simply carried out from a somewhat different set of premises. The course of action they prescribe may be so self-evident to the organization's members as to make a great deal of strategical deliberations and conscious course setting superfluous.

### 6.6 RELATING TO AN ENVIRONMENT

An organization's relationship to its environment may most immediately be analyzed in terms of its openness or closedness, that is, the degree to which it is engaged in exchange with its environment or striving to cut itself off it, respectively. Rosabeth Kanter's research, already referred to in the previous chapters, comes closest to a model of the closed deviant organization. Successful reproduction is achieved through a close watch of the organization's boundaries and enhancement of commitment. A.L Wilkins and W. G. Ouchi, in outlining the preconditions for clans being established, advocate a partial isolation (or, rather, decoupling) under the organization's formative stage and emphasize the importance of buffer characteristics (1983:474)[211]. The slack in environmental dependencies that such features introduce is considered vital in the clan organizations' formative stage[212]. "Mature" clans, though actively involved in the market, would normally preserve some of these protective strategies, especially where mobility of personnel is concerned. Nearly at the other end of the continuum, Bjarne Herskin (n.d.) presents a model of an organization that is totally devoid of boundary defences. Environmental strains are transferred in this model into internal ones, and the locus of coping is placed, accordingly, exclusively within the organization (see section 5.6).

Openness and closedness versus the environment need not be treated as mutually exclusive. Both policy strains can often be observed to appear simultaneously in the same deviant organization. That recluse organizations may find themselves forced to seek contacts and enter transactions with the environment, is intuitively clear (Pfeffer and Salancik, 1978:2). However, the obverse case, of predominantly open organizations showing reclusive traits, can also be observed, as the following statement, taken from the study of a patently open organization form, the early consumer cooperative movement, may illustrate:

> Whereas the long tradition of state socialism and of political action was for changing society as a whole /. . /, the cooperator attempted to take himself out of society, to seek his own solution without troubling with those who would stay behind /. . /. "Co-operators", stated Dr. King in 1828, "ask nothing from anyone but to be left alone, and nothing from the law but protection"/. . /. "The modern co-operator", concluded Ernest Aves, "is.. more than any other, trying to carve out from the whole a sphere that shall be determined by his own scheme of things". (Pollard, 1967:110)

The lingering vision of a cooperative retreat (Pollard 1967) however impractical, makes sense on the theoretical plane. As organizations commonly integrate *activities* rather than whole individuals (Pfeffer and Salancik, 1978:30; Scott, 1981:103), their boundaries run, as it were, not merely *between* individuals but *through* them as well. The more of an individual's activities that take place within the organization, the higher this individuals' degree of integration in it (Allport, 1934; Allport, 1962) and, accordingly, the less traffic that would be required with the environment. Consider the following account of the early stages of the kibbutz movement: "The kibbutz regards itself as a socialistic cell in a capitalistic society. When the Kibbutz movement started, it aspired to solve this ideological-economic problem in two ways: through maximal detachment from the capitalist market and by reaching autharky [economic self-sufficiency] in supplying goods to its population /. . / Thus, direct contact with the market would be prevented" (Peleg, 1982:7).

An elegant theoretical formulation that addresses the openness-closedness dimension is suggested by Amitai Niv's (1976; 1977/1978; 1980) research of kibbutzim and American communes: Generalizing his findings, Niv concluded that deviant organizations' relation to the environment can be refined into two ideal types. These ideal types resolve, each in its way, the basic dissonance between the belief in one's way's intrinsic worth and the fact that this cherished way is deviant to, and rejected by, the environment. Each type integrates philosophical and normative assumptions as to the organization's role and the environment's character with concrete rules of conduct. Roughly speaking, the idealized choice is between:

1. "Model" ideal type: self-imposed isolation from the corrupting environment, inevitably leading, if carried out to its extreme, to stagnation
2. "Pioneer" type, committed to societal change and, accordingly, intensively engaged in its environment. The intensive exchange

terminates in the organization's assimilation, its distinctive "normative order" lost (see Hannan and Freeman, 1977:935).

Strict adherence to any of the two ideal types would bring about the organization's demise or assimilation, just the fate predicted by Webb. However, claimed Niv, these types mark the extremes between which successful strategies can be formulated. The secret of survival lies not in faithful adherence to an ideal type, but in "impurities". The departures from ideal type in real-life successful organizations "may, in fact, represent a set of survival mechanisms" (1980:390)[213]. Predominantly open organizations would be advised to screen off certain types of inputs; predominantly closed ones, to selectively open themselves to others. An organization's boundaries ought to be permeable, but not indefinitely so. Inputs are filtered, countered, and to some degree transformed in the act of boundary spanning. The precise prescriptions would vary, though. Thus, keeping to Niv's research subjects, the Hutterite communities maintain a ban on television sets (Hostetler, 1977), whereas kibbutzim do not. However, it is symptomatic that, although the introduction of television sets into kibbutzim lagged considerably behind the Israeli population at large, the kibbutz movement has assumed the uncontested lead in the establishment of local cable television networks and in production of community broadcasts, as soon as the appropriate technology materialized (Shinar, 1987).

The maintenance of boundaries would also tend toward a compromise between a strict demarcation, in keeping with the "model" type, and a nebulous continuum, which would be expected of a pioneer-type organization and is, in fact, suggested in Bjarne Herskin's model, above. Boundary lines, in the organizations studied by Niv, are extended into boundary zones, that function as intermediate environments. An important role in the formation of such intermediate environments is assigned to federative frameworks, an issue discussed later in this chapter.

## 6.7 CHOOSING AN ENVIRONMENT

Closedness stands, in principle, for self-sufficiency, or internal substitution of resources, and openness for their procurement in transactions with the environment. "Type impurities" both in open and in closed organizations can be seen as binary configurations of resource-procurement strategies. By determining which resources are to be procured from the environment and which not, an organization creates a rudimentary definition of its environmental niche. As noted in chapter 5, access to discrete resources would often be conditional on meeting specific constraints or would entail internal side effects. Taking such price tags into consideration, an organization may either design some creative ways of dealing with and minimizing such constraints or attempt to cut off the dependency in question, through reliance on its own resources.

Assorting a specific set of resources that an organization would choose to be dependent on and their best suitable supply sources as far as imposed constraints are concerned amounts, in effect, to environmental micro-design. Formulating its resource needs and choosing its exchange partners, an organization does, to a not insignificant degree, choose its environment (see, for example, Selznick[214], 1949; Hedberg, 1974; Starbuck et al., 1978). In practice, such choices will be effected through choices of location, incorporation form, technology, products, banking contacts, and so on.

The capability for environment design and modification is normally studied in relatively powerful organizations[215]. Smaller and relatively powerless self-managed organizations can, in fact, influence their considerably more circumscribed environments as well. In doing so they may be drawing upon resources that lie beyond detection or out of reach for the bigger ones[216].

Micro environments may contain a wealth of resources that are hard to detect for bigger organizations. To take a somewhat odd example; just regulatory standard setting state interference, commonly assumed to impose isomorphism and eliminate diversity (Meyer and Rowan, 1977), may actually increase it (Hannan and Freeman, 1977), through adding new constraints to the already existing ones and creating a considerable degree of "understood complexity" (Hirschman, 1981:265) on the local level. Leif Lindmark (1983), dealing with the potential leeway for local initiatives in Sweden, stated: "The complex flora of aid measures and institutional actors on the local scene increases the local actors' freedom of action, and makes 'bottom up' strategies feasible". Local resources may either be concealed by local complexities, or spread in such a manner as to make bigger organizations' advantages of scale irrelevant. Granted, such environmental configurations would be potentially unstable: None of the powers that be would have any interest in preserving resources it cannot as much as notice.

The self-managed organization may also be uniquely equipped to tap certain resources that normally lie beyond its competitors' reach. If we follow Hannan and Freeman's ecological notion that "the greater the similarity of two resource-limited competitors, the less feasible it is that a single environment can support both of them in equilibrium" (1977:943), the most reasonable course of action for self-managed organizations would be to diversify their resource dependencies to domains that lie beyond those of their potential, conventional competitors.

The fact, mentioned earlier, that boundaries often are drawn through people (in our case, members) implies that these members' external activities may be considered the organization's most immediate environment, to be drawn upon in need[217]. An organization may, in other words, maintain access to its rank and file members' "private" resource reserves. Self-financing on one hand, and the phenomenon of involvement on the other hand, are two disparate examples of ways in which such resources (private savings and private time and creativity, respectively) may be mobilized. Member's private friendship and kin-ship networks may also be called upon, under some circumstances, as a channel in such resource drives or as a means of establishing outposts in the environment. In a sense, such access to resources in the immediate environment can be seen as a highly economic way of maintaining slack resources, something that a small organization in a turbulent environ-ment stands clearly in need of (Hannan and Freeman, 1977).

Lacking power to make permanent the results that its micro-envi-ronmental design would yield, a deviant organization's environmental niche can neither be stable nor secure. To the extent they are accidental by-products of administrative or political decisions negotiated by other, "heavier" parts, commonly lacking consideration for "our" orga-nizations' existence, such environmental niches would also be exposed to considerable turbulence. In this sense, the self-managed organization will often be living dangerously. This is amply illustrated by the history of the British building guilds (digested from Oakeshott, 1978:71).

> "The episode of the Building Guilds is like a very brief short story. It has a perfectly recognizable beginning, an unmistakable end, but very little by way of a middle" The building guilds owed their birth to the introduction in 1920, by the Lloyd George cabinet, of new payment arrangements for construction of public housing. "Generous provisions for interim payments against work in progress were put into the contracts, so the financial needs of the guilds were relatively modest. Moreover, since the contracts were effectively drawn up on a cost-plus basis /. . / loans could be advanced to them at virtually no risk". Another administrative decision has promptly put an end to these con-ditions: "In the summer of 1921 the policy of Lloyd George's government abruptly swung away from these subsidized cost-plus contracts. They were discontinued. So were the provisions for interim payments". The guild initia-tive collapsed in 1922. The guilds were never given a chance, at any stage of the proceedings, to participate in some way in the decisions that were to determine their existence.

A flexible structure, tended to by rotation and internal mobility (see sections 3.5.1-3.5.3), and the possibility to mobilize external resources in emergencies, through linkages to community, neighbourhood, or subcul-ture networks, are often the best insurance policy such organizations can hope for. These abilities can be of vital importance in weathering the collapse of one environmental configuration and in establishing a new one. As a last resort, the option of choosing one's environment may even be exercised in its most literal sense; Some of the American communes studied by Niv and Kanter have in fact, changed physical location in the course of their history, Dove Cote (pseudonym), the Hutterite commune studied by Niv, being, in fact, a *sixth* start for the movement (1976:312). A principal readiness to take such a step once again, if necessary, is still evident in the commune: "T of Dove Cote: 'It [the relations to the environment] can change, and we have to prepare ourselves for this possibility. If needed, we are ready to leave behind all we have here and go back to the woods'" (Niv, 1976:312).

A similar feat was recently performed by the Uruguayan Communidad del Sur production collective, now located in Stockholm. Founded 1955 in Montevideo, Uruguay, the collective was forced 1975 into exile by the military regime's persecution. After a brief and unsuccessful trial period in Peru it reestablished itself in Stockholm. A printing press and a publishing house were established in 1980 and are in operation till this day. With the collapse of the junta, some of the members were sent to Uruguay and are working on new cooperative initiatives there[218].

Such a relocalization would, however, come harder for member-based organizations than for corporations, and may, in fact, be considered as membership's supreme test. It would, thus, only be taken as an ultimate measure. Under normal and more manageable circumstances, the tendency would rather be to find some new *modus vivendi* with the powers that be, most evidently with sources of capital and with the state, using community support for leverage.

## 6.8 ECOLOGY AND POWER: THE DILEMMA OF SIZE

Environmental approaches' chief contribution lies in the powerful tools they offer for understanding of the forces that shape and maintain populations. The models offered generally manage to avoid the normative trap of presenting the reality they explain as being in some way intrinsically desirable. As long as they keep a high abstraction level, they do indeed open some interesting possibilities where the generation of alternatives is concerned. Since all of the models considered tend to abstract from issues of history, power and meta-power (power to modify environmental parameters; see Burns, 1976), these openings are left unexplored. Consequently, when focusing on existing population configurations, they tend, to see the present as virtually inevitable (see Perrow, 1979:237ff). We may, then, to paraphrase Dr. Pangloss, not be living in the best of all possible worlds, but yet, the world we live in is the only possible one there is.

The ecological perspective largely takes the environment as exogenous: "the great majority of organizations are not large or powerful. Dominant organizations set conditions of existence for the small and powerless, and they [the conditions] must be incorporated in any analysis" (Aldrich, 1979:218).

Changes and fluctuations are generally treated as properties of the field, rather than as manifestations of the exercise of power. Some understanding of the operation of power on and within environments, of a sort that the ecological perspectiv cannot provide, is a *sine qua non* of any attempt at strategy design.

Powerlessness has been somewhat of a major theme in our discussion thus far. It also seems to be a basic quality in most SM organizations' existence. One important reason for such organizations' powerlessness is their often consciously maintained small size.

For organizations, size seems to be a basic precondition for achieving any degree of power or political weight. "All other things being equal, a large organization will have more real political and economic clout than a small one" (Rothschild and Whitt, 1986:95). The size requirements for achieving prominence would vary with the relevant arena, be it local, regional, national, or multinational, and with the sort of competitors and partners to be found there. The principle, however, would remain the same: below a certain size, an organization would simply remain unnoticed.

Growth is, thus, a first step on the way to power. Unfortunately, this obvious path is far from unproblematic for SM organizations. To start with, SM organizations often show a built in reluctance to grow[219]. Their resistance is in part technical and directed against growth in itself: The selective recruiting procedures used by SM organizations are not suitable for handling big flows of aspirants, socialization of new entrants is a slow process, and one is generally aware of the risks that too rapid a dilution of the existing body of members would entail. Underlying the seemingly pragmatic objections to growth, we often find a principal objection to size, growth's objective. Joyce Rothschild and Alan J. Whitt found that a significant portion of cooperative members believe that there is an optimal size for cooperatives. These members tend to consider their cooperative's present size as the optimal one, regardless of what this size actually is (1986:93).

A belief that size is detrimental to democracy, participation, and immediate personal relations between members is commonly shared by practitioners and students of self-management. It is convincingly expressed by E. F. Schumacher (1974) and by Thomas Baumgartner and Tom R. Burns (1979) for the case of self-management, by Joyce Rothschild and Alan J. Whitt (1986:91-95) for worker cooperatives, and by Victor Pestoff (1979) for cooperative organizations.Tadeusz Kowalak, in a survey of Polish worker cooperatives found that "democracy is inversely proportional to the size of the cooperative, and it seems to be a rule, in spite of several experiments being made to avoid the consequences of that rule" (1981:22).

The dilemma facing the SM organization is obvious: power or identity. The collectivistic organizations in Rothschild and Whitt's sample seem to have voted for identity: "In choosing a democratically manageable size /. . / co-ops may have to face the dilemma of trading a degree of impact on the larger society" (Rothschild and Whitt, 1986:95).

Conventional cooperation, on the other hand, has obviously chosen the other alternative: To be more effective in its pursuit of power and societal change, cooperation has been willing to dilute considerably or outright sacrifice its members' place (Pestoff, 1979; Bager, 1988), and thus its identity.

Looking for possible ways out of the dilemma, it may be useful to give the issue of size a closer examination. Interestingly, although the relation between growth and the quality of self-management in any given organization seems to be consistently negative and well documented, no absolute size limits were ever established empirically:

> Although it is certainly reasonable to suppose that some large number would be too cumbersome for democratic groups, it may be impossible to determine a particular threshold beyond which democratic control yields to oligarchic control. Over the centuries philosophers and political theorists have posited an upper limit, yet no consistent number has emerged from the record /. . / This leads us to believe that there may be no single cutoff point concerning size, but only a curve of diminishing returns – a slow erosion of democracy rather than a single break. (Rothschild and Whitt, 1986:92)

In other words, different SM organizations each would seem to have its own size limit. The point is well illustrated in the case of the kibbutz: The founder members of Degania, the first kibbutz established in 1910, have from the outset decided to split the kibbutz, once it becomes too big to sustain intimate relations. This decision was also followed in due time with the establishment of Degania B. The size limit was then believed to be around 20 members and was soon exceeded by later kibbutzim. At the other extreme, the Meuchad movement has advocated a big and growing kibbutz, with thousands of members (Cohen, 1972), but this objective has hardly ever been met. Hakibbutz Haartzi, in its turn, has advocated an "organic kibbutz size" of about 100 members and has actually adhered to it in practice for a long time. At the moment, both practice and theory appear to converge on a size range of 250 to 600 members, although even bigger kibbutzim do appear to be performing tolerably well, despite typical problems of size.

To the extent that a size limit can be established at all for SM organizations, it would seem that it would be affected by the following organizational variables: a. rate of growth, b. the nature of relationship between members, c. internal organization.

Organizations that attain their size through gradual, "organic" growth may have a higher size limit than organizations that grow rapidly or were initially formed on a big scale. Organizations that build on, and presuppose intimacy, such as collectives, would have to remain quite small. Organizations that from the outset count on involving only a limited portion of members' time and interests (e.g., consumer cooperatives) can sustain a (relatively) bigger size while remaining reasonably well self-managed.

The question of internal organization offers the broadest range of possibilities, the loose label of "organization" permitting of a nearly infinite variation of internal arrangements. Intuitively, it is possible to suggest that closely coupled organizations, operating as a single unit, would have to remain small, if they are to retain their self-management. Loosely coupled organizations, on the other hand, would be able to maintain self-management as long as (a) the size of subunits is kept down and (b) a reasonable way of aggregating these subunits' actions, while preserving a wide-ranging autonomy, is found. Growth, in such cases will be effected through establishment of new subunits. They can either be started from scratch in new areas of activity, come into being through splitting of existing units once they have grown beyond a certain size (see Baumgartner et al., 1981), or, finally, can evolve through the weaning of groups that have evolved in an intrapreneurial process within existing subunits.

Organizations that evolve along these lines would, in a manner of speaking, represent an inversion of the established organizational order of things. Formally subordinate subunits in the organizational sense are turned, in such an organizational setup, into *primary units* in a loosely composed whole.

The developmental path suggested above could be regarded as a program of *federalization*. It is, in essence, the converse of the process of consolidation of federations into unitary organizations, known from the literature (Abrahamsson, 1977; Nilsson, 1986; Stryjan, 1988). The best example thus far of a single SM organization evolving into a federation is probably that of Mondragon[220]. Models of federalization processes could be of major interest in outlining development paths for SM organizations and, not the least, in designing the conversion of bigger organizations into SM forms.

### 6.9 POWER AND META-POWER:
### FROM ISOLATED ENTERPRISES TO FEDERATIVE FORMS

When discussing the modification of environments, it may be useful to distinguish between the concepts of power and meta-power. *Power* is exercised by and on organizations that co-occupy the same environment, with the primary aim of changing the competitive balance within it (most typically, through exclusion, raiding, predatory pricing practices and the like[221]). *Meta-power* (Burns, 1976) is exercised upon environmental parameters, with their modification in sight.

The power problematique may yet, be accomodated, if uneasily, into an ecological framework, for instance, by ranking power as an environmental resource, a solution hinted at by Hannan and Freeman. Issues of meta-power lie, almost by definition, outside it. In an important sense, the ecological perspective deals with the mechanisms through which meta-power operates on populations (e.g., what happens with the fish population when somebody opens the pond's sluice port), and the intended, as well as unintended, results this yields.

The distinction between power and meta-power is important in understanding eventual differences in strategy between single organizations and federations. At the single enterprise level, we deal mostly with issues of power and, more often than not where the deviant organization is concerned, of power as seen from the angle of the powerless. Outcomes of meta-power application are taken as a given, since deviant organizations seldom possess any access to meta-power, or influence over actors that may wield it. From the single, isolated organization's angle, the (institutional) environment would then be viewed as primarily a fact of life.

What cannot be achieved by any single small organization may well be within reach for organizations acting as a group. Jeffrey Pfeffer (substantially underestimating the single organization's resilience) remarked:

> Aldrich (1979) and J Freeman (1982)[222] have implied that the potential to alter the environment to manage external dependence is a capacity possessed primarily by large organizations and, thus, that resource dependence is a theory applicable primarily to only relatively large organizations. This view would probably be true only if organizations exerted influence in solo. However, there are numerous examples of small organizations banding together in associations and achieving substantial control over their environments. (1982:198)

Federative strategies (Jordan, 1986) may provide a highly appropriate substitute for growth, as far as access to power and advantages of scale are concerned, to organizations that would rather remain small. Jonnergård (1988:340) defined federative organizations as follows: "A federative organization is an organizational form where independent organizations gather together and create one or more units (central units) which are supposed to fulfil some common needs of the founding organizations and to foster collaboration /. . /. At the same time, the member organizations /. . / keep their independence and self-governance in important areas" Once, and if, isolation is broken, by way of federation formation or network linkups, the issues of power and meta-power, largely irrelevant in the discussion of the single organization, become adamant. What for the single organization has constituted an ecological constraint may in a federative perspective become an item in an agenda for change.

A brief outline of possibilities that federative strategies offer is presented below. It concentrates on on existing examples, as seen from the angle of the single "member-organization" angle, and not on future scenarios. It is dominated by examples taken from the kibbutz movements and the Mondragon federation, probably the most developed and certainly the best documented federative organs of this sort.

a.    As a tool and resource in legal suits, taxation issues, etc, and as a lobbying group for new legislation or modification of existing one[223]. The degree of involvement in legislation need not reflect the organization's power but may, instead, be a way of mobilizing and binding sympathetic powerholders through single-issue campaigns. Thus the ICOM group's involvement was keyed to passing of concrete legislation in the British Parliament, and the same may be said about actions of American supporters of self-management (see Gunn, 1984; Blasi and Whyte, 1980) in promoting the Employee Stock Ownership Plans legislation (though the latter is rather a case of a political lobbying group not directly connected to any organizations). The kibbutz federations have instead used their proportionally heavier weight to minimize legislative regulation of kibbutz affairs.

b.    As a source of "committed financing". Since organizations are highly vulnerable to pressure in their formative stage, committed financing would play a key role especially where establishment or conversion of new units is considered (see Wilkins and Ouchi, 1983:474). The central role of the Caja Laboral Popular in the Mondragon group is well-documented (Oakeshott, 1978, Campbell et al. 1977; Thomas and Logan, 1982). The Caja's perhaps most exceptional feature is that it functions to channel external resources (community savings) into co-operative investment. The kibbutz movements never established their own bank and relied instead on close contacts with established ones[224]. However, each movement maintains financial institutions to manage its own funds. The presence of such institutions highly enhanced the single kibbutz' creditworthiness in the past. The movements' funds do often play an important role in aid programs and rescue operations in existing kibbutzim and, indirectly, kept up the member organizations' solid reputation. The importance of mutual aid has increased dramatically in the 1980s, as a result of considerable turbulence in the economy and political tensions with the right-wing dominated Treasury (Tsur, 1987).

Financing of rescues and takeovers of closing enterprises was also provided on a wide scale by the Italian cooperative federations, most notably by the Lega (Oakeshott, 1978:152ff). Some aid to new cooperatives, though, due to economic limitations, on a considerably smaller scale, is also extended by the ICOM group (Oakeshott, 1978; Schumacher, 1974). The kibbutz movements, by comparison, have largely relied on external financing in establishing new kibbutzim.

c.     As a forum for exchange of organizational know-how, an "experience clearinghouse" supplying information on successful modes of creative adaptation to arising problems or novel situations. In a sense, such a forum mediates between ideological premises, which it helps reformulate, and practical, often environment-caused constraints. Within the kibbutz movement innovations are predominantly spread by diffusion. The movement's central role in the context is that of "being there", as a hub or linking-pin (see Aldrich, 1979), for exchanges between members and office holders from various kibbutzim (Blasi, 1982). Consulting services are available on a member organization's request, and certain standards are set, primarily regarding consumption and education. These standards are seldom backed by any sanctions. Their acceptance is to a great degree motivated by avoidance of transaction costs an independent standard setting would have implied. At the same time, the setting of standards in key areas makes kibbutzim more directly comparable with each other and thus facilitates diffusion. Kibbutzim may thus find it easier to mimic each other rather than successful organizations elsewhere.

The staff role of the central service organizations is more pronounced in the case of the Mondragon federation. Unlike the kibbutz federations where the entire staff is "loaned" from respective kibbutzim, the operations of Mondragon are carried out on a professional basis. A considerable administrative skills differential exists in this case between member organizations and the Caja's enterpreneurial division's staff. The division's operation is, nonetheless, guided by strong stress on the cooperative's autonomy (Campbell et al., 1977). The Italian Lega as well does provide a considerable degree of organizational help and know-how, especially in cases of takeover and conversion (though, as Oakeshott [1978] suggested, at times in a somewhat high-handed manner).

d.     As a recruiting organ: This is a twofold function consisting of (a) long-range activities aimed to maintain and service the recruiting base, already illustrated in the case of the kibbutz above, and (b) actual recruitment and screening of applicants. In the kibbutz case, the recruitment base has, historically, been tended for through political activity and propagation of ideas in the population at large on the one side and through the institutionalized frameworks of youth movements, in Israel and abroad, on the other side. The absorption departments of the respective movements deal also with scanning and direction of single applicants to kibbutzim[225]. Overall growth of the movement, through establishment of new kibbutzim, is handled exclusively by the federations, not the least because the resource allocations, most notably land, that such expansion requires can be met only through political negotiations.

Mondragon's as well as the Italian Lega's federative recruiting activities concentrate on recruitment of new member-organizations (Bradley and Gelb, 1982a), either through aid to new enterprises or through conversion of existing ones. Recruitment of individuals is predominantly tended to by the member-enterprises. The federation's active involvement in politics and social welfare in the community (ibid.) plays an important role in the maintenance of the federation's recruiting base.

e.    In the specific kibbutz case, the federative organizations also provide a great deal of the infrastructure for communal and social services, which are thus supplied on the kibbutzim's own terms. A somewhat less extensive system of education, health, and welfare services was also developed by the Mondragon group (Campbell et al., 1977). Such an expansion of the self-managed sphere creates the preconditions for establishment of more complete micro-reproduction circuits that are less reliant on environmental inputs and, thus, less turbulence prone than the single organization's sources of resource supply[226]. At the same time, such an expansion poses some interesting theoretical questions regarding the environment-organization relationship, inasmuch as it can be employed both as a means for self-isolation from the immediate environment, as is the case to some extent in the kibbutz movement (see Rayman 1981), and as a means of increasing integration in local community, as the case seems to be in Mondragon.

The difference between single organizations and federations' scope of action appears, when seen from the single organization's angle, to be more a matter of degree than of sort. Federative organizations deal, normally with the same problems their (would-be or actual) members grapple with, though shifting them to a higher level, as table 6.1 (next page) illustrates. The theoretical framework presented in this book provides us with no tools to deal with self-managed organizations as wielders of power over their environment. The issue seems also, under the circumstances, to be academic.

**Table 6.1    Coping with Environmental Pressures
at Micro and Macro Levels**

| type of pressure | Level of coping: single organization | Macro/federation |
|---|---|---|
| COERCIVE | legal 'decoupling' | influence over legislation |
| | | legal services |
| | PR (local) | Lobbying |
| | contact network to financing organs | own or sympathetic financing organs |
| | | (ev) marketing outlets |
| MIMETIC | Distinct culture | Emulation models |
| | Innovation/creative adaptation | Organizational R&D |
| | selective search for models | Experience clearing-house, education |
| NORMATIVE | Internal recruitment | "manpower services" |
| | Selective recruitment | contact with recruiting base |
| | | Schooling system. |
| | extensive "on the job" training. | Professional services and counseling. |

To the extent that extrapolation is at all possible, an eschatological scenario for a societywide change, to be derived from this framework, would be a one of *colonizing* society rather than of forcefully changing it: "the story of a peaceful revolution"[27]. The central role, in such a scenario, would be reserved for the single organization, acting, though, as a part of a federation or a movement (see Jobring, 1988), bound with it by ties of shared values and perspective (Jonnergård, 1988:345) and drawing on the support of the federation's aggregated resources and common organs. The complex interplay between autonomy and interdependence is a central issue in the federative problematique:

> The unique characteristic of a federative organization is /. . / the mutual dependence and independence of units within the organization due to the simultaneous (central) coordination and member self-governance. This creates complex relationships within the federative organization /. . /. The autonomy of units within the federative organization is said to depend upon the allocation of competence, balances of power between the organizations's parts, and the possibility for units to leave the federative organization. (Jonnergård, 1988:340).

The aggregation of organizations into federative forms is not problem free. The dual nature of the federative organization, as an organization in its own right (and, furthermore, a one of considerably more weight than any of its constituents) and as an intermediate environment normatively subordinated to member organizations' needs. This would necessarily create considerable ambiguity: "The federative organization is a *borderline* organization. /. . / [It] is both an inter- and intraorganizational system, with freedom for the participants to define their belonging to different parts of the system. This explains the confusion about authority and responsibility" (Jonnergård, 1988:345).

Besides, the federative organization's relations with the environment would raise, on an aggregate level, problems of concerted action and problems of isomorphic pressures, which considerably resemble the ones dealt with in this work, on the single-organization level. Coping with isomorphic pressures, and maintaining the complex internal balance, would presuppose an ongoing reproduction process, not unlike that outlined in this work for the single organization. A reproduction model of this sort, applying some of the key ideas in this book, was recently proposed by Karin Jonnergård (1988:303ff, 345)[228]. It opens a promising direction of research, but stands, still in need of further refinement. In its present form, the suggested model focuses solely on a somewhat schematized interaction between an apex organization and isolated member (primary) organizations, and abstacts both from interdependencies and reciprocal peer relations between primary organizations and from the role played by *physical members* in primary organizations in the reproduction process[229].

Primarily interacting with its member-organizations, rather than with individual members, the federative organization is dependent on individual members' inputs, as long as its constituent organizations are being steered by their members. This fact should be talen into consideration in further theory construction. However, members' corrective inputs in the federative organization would be mediated, rather than direct, and thus run the risk of becoming attenuated to the point of incoherence. The twin challenge federative organizations face in their interaction with their membership, is that of reproduction of a member competence that is equal to the task of steering a federative organization, and of maintenance of channels for corrective inputs, whereby such competence can be drawn upon. No scenario for the change, or betterment of, society can count on organizations, federative or otherwise, being reproduced by other organizations alone. Models that can link members in primary organizations, and the federative, second-tier organizations that their primary organizations form, ought, therefore to be an important item on the agenda for future research.

## 6.10 SUMMARY

This chapter has examined some theoretical aspects of the relationship between the self-managed organization and its environment. It opened with an examination of organization-theoretical approaches, that deal with organizations' relationships to the environment (Table 6.2)

**Table 6.2    The Organization and Its Environment:**
**A Schematic Summary of Theoretical Approaches**

| Authors/approach | central mechanism | MATCH* | possibility of deviance |
|---|---|---|---|
| Hawley (1968) | adaptation | Yes | Unthinkable |
| Hannan and Freeman (1977) | competition adaptation | Yes | theoretically conceivable, not dealt with |
| Meyer and Rowan (1977) | adaptation | No | possible but problematic |
| DiMaggio and Powell (1983) | adaptation | No | as transient phenomena |
| Kanter (1972) | adaptation | No(?) | focus of study |
| Aldrich (1979) | competition | Yes(?) | unclear |
| Pfeffer (1982) Pfeffer and Salancik, (1978) | competition | Nc | possible, if environment can be manipulated |

* stands for: is external efficiency (efectiveness) equaled with internal efficiency.

The approaches surveyed differ in their respective evaluations of the degree of the environment's "systemness" and of the single organization's resilience. They do, however, share the basic view that organizations are steered by their environment.

Without questioning the environmental approaches contribution for the understanding of conventional organizations, it is still possible to claim that the malleability of conventional organizations is not due to "imperativity" of environmental demands but rather to the fact that conventional organizations, unlike deviant ones, have no reason whatsoever to resist them. The deviant organization's relationship to its environment would, instead, be one of coping with environmental pressures so as to preserve its identity.

Viewed from the angle of ecological theory, deviant organizations could survive only as interstitial phenomena, subsisting on the environment's field imperfections. They may then be living dangerously, indeed, but nonetheless, it is claimed here, that they may live quite well, negotiating environmental obstacles, and taking advantage of the options for choice and modification that an environment offers. By selectively adjusting their resource requirements to the opportunities the environment offers and by establishing innovative supply channels, such organizations would be, in fact, engineering their own environment niches.

The single organization would lack power to make permanent the environment it constructs. This vulnerability is, however, compensated for by a higher degree of flexibility and by the ability to mobilize additional resources under emergencies, drawing upon either its members' reserves or their contact networks. These capabilities are built, as it were, into the self-managed organization's mode of functioning. In a sense, then, the self-managed organization's "deviance" both exposes it to environmental instability and helps generate the means by which the problems that instability generates can be overcome.

Organizations wishing to increase their power normally choose the path of growth. Conventional patterns of growth can, however, easily jeopardize a SM organization's identity. A strategy combining growth with federalization may provide a practical solution to this dilemma. Federative strategies may also be pursued by small organizations, banding together to form a federative whole. The promise of such strategies is illustrated by a brief review of concrete application fields, most notably, within the kibbutz federation and Mondragon. Aggregation of organizations into federative structures is not problem free. A better understanding of the problems involved in the complex balance between dependence, interdependence, and independence in federative organizations and the question of such forms' reproduction ought to be placed on the agenda of future research.

# 7

# REPRODUCTION AS A
# THEORETICAL TOOL

## 7.1. INTRODUCTION

In this chapter, we leave the discussion of self-management, and address some of the reproduction perspective's broader implications. On a theoretical level, this work has explored a conjunction of two fields: organizational theory and self-management. Can conclusions and insights drawn from this fairly specific case be generalized? Given that the theoretical point made here, namely, that self-managed organizations ought to be understood in terms of reproductive processes, is accepted as plausible, the following questions can be posed:

a. Is organizational reproduction a phenomenon particular to SM organizations, or can a reproduction perspective be applied to all organizations?
b. Can it yield useful insights even when applied to organizations that can hardly be said to be self-reproducing?
c. Is self-management possible only in one specific sort of organizations or can it be implemented in any organization?

Some tentative answers to these questions are discussed below. Mirroring the structure of the book, the discussion starts with the a review of the perspective as a whole, proceeding to more specific applications, and ending with a review of the organization-environment relationship. The attention is directed, at each stage, to linkages with organization theory and to possibilities of generalizing the theoretical findings and applying them in more conventional setups.

## 7.2. A RESTATEMENT

The primary aim of this work has been to outline a theoretical perspective on self-managed organizations. Previous research of such organizations has, to a considerable degree, tended to focus on the eventuality, or even inevitability, of their failure. The approach outlined here attempts to establish a perspective that would depart, instead, from such organizations' mode of functioning and to explain cases of success rather than failure.

Another common tendency in the research of self-managed organizations has been to see them as basically conventional organizations, *owned* by their workers. In this work, ownership was seen as just one way by which individuals can become affiliated with organizations. The examination of the role of ownership, undertaken in chapter 2, suggests that self-management research should proceed from the a concept of *membership*.

A membership-based model of organizational reproduction was outlined in chapter 3, for the specific case of self-managed organizations, and developed in the remainder of the work. Organizational reproduction is primarily carried by the organization's members and through the organization's daily routines. Self-management's core process centres on reproduction of the organization's active membership. Somewhat schematically, the process can be summed up as a loop, in which members continuously shape and reshape their organization and are, in turn, also being shaped by it.

Organizational reproduction is examined stepwise in the successive chapters, each chapter starting from and applying a reproduction model to an increasingly complex theoretical model of organization. Each step involves an examination of the relevant approaches in organization theory that can be used to deal with the problems at hand. This examination provides a linkage with mainstream organization theory and a vantage point for evaluation of organization theory's limitations as well as of its possible application to the case of self-management.

The discussion opens with a grossly idealized model of organizational decision-making and design; an organization whose design is explicitly and unambiguously decided upon in a formal process. A notion of organizational fallibility is introduced in the next step. Failures, errors, and shortcomings are inimical to organizational functioning, and the road from decision through implementation to outcomes is far from straight. A considerable portion of an organization's energies would normally be devoted to correcting and managing the consequences of old decisions, not to making new ones.

It is in this "unglamorous" context that we should view the full import of members as bearers of their organization. Members do more than merely follow directives or chime in on formalized occasions of decision-making as formal participation theories would often expect them to. Their prime contribution should be sought in the perpetual and decentralized activities of troubleshooting and correction, directed both inwards, to remedy or prevent deterioration in their organization, and outwards, to help push it through periodically encountered environmental quicksands.

Organizations differ in the degree to which they permit members to involve themselves in the organization's problems. The way an organization manages and responds to different modes of members' inputs decides, in the long run, its demographical composition and its members' level of competence. Different organizational structures would give rise to differing paths of organizational change. Seen from our perspective, degeneration, a central concept in SM research, is just one such possible path. It is the combined result of mismanagement of members' corrective inputs and of demographic deterioration. Degeneration and organizational futures in general are, however, not predetermined. The constraints that an organizational structure imposes may be transcended, modified, or replaced by agent-members acting to change their organization.

Organizations exist in an environment and subsist on resources. While dealing with its internal problems, an organization is also called upon to secure the resources necessary for its continued existence and to manage environmental pressures. The self-managed organization's specific pattern of resource dependence, reviewed in chapters 5-6, would be somewhat different from the one generally applying for conventional organizations. Differences would be due in part to such organizations' marginal position and in part to their deviant quality requirements. The SM organization's preferences as to quality, level, and even timing of demand for resources are subordinated to the requirements set by the reproduction of its membership. It would, for example, invest after getting hold of appropriate new members, unlike the conventional firm, that would proceed to hire new workers after getting hold of capital.

Like other deviant organizations, a SM organization would encounter difficulties in ensuring a supply of the resources necessary for its reproduction and in accommodating staple resources whose supply is societally guarantied. Deviance also exposes it to environmental *isomorphic* pressures to step back in line and and renounce its identity. The organization's policies of coping with such environmental pressures amount, in fact, to construction and maintenance of an own environmental niche. Environmental engineering undertaken from a position of powerlessness, SM organizations' common lot, requires considerable resourcefulness. Moreover, the arrangements involved in creating such environmental niches would often be provisional and dependent on external goodwill or on chance configurations. The reproduction of self-management would have to be managed in a basically unfriendly and unstable environment. Self-management, however, also generates the flexibility and internal resources necessary for managing such self-chosen conditions of high uncertainty, not the least through mobilizing members' involvement and personal resources to the task.

### 7.3 EXTENDING THEORY: REPRODUCTION AND THE "CONVENTIONAL" ORGANIZATION

Are reproductive processes worth examining in all organizations? The question is complex. Intuitively, it is indeed possible to observe rudimentary (or, perhaps, vestigal) reproduction loops in most organizations. Nearly all organizations recruit and select their own personnel, subject it to organizational socialization, and are immediately dependent on this personnel's performance. Furthermore, individual agents within an organization would often engage in attempts to institute self-reproducing, repetitive patterns at different levels in the organization.

These elements would not add up to one complete and full-fledged reproduction circuit. To start with, the degree of reliance on "staple" agents and resources, supplied by surrounding society, would be high in most organizations. Primarily, an organization would act as a free rider on macro-reproduction processes, replicating, with minor deviations, some of their links and, thus, introducing some singularities into the societal flow.

The picture may be seen in terms of a continuum; at one end we will find "egocentric organizations" (Morgan, 1986:243): deviant and/or self-managed organizations that do, to a large extent, tend to their own reproduction. The other extreme will be occupied by "organizations without qualities", to paraphrase Robert Musil; faceless organizations (say, a randomly assembled platoon of conscript recruits) that are almost totally reproduced by society. As we move along the continuum from deviant organizations to conventional ones organizational identity fades, and the prominence of reproduction processes decreases, with reproduction loops fading into the background. The organizations studied lose their distinctiveness. In studying a related issue, that of organizational cultures, A. L. Wilkins and W. G. Ouchi concluded: "We claim that the existence of local organizational cultures that are distinct from more generally shared background cultures occurs relatively infrequently at the level of the whole organization / . ./ in some organizational settings there seems to be less unique culture than in other settings" (1983:468).

Studying organizational culture presupposes that such a culture indeed exists. Otherwise, it would merely become a somewhat roundabout way of gathering information about the surrounding culture that the organization is immersed in and reflects. Studying reproduction may be fruitful in all the cases. The quality of information generated by such study would change, though, as we move along the continuum from highly organization-specific at one end to information and hypothesis generation about society at large at the other end.

On a somewhat more abstract level, the application of a reproduction-oriented perspective can enhance our ability of seeing organizations in non-linear terms. To quote Gareth Morgan (1986) on the matter: "we are encouraged to think of change in terms of loops rather than lines, and to replace the idea of mechanical causality — e.g., that A causes B — with the idea of mutual causality, which suggests that A and B may be codefined as a consequence of belonging to the same system of circular relations" (p. 247). In this way, the organization, its internal reproduction process, and its relationship with its environment can be seen in terms of an interpenetration of circuits, whereby elements in one circuit can be integrated in other ones that span the organization's boundaries. Interpenetration can at times be regarded as a case of environmental intrusion into the organization, though the opposite situation also can be considered. Dominant plants in small local communities, as well as big corporations in national environments, would often tend to colonize their surroundings, integrating the environment into their own reproduction circuits. Small organizations in small communities would strive for mutual harmonization, preferably on their terms. The degree of inter-connectedness would vary, depending to a great degree on the organization's preferences.

### 7.3.1 REPRODUCTION AS A GENERAL PERSPECTIVE

In applying a reproduction perspective to organizations at large, we should keep in mind that we will be exploring but one particular aspect of the organization in question. Morgan's (1986) metaphor approach provides a suitable frame of mind for such an exercise: "Any realistic approach to organizational analysis must start from the premise that organizations can be many things at one and the same time" (1986:321). A reproduction perspective, seen in this way, would be one more metaphor to be resorted to when useful. Applying it to the rudimentary reproduction loops that are likely to be found in conventional organizations, the observer would be able to identify weaknesses as well as open opportunities. On the problem side, the perspective helps to identify gaps in reproduction loops that are not satisfactorily bridged neither by internal resources nor by resources available in the environment. It can also expose incongruities between links in the process at places where different actors seem to be bent on reproducing each his own organization. On the opportunity side, it can help in localizing new sources and categories of resources and groups that could potentially be involved in the organization's activities.

By linking flows and structure, a reproduction perspective also helps to set demographical phenomena and "manpower policy" issues in new light: Is the organization socializing new members for staying in the organization or for leaving it? Who is recruiting new "members" and how are old ones shed? Are managers removed, rotated, or sucked out of the system by social mobility prospects outside it? Finally, the improved understanding of the role of organizational routines that the perspective provides can enhance evaluation of organizational interventions and changes of routines, for example in cases of decentralization, rationalization, and cost-cutting drives, and improve predictions of the consequences that planned organizational intervention and redesign can yield.

### 7.4 MEMBERSHIP AND REPRODUCTION

The concept of *membership* is central to the reproduction perspective outlined in this work. As far as theory and practice of self-management are concerned, the most important conclusion of this work is, indeed, that the primary concern of a self-managed organization is with its own membership (Stryjan, 1987).

Naturally, the nearest field of application would be other member-based organizations, primarily other forms of cooperation and, with some reservations, social movements and political parties. At the least, the perspective could serve as a tool in a study of historical development, providing an explanatory framework both for trends of degeneration and for periodically occurring "fundamentalist" revivals – at best, as a starting point for a critical theory for this particular, often underestimated, mode of human organization.

Organizations of this type often consist of an apparatus, manned by a minority of members, or even by paid professionals and non-members, that handles daily operations. Most members participate to a limited degree in the running of this apparatus, though they may, nonetheless, have daily interactions with their organization (e.g., shopping in consumer coops). Although seemingly decoupled from "their" organization, members in such organizations would nonetheless have an important part to play, primarily through sporadic inputs of a corrective character. The key notions, in this case, just as in the discussion of SM organizations in chapter 4, are those of individuals relating and responding to their organization and of those responses serving as corrective inputs in the organization's stering. A basic repertoire of such inputs, developing and reinterpreting the work of A. O. Hirschman, was outlined in chapter 4. It consists of four modes: involvement, protest, loyalty, and exit. All four modes are, in principle, available (though not necessarily held in high esteem) in any but the most repressive organizations. The actual propensity to employ any of them would be a product of a complex interplay between demographic characteristics, ideological premises, and elements of organizational structure.

Members' ways of relating to their organization, and their repertoires of action, in the case of consumer cooperatives and other member organizations, will be formed and reproduced in their encounters with it (Stryjan and Mann, 1988). Those encounters will be much more sporadic than in SM organizations proper, and members would be external to their own organization, with their chief involvements laying elsewhere. Reproduction circuits would, in this case, be drawn across the organizations' boundaries, with members cast in a unique role of a link between the organization and its environment. This proposition is considered in the next section.

Membership can be expected to enhance involvement and protest by providing legitimation for their exercise. Well-functioning membership-based organizations can also be expected to provide better structural preconditions for their expression than do conventional organizations. However, since the propensities for being involved, or giving vent to dissatisfaction, are, after all, basic human qualities, the interest in involvement is hardly restricted to students of cooperative or self-managed organizations. The popularity and, consequently, the looseness of usage (commented upon in chapter 3) that the membership concept enjoys in organizational theorizing bears clear witness to this interest.

A great deal of "post-taylorist" work sociology and business management from Elton Mayo and onwards has addressed itself to the problem of harnessing involvement in the organization's pay. To be sure, the guiding assumption is, all too often, that involvement can be refined, so that inconvenient side effects, such as protest or prying in management's, owners', or leaders' affairs, are eliminated. As such, these approaches often tend to be manipulative or implicitly selective (e.g., Herzberg, 1966[230]).

Is it possible to obtain "quasi-membership" even in organizations that lack formal membership? To paraphrase the old quip, we may, indeed, "be having some of it all of the time, or all of it for some of the time". Maintaining a permanent and comprehensive member-like commitment in a non-member-based organization is an unlikely feat. Some diluted feeling of affinity and mutual obligation exists, probably in most halfway decent organizations. Individuals may then be acting in some degree toward the organization *as if* they were members in it, and their assumptions, though counterfactual, have to be taken seriously by the organization analyst. The maintenance of such patterns over time would depend on a degree of reciprocity on the organization's side, with the organization personified, for the purpose, by executives or other relevant others in position of authority. Paternalistic organizations may, if not all too authoritarian, successfully follow and develop such a quasi-reproductive pattern, and so do clan-like organizations, discussed in chapter 3.

The second case, of mass involvement, best illustrated by cases of worker mobilization in a crisis (Baumgartner et al., 1978), is certainly the more spectacular of the two. States in which external control is absent, benevolent, or passive, and the workforce united by a single purpose do occur periodically in organizations. They often arise in the context of crisis, but they may also be induced by management or leadership as an element in company drives, such as the celebrated "SAS spirit" (Peters and Waterman, 1982). In such states, be they genuine or contrived, at least a portion of the workforce or, for that matter, the clientele of a favourite grocer in trouble would be acting as bona fide members. External control normally reasserts itself once the crisis is over or the drive's objective is achieved. The perspective outlined here may be of use in understanding such states, the boundaries of their maintenance, and, finally, the *ennui* arising once they draw to their inevitable close. Such applications would be counterfactual. They require a degree of watchfulness as to both such states' transience and the inherent possibility of manipulation.

### 7.5 MEMBERS, RESOURCES, ENVIRONMENTS

As far as relations with the environment are concerned, the theoretical problem dealt with in this book is that of organizations' freedom of action in unfriendly environments. As far as separate organizational techniques of managing environmental dependences are concerned, the approach developed here is an application of existing models rather than a new and different one. However, the core technology that the SM organization is striving to protect is a social one. Accordingly, the SM organization integrates conventional techniques into a strategy aimed at preserving its identity. At the same time, it also draws on its identity, employing it as a major resource in coping with the environment.

Stretching organization theory to accommodate these notions would improve our understanding of the way organizations cope with their environment. It can provide us with better models for understanding "egocentric notions" that may be entertained by organizations and the way in which they are preserved[231]. As far as environmental strategies are concerned, the difference between such organizations and SM ones can, in many cases, be seen as one of degree and not of kind.

Special relationships developed with suppliers of particular resources, be it permanent subcontractors, law firms, or the locality's technical high school, are an important element in SM organizations' environmental design. They may, in fact, be seen as reproductive loops of sorts, binding the organization with choice portions of its environment. Such reproductive linkages can also be observed in conventional firms. An important role in such relationships can be played by inter-organizational personnel flows. Such flows can be circular, as is often the case in relationships between corporations and universities. They may also be one-directional: the advancement of retired senior executives in Japanese corporations to positions in major banks (Ouchi, 1981) is an interesting example for the latter.

An organization's boundaries, as noted in chapter 6, pass not merely between members and non-members but also through members. Members' "extra-organizational" activities, ties, and resources ought thus to be seen as an important segment of the organization's immediate environment. This becomes evident once we consider the way members' resources and their "private" environmental linkages can be used by an organization in coping with its environment. On facing a crisis, or a forced rapid reorientation, the SM organization has the option of calling upon its members' private capital, time, knowledge or friendships. These resources may be utilized both as externally stored reserves of "organizational slack" and as non-market linkages to the environment, useful in tapping and mobilizing external resources in the surrounding community.

Consumer cooperatives and other member-organizations, such as associations, movements, or political parties, present an interesting example of an organization-membership-environment triad. With the organization's activities carried by a professional apparatus, members in such organizations would find themselves in a particular position, straddling, as it were the organization's boundary. Naturally, they come to play a role of an important two-way link between the organization and its environment, shaping markets (in the case of consumer cooperation), bringing in new members, and also mediating environmental feedbacks and grassroots preferences back into the organization by way of corrective inputs (Stryjan and Mann, 1988).

Members' contribution as a boundary-spanning link is dependent on the way an organization manages its relations with its members: "The extent to which these twin roles can be practiced will depend on the positioning of members on the organization-environment divide, which will vary between societies and from one period to another. Societies with weak membership ties will have difficulties in mobilizing them [the members] to modify their environment. Members not familiar with with their own organization will lack the ability to provide relevant information" (Stryjan and Mann, 1988:124).

Active membership ought to be seen as a central element of a cooperative organizations' adaptivity to changes in its environment. In evaluating possible structures for cooperative organizations, much more attention should be devoted to the ways in which structure can facilitate or inhibit the organization's contact with its members than is the case today.

The role of members' or work-floor employees, as the case may be in an organization's resource-procuring strategies, can be suggested as a point of departure for an organizational typology, sorting organizations by the locus of their interaction with the environment.

Roughly speaking, it would be possible to distinguish two main clusters of organizations: those that attempt to concentrate all significant exchange to their apex and those that conduct a significant portion of their environmental exchange through their "base", respectively. "Tayloristic" organizations, striving to manage all flows from a command centre, could stand as a nearly ideal example of the top-relating category. "Hunting and gathering" organizations (Stryjan, 1989), of the sort discussed in chapters 5-6 of this book, could be expected to relate to their environment through their base, or their footsoles, as it were.

As the case of Taylorism illustrates, an organization's mode of relating to the environment is to a large extent a matter of ideology and, thus, also of choice. However, environmental contingencies also play an important role. What resources are relevant for the organization, and where are they to be found, would depend on choice of technology and product and on the structure of relevant markets. Understanding these constraints can help us in delimiting promising areas for future development of self-management and other organization forms that are responsive to their rank and file workers' inputs.

Members of the workforce in most organizations are normally able, nearly by definition, to draw in resources from the organization's immediate local environment. In some cases, however, such resources would simply be irrelevant. Extremely capital-intensive lines of enterprise would be one clear example: one cannot seriously expect the management of a nuclear power plant or a big chemical industry to allot first priority to relations with its primary environment. The same would apply for industries producing for highly politicized markets, such as today's shipping industry, where orders are scarce and often politically steered, or the aerospace and weapon systems industries, where they are merely politically steered. Regardless of ideological attitudes, commercial organizations in certain branches would, by the nature of their branch, be infinitely more dependent on their managements' political acumen in managing relations with the state and with other big organizations than on any resources that the workforce may prove able to draw into the organization. The same would apply to non-profit organizations in a political system where most resources are channeled through a state bureaucracy.

The lines within conventional industry appear fairly obvious, with big and advanced industry gravitating toward increasingly top-steered forms of exchange with the environment and only relatively backward sectors providing a promising ground for workers' contribution and thus also for self-management. However, the picture changes dramatically once we apply our tentative typology to other important sectors in a modern economy, such as enterprises in knowledge-intensive and service branches and activities within the scope of today's welfare state.

Knowledge-intensive enterprises offer the most clear example of an organization's dependence on its members' resources. Simply stated, an enterprise with a considerable portion of its capital locked in employees brains can hardly afford being unresponsive to its workers' inputs. Such enterprises provide the most interesting ground for experiments with novel modes of organization and, one hopes, also a potential expansion field for self-management.

Enterprises in the service sector, together with care organizations within the scope of the welfare state, form yet another category of interest. In organizations of this type, a vital part of the knowledge of the "market" the organization is active in is generated on the client-organization interface that is manned by work-floor employees. Speaking in hierarchical terms, this knowledge is preserved at the bottom of the organizational structure. Care organizations, similiar in many respect with service ones, illustrate an additional point: the organization's legitimacy, crucial for the pursuit of resources in the political system, is mainly generated at the patient-organization interface. Both service and care organizations can and ought to be understood in terms of reproductive processes, linking the organizations' frontier — and the employees manning it — with the relevant environment. The employees' pivot position in such organizations may accordingly make them into suitable bearers of future self-managed alternatives.

## 7.6 SUMMARY

The aim of this work has been to outline a new theoretical perspective on organizations. This was done with a particular aim in mind: a better understanding of self-management and self-managed organizations and, thus, an indirect aid for the practitioners, however imperfect, of self-management. The most important conclusion of this work, as far as practitioners are concerned, is that the central concern of a self-managed organization is with its own membership. This basic premise is all-too-easily forgotten in organizations in which the most apparent threat is environmental.

As any other tool, perspectives, once developed, can be applied in a variety of ways, besides the one originally intended. Some were suggested in this chapter. Any of them would presuppose a great deal of adaptation and improvement in this rudimentary tool.

Naturally, the nearest field of application would be other member-based organizations, primarily in other forms of cooperation and, with some reservations, movements and political parties. At the least, it could serve as a tool in a study of historical development, providing an explanatory framework both for trends of degeneration and for periodically occurring regenerative surges. At best, as a starting point for a critical theory for this particular, often underestimated, mode of human organization. The perspectives prime advantage over a great deal of existing cooperative theory and rethoric lies in the attempt to provide some matter-of-fact answers to the question that perplexed consumer cooperators repeatedly pose: What are members for?

Two possible applications can be conceived of within the broader domain of "conventional" organizational researchapter First, the modes of application and reinterpretation of different theoretical approaches experimented with in this work could, one hopes, stand on their own as minor contributions to the respective approaches. Second, applied as a metaphor (Morgan, 1986), the reproduction perspective can set in relief an important aspect of organizations that tends to get lost in more piecemeal treatments. The stress on mutual causality and circular processes that the perspective introduces into organizational analysis facilitates understanding of demographical change in organizations and of the complex links between organizations and their environment. Clarifying the role that the organization's work floor can play in organizations, it also helps to point out potential fields for implementation of self-management.

Within social theory, the perspective developed here is, in fact, an indirect restatement of some of structuration theory's propositions in the language of organizational theory. As such, it may improve the understanding of the mechanics of reproduction and augment the middle level links of the theory. Focusing inwards it does not, and cannot by its nature, provide answers as to such micro-circuits societal impact and relevance. These answers should be sought within structuration theory proper. Nonetheless, it is hoped that the qualities self-management enhances could contribute to a better society, granted a society that is responsive to its members' qualities. Until this happy state of affairs is reached, self-management can only be treated as a particularly captivating and worthy way of achieving consequences that, intentions notwithstanding, are all too often doomed to remain unintended.

# NOTES

## Chapter 1

1.  Stodolsky's formulation is clearly inspired by Adizes and Borgese's more ambitious one for society-wide self-management (1975:4).
2.  The project title is an acronym of Ekonomisk Demokrati, Löntagarägda Företag och Arbetskooperativ (economic democracy, wage-earner-owned enterprises and worker-cooperatives).
3.  A statement amply echoed by Gunn (1984:9): "The term *worker's self-management* has been used in the United States in various and conflicting ways". The term *producer cooperative* is used by Abell, above, as a synonym for worker cooperatives. It is used by other authors as a specific label for farmers' cooperatives. This confusion well reflects the conceptual tangle in this research field.
4.  The religious kibbutzim, forming two small but distinct clusters, are ignored here to simplify the discussion. Constituting an insignificant minority, they are seldom addressed by the abundant literature on kibbutz research.
5.  This issue was dealt with in some length in Stryjan (1984b).
6.  The volume of research literature on the topic probably surpasses that written on any other form of self-management. Shur's (1981) English bibliography of Kibbutz research covers more than 1,000 titles.
7.  Webb's criteria for choice of population, as well as the degree of inclusiveness, have been questioned by Derek Jones (1976:39). See also note 12.
8.  As major Labour ideologues, grounders of "The New Statesman" and of the London School of Economics.
9.  The term *custom* denotes demand, or potential market. Webb's material is to a great extent dominated by job-saving enterprises in crisis-struck branches. In this category her remarks (1891:152) are still relevant.
10. Conforth (1983) found that the emphasis in the Webbs' work clearly shifts with the years from "environmental" toward the "structural" reasons for failure described below.
11. The same conclusions are repeated 30 years later: "No self-governing workshop /. . / has yet made its administration successful on the lines of letting the subordinate employees elect or dismiss the executive officers or managers" (S. Webb and B. Webb 1920/1975:166). Also: "the principal and almost invariable cause of their failure has been the inability to maintain, either the necessary workshop discipline, or any continuity of industrial or commercial policy, by a

management that is chosen and controlled by those to whom it has to give orders" (ibid.:48n.; A verbatim quotation from a 1914 article).

12. Jones (1976) suggested that Webb's conclusions were overdriven even at the time they were first presented (1891), probably as a result of a careless, if not outright tendentious, choice of population (ibid:53; see also p. 35). Moreover, these conclusions, though often repeated, were never again seriously tested against the population, although a change in population characteristics seems to have occurred in the 1880s, making Webb's description obsolete. It is worth noting that out of the eight "insignificant" enterprises listed by Webb, two could still be found in operation in 1973 (Oakeshott 1978:66), together with at least two more that were dismissed by Webb as already degenerated by 1891. See also Campbell et al., 1977. Paradoxically, Derek Jones' preoccupation with disproving an empirical study, nearly a century old, bears best witness to the grip of Webb's approach. Unfortunately, fighting a bad reputation with facts is no easy task.

13. These alleged contradictions, besides giving a ground for critics of the idea, have also been absorbed, more or less smoothly, into the work of its supporters. The contradiction between ownership and labour stands at the core of Vanek's (1975a) cooperative self-extinction forces, uncritically accepted also by followers of "alternative" organization models as Lichtenstein (1986). The contradiction between market and principle was recently given a persuasive environmental reformulation by Clarke (1981,\1983) and an economic one by Miyazaki (1982). Finally, the postulate of a contradiction between democracy and efficiency, somewhat tarnished in the 1960s, is nonetheless accepted at face value by Rothschild-Whitt (1979). It was recently reformulated by Abrahamsson (1986) in a rather simplistic application of Williamson's (1975) approach.

14. Compare Stryjan 1984a. Compared to the (relative) proliferation of comparative "twin" studies, whose null hypothesis is that SM organizations perform less well than conventional ones, comparative studies *within* the population charting the impact of different organizational features are relatively rare.

15. All are quoted extensively in chapters 5-6 of this book.

16. Acts requiring such complex theoretical explanations may, in fact, be fairly simple and often unreflexive. For example, managing a household budget involves managing consequences of inflationary pressures, agricultural policies, budget constraints, and family politics. What complicates the case when dealing with deviant organizations is that considerably less of these factors can be taken as a given or predicted from aggregate data.

17. Two applications of structuration theory to organizations have been tried thus far within organization research: Departing from a rudimentary agent-system dichotomy, both approaches simply insert organizations into one of these two slots:

a.    Organizations as agents (DiMaggio and Powell, 1983; see also chapter 6 in this book). This approach concerns itself primarily with the environment and its impact on organizations. Institutionalization processes are seen as ongoing processes of structuration of the organizational field. Interacting with their environment, organizations generate constraints (norms of institutional conduct) that increasingly limit organizations' freedom of action. Agency is seen as a one-way enterprise, successively building up the walls of the institutional "iron cage" (a term borrowed from Weber, 1930/1976).

b.    Organizations as systems (Ranson et al., 1980). The entity to be reproduced in this somewhat mechanical application of Giddens' system reproduction model is "the organization". The environment enters in only as a source of constraints.

The first of these applications provides some useful insights into the organization-environment relationship. It places, however, an all too one-sided emphasis on structural constraints, abstracting from the fact that structures can also be understood in terms of resources, an approach that empties the concept of agency of its meaning. The second approach largely abstracts from the fact that organizations are, in fact, embedded in systems and thus offers no convincing explanation as to why agents (the term actually used is *actors*) should take the trouble to reproduce it at all.

## Chapter 2

18. See Gabrielsson, 1980; Jansson, 1983; Bucht et al., 1976; Lindqvist and Svensson, 1982; MAC-MAREV 1982.

19. That is, figures in the organization's constitution or charter; see Abrahamsson, (1986:268; 1975:26)

20. Typical in this respect is Abrahamsson's undifferentiated usage of the two terms: *wage-earner owned*, and *wage-earner-steered* enterprises (löntagarägda and löntagarstyrda, respectively) in Abrahamsson, 1986. Similarly, Lindqvist (1986) operated with the twin concept "member-owned" and "member-steered", without clarifying the implications of the term *members*.

21. Under the name "arbetarproduktionsföreningar", a term closely reminiscent of the English "associations of producers". For a historical study of early worker cooperation in Sweden see Jobring, 1982; Jobring and Ottermark, 1982.

22. See Stryjan 1984b and references there.

23. The acronym stands for Ekonomisk Demokrati, Löntagarägda företag och Arbetskooperativ (Economic Democracy, Wage-earner-owned enterprises and Worker-cooperatives). The project was led by Anders Broström.

24. As to the usage of the term *pragmatic*, see Granrose and Hochner, 1985.

25. In three of the cases buyout was actually initiated by the former owner, and in another four cases the former owner played a major role during the process of takeover.

26. Leading, in one of the cases (STONE) to termination of worker ownership in 1985.

27. The board convenes more often (six to eight times a year is a normal frequency for this group, compared with a reported normal frequency of between one and three meetings in small industrial firms at large [Boman and Boter, 1979; Andersson and Lindroth, 1979]), is larger (between five and ten members, most commonly six to eight, as compared to three to four board-members in conventional small firms [ibid.]), and discusses the operation of the firm in more detail. In 49 percent of the firms investigated by Boman and Boter the board has no, or minor influence over the operation of the firm (Noted by Ann-Britt Hellmark in Stryjan and Hellmark, 1985).

28. In fact, the most active board in the sample presides over the least participative of the enterprises (JUNO; see description in appendix to Stryjan and Hellmark, 1985).

29. Before the change in ownership 13 out of 19 firms had piece-rate. After takeover, five firms abolished their former piece-rate system (two changed to equal wages), and one moved from "straight" to "mixed" piece-rate (a pay-system consisting of a fixed and a bonus part). "Straight" piece-rate is now in force in two firms and in another two some tasks are paid this way. "Mixed" piece-rate is in force in five firms (including the two where also "straight" piece-rate also is in force). Equal wages have been introduced in four cases.

30. Federal tax benefits, a substantial incentive for the schemes' spread were introduced in 1974. However, the basic idea was formulated by L. O. Kelso and Mortimer Adler (in a book appropriately titled *The Capitalist Manifesto*) as early as 1956. The first leveraged buyout based on these principles was engineered 1958. Some ESOP-type schemes are noted as early as 1916 (U.S. General Accounting Office, 1986).

31. Klein and Rosen (1984) estimated the number at no less than 7,000. The U.S. General Accounting Office (GAO) presented a more conservative estimate, assessing the number of active ESOPs in 1985 at 5,188, totaling about 7 million employees and $18.6 billions in assets (volume estimated from 1983 returns).

32. "ESOPs: Revolution or a Ripoff". *Business Week*, April 15th, 1985.

33. "ESOPs: Revolution or a Ripoff". *Business Week*, April 15th, 1985.

34 Gene Daniels: Interview with Gene Redmon, union local president, and Chuck Mueller, chief steward at Rath Packing Co., appropriately titled "Lost

Dreams". Interviewed and interviewer appear jointly as authors in the Labor Research Review table of contents and therefore also on the reference list.

35. Taken, with slight modifications, from Stryjan (1983b:253), a study of degenerative processes in the kibbutz organization. See also Abrahamsson, (1986:106).

36. The following caption (from a magazine feature amply titled: "ESOPs: Revolution or a Ripoff") provides an extreme illustration of the Dan River settlement's results:

In Danville, Va, about 8000 employees own 70% of textile manufacturer Dan River Inc. through an ESOP; but they have no voting rights or other voice in the business. Control is held by managers and outside investors who together hold 30% of the company [bought for approximately four percent of capital]. Complains union official Kim A Meeks; "The company stamps its cartons with a big 'D' and 'employee owned'. But most of the people realize that they don't own anything. They're just paying the bill for these big management people to own the company" (*Business Week*, April 15th, 1985).

37. Burnham, 1941; see also Williamson, 1975. A formally parallel argument, putting the stress on professional competence and placing the locus of control in a "technostructure" was developed by Galbraight (1967).

38 Abrahamsson's reasoning echoes that of Sidney and Beatrice Webb in their analysis of Trade Union democracy (1897). It is interesting to note that the Webbs are perfectly willing in this case to endorse an organizational development that, in the case of worker cooperatives, they branded as degeneration.

39. "We may see the situation as one where many small holders of venture capital free-ride on the monitoring contribution of the five percent [controlling interest] holder" (Eidem, 1982:43; translation mine).

40. Hindley (1970) suggested that observable "control gaps" should be attributed to imperfections of the "corporate control market".

41. An additional possibility is that of collective exit, that is, of workers deciding, individually or collectively, to sell out. The VAG case (Zwerdling, 1980; Rothschild-Whitt and Whitt, 1986), of workers selling out (at profit) to an outside bidder that has promised to oust the sitting management board, is a typical example of such a development. See also Long, 1982. A step of this sort, though perfectly logical from the shareholders' point of view, loses the problem of management by terminating the worker-ownership arrangement.

42. "That steering and control functions become professionalized need not imply that control is transferred from owners to administrators. It is true that this shapes preconditions for bureaucratization; whether control really shifts into the executive's hands or not is quite another matter" (Abrahamsson, 1986:159; translation. mine) Abrahamsson concluded also that the greater "political" competencies that directors are now called to develop may prove useful in their eventual quest for control. Instead of pursuing the point, he concludes the paragraph with a rather cryptic statement: "This problem falls under the bureaucracy heading, i.e., it is a case of an usurpatory executive" (ibid.).

43. As to internal and external monitoring, see Eidem, 1982; Abrahamsson, 1986:126.

44. Sjöstrand, however, does not subscribe to the mandator approach.

45. For a thorough literature review of such research see chapter 12 in ldrich (1979).

46. A somewhat different enumeration of rights included in the full concept of ownership was suggested by Abell (1983:89). The rights in this list are more sweepingly formulated, but on the other hand, limitations and duties connected to ownership are treated as an integral part of the rights' packet.

47. This is not meant to carry the normative message implied by Furubotn and Pejovich and other property rights proponents, that a system carrying fewer restrictions is somehow better than one with more.

48. It is interesting to note that property right theorists have a pronounced weakness for examples dealing with land usage, land being perhaps the only asset in

existence that is infinitely divisible. No examples ever deal with as traditional — but less divisible – forms of property, such as fishing boats or irrigation schemes.

49. For an exhaustive discussion of the interest concept, see Hirschman, 1977.

50. Adapted from Stryjan and Hellmark, 1985.

51. As to "primitive" concepts, see an interesting discussion (departing from the concept of commitment) in Becker, 1960.

52. Commonly, such criteria would be formulated as: $N$ is a member *if* A or $N$ is a member *if* A *and* B. Criteria of the form "*if* A *or* B" are avoided.

53. Abrahamsson polemized, in this case, with Albrow's onslaught on the concept of bureaucracy that is based on a rationale identical with the one Abrahamsson himself employed here.

54. It has to be noted that the term *member* is often used in ethnomethodological literature as a shorthand for *member of society* (see, for example, Garfinkel, 1967; Leitner, 1980). Thus the requirement formulated here of a definite, bounded membership is met also within ethnomethodological theorizing, if in a somewhat attenuated way.

## Chapter 3

55. The reasoning here mirrors Giddens' (1984:24) argumentation at the system level.

56. In itself, the problem of maintaining participants' affiliations can be considered a particular case of the wider problem of making participants keep their obligations This problem has been addressed by a wide range of theorists, with Weber's legitimation and Etzioni's compliance concepts standing out as the central contributions. The monitor concept within the theory of the firm can be seen as a particular application to the case of (Etzioni's) calculative compliance.

57. It should be remarked that mainstream research within industrial psychology and sociology tends to focus on personal and interpersonal behaviours and attitudes rather than on organization-directed ones.

58. Fletcher argued in his article for the primacy of ideology over structure. By so doing he merely added one more invariable to the scene. The direction chosen in this work is, instead, to trace interrelations between the two as they are being enacted by the organizations' members.

59. A caveat is required here: Giddens' formulations address themselves expressly to the aggregate (macro) level. An application to single organizations, of the sort attempted here, though reconcilable with structuration theory, is somewhat problematic. See also section 1.2.3.

60. Ranson et al. (1980) suggested that the choice of relevant concept of structure is a function of the time perspective adopted: "the closer the 'horizon', the more visible the actor but constrained by his context; in the longer time perspective, actors become less 'visible', but their frames of meaning, the product of their structuring, more determinate. Constituted structures have become constitutive".

61. "First, the individual is in a position in which his decision with regard to some particular line of action has consequences for other interests and activities not necessarily related to it. Second, he has placed himself in that position by his own prior actions. A third element /. . /: the committed person must be aware that he made the side bet" (Becker, 1960:36).

62. Adapted from Stryjan 1983b:250. In a similar vein, Grusky (1966) commented, in the case of women executives: "The lack of available opportunities at a similar status level should function to provide strong commitment to the company" (p. 502).

63. Kanter (1972) found no instance where an externally caused difficulty or crisis could be unequivocally said to have rendered communal survival technically impossible. Any of the ordeals that have "objectively" terminated some communes (economic crisis, famine, epidemics, natural disaster, and so on) have been survived by other communes.

64. The issue has nearly been defined away in mainstream self-management research. An often-preached assumption advises us to expect increased motivation, decreased need for control, and so forth, the moment ownership has been transferred to workers. Clarke (1983:9ff) brings up the uncomfortable closeness of this somewhat simplistic view to official Soviet dogma.

65. Later research is marked to a considerable extent by a growing divergence between an increasingly sophisticated theoretical interpretation of the concept and empirical tools that, in fact, merely operationalize either a desire to stay in one's work place or, at most, positive oral evaluation of the company. This has actually led Steers (1977) to suspect that the research actually done amounts to talking about commitment while measuring loyalty.

66. More general applications of the model to other types of organizations are discussed in chapter 7.

67. First presented in Stryjan 1984b.

68. Wherever formal decision-making takes place. Formal policy setting and major reorganization decisions often take place in general assemblies or corresponding organs. Other locii where formal decision making takes place (committees, departments, and so on) often vary from one organization to another. The stress here is, for obvious reasons, on decisions that in some way affect organization design.

69. See Giddens, 1984:26.

70. Dealing with a post-factum analysis of an aggregation of members' free choices over time, as Kanter does, this can hardly be considered a problem. However, one may wonder whether the members of these successful communes Kanter analyzed would ever have reached their correct decisions were they not blissfully ignorant of her analysis.

71. Similar qualifications can be raised regarding Rothschild-Whitt's ambitious effort (1979) to outline Weber's "missing type": "an attempt to delineate the form of authority and the corresponding mode of organization that follows from value-rational premises" (p. 510). Rothschild-Whitt departed explicitly from Weber's definition of value-rationality: "The orientation of value-rational action is distinguished /. . / by its clearly self-conscious formulation of the ultimate values governing the action and its consistently planned orientation of its detailed course to these values" (1978:25). By so doing, Rothschild-Whitt subordinated the *practice* of organization design to Weber's intransigent *analytical* requirements of constant vigilance and full discursive accountability. These requirements well exceed what any real-life organization could be expected to bear. The focus in this work is, instead, on routine action and practical consciousness (Giddens, 1984), two categories largely omitted by Weber.

72. For an account of such path-seeking in the case of the kibbutz, see Spiro, 1970.

73. Compare Ouchi, 1980. Pfeffer, adapting Kuhn's (1962) notions for the organizational context, stated that an organizational paradigm would include: "the beliefs about case-and-effect relations and standards of practice and behaviour, as well as concrete examples of these, that constitute how an organization goes about doing things" (Pfeffer, 1982:227-228).

74. See Stryjan, 1986, 1987, where the concept was employed in a discussion of cooperative planning. Some correspondence, which will be discussed further in this chapter, exists between this approach and Ouchi's (1980) notion of an organizational paradigm.

75. Ouchi's approach is influenced to a considerable extent by the Japanese corporation. Similarities and parallels between the Japanese corporation and the Israeli kibbutz, in regard to individuals' (employees and members, respectively) relation to the organization and their career paths, were pointed out by Golomb (n.d.).

76. Miyazaki (1982, in an otherwise insightful economic model of the SM firm) gave the issue yet one more absurd twist: since equality is assumed in the model, lay-offs are expected to occur randomly throughout the organization.

77. Arithmetically, an expectancy of future benefits is a multiplication product of calculated benefit by the probability the participant has of being around to partake of it. The lower this probability, the shorter the time horizon.

78. It is worth noting that the seriousness of the commitment that taking in a new member would imply under these circumstances may yield a somewhat problematic corollary to the assumption, namely, a reluctance to employ mew workers (see Jackall and Levin, 1984a:11; Fletcher, 1976:184).

79. It is perhaps symptomatic that CLIFFS, the most participative enterprise in the EDLA sample (briefly presented under a heading "A sunshine case" in an appendix to Stryjan and Hellmark 1985) was the only case in the sample in which management clearly stated that job sharing, rather than any of the above alternatives, would be chosen if the need for desinvestment ever arose (interview material, courtesy of Ann-Britt Hellmark, and my own interview material).

80. A model of the kibbutz, incorporating creation of work in the objective function, was, however, constructed by Ben-Ner and Neuberger (1979a, 1979b). A notion of an employment contract is also incorporated in Miyazaki's model (1982).

81. An interesting study of the operation of such controls in the case of labour (re)allocation in a kibbutz can be found in Shepher, 1983.

82. Such practices may be borrowed, or simply inherited by the cooperative, and accepted as part of the natural order of things, a conventional wisdom that is all-too-seldom questioned by research. Conforth (1982:21) related: "one representative [workers' representative to board] recalled that they had persuaded the manager not to sack someone". Neither the author nor the informant seem to question the manager's right to do so had he remained unpersuaded.

83. Domar's model, developed originally for the Russian collective farm, "demonstrates" that individual motivation is incompatible with collective reward, since a motivated participant will be rewarded only by the $n$th part of his effort's result, $n$ being the number of participants. The approach here closely reminds of Olson's (as to collective action).

84. An interesting and highly comprehensive community-service package of the sort is described by Gavito et al. (1986), in the case of the Mexican Cruz Azul cooperative cement plant.

85. Flexibility imposed from above, without being legitimated by needs that are clear to those commanded about, would probably generate opposition and be eventually sabotaged from below (see Stryjan, 1983b).

86 Establishment of personal domains and inter-team or department rivalries, turns reciprocal relations into zero-sum games. A study of such developments in the relations between kibbutz production branches was presented in Stryjan, 1983b.

87. The problems of "horizontal" splits (between hierarchical levels) and "vertical" splits (between departments, work groups or production lines) are almost endemic to a defensive takeover situation, since the "new" enterprise automatically inherits the old organizational blueprint, with its built in domains and entrenched rivalries. These strains may be bridged, for a while, by initial enthusiasm. The honeymoon period may be marked by increased mobility and organizational flexibility (see, for example, Fleet, 1976:175; Oakeshott, 1978:119; Lichtenstein, 1986). These qualities tend to wane with time, gradually being replaced by reemergent traditional patterns.

88. For example, through the agency of externally recruited management or organization consultants. This issue is discussed in chapter 5.

89. American 19-th century communes, studied by Kanter and by Niv, are somewhat of a boundary case, often combining, as it were, democracy in daily affairs with deference to a religious founder figure. It would seem that successful communes have managed to maintain a skillful division between guidance and governance, with the religious leader as a source of general guidance and a benevolent court of last appeal.

90. A situation that is not uncommon, though by no means universal. Kibbutzim, and monastic communities are known to have enjoyed, in certain historical periods, a considerable prestige in their respective social contexts.

91. The cumulative impact of such choices was examined, under the label *drift* in Stryjan, 1983b. The issue is discussed in some length in chapters 5 and 6.

92. Somewhat in keeping with the restrictive notion of "principle": "A principle is a rule of inaction giving valid and general reasons for not doing in a specific instance what to unprincipled instinct would seem to be right" (quoted after Mills, 1959:285).

93. The following paragraph is abstracted from "A Reply to Prof. Rosner" (Stryjan, 1984a), a reply to Leviatan's collaborator's rejoinder to Stryjan (1983b). It is unclear whether the data Leviatan discusses were collected by him or by Rosner.

94. A feeling that "this is my enterprise", frequently stated in the replies in the EDLA interviews, is only marginally connected to formal ownership arrangements. It seems rather to be grounded on one's perceived importance and the ability — whether actually exercised or perceived as potentially within grasp — to affect the course of things. Typically, the only complaints as to the worker-owners "not shouldering their responsibility" heard in the EDLA study came from one of the least participative firms (STONE), which eventually ceased being worker-owned.

95. This is the predominant pattern observed in the Swedish EDLA sample enterprises. See Stryjan and Hellmark, 1985.

96. See Habermas, 1976.

97. This constraint (of the multitude of decisions) is considerably more serious than the talk-time constraint (number of participants) raised by Dahl and repeated by Abrahamsson.

98. This claim can be tested when controversial issues are at stake: proposals may be returned to a committee for reformulation (and further search for consensus). When decisions judged divisive are decided by a close draw, it is often the practice to suspend the decision and arrange for further discussion.

99. In the sense of simultaneously occupying super- and subordinate roles in different and parallel contexts (see Lissak, 1969). Similar patterns were also observed by Rothschild-Whitt (1979).

100. For the distinction between "strong" and "weak" hierarchy, see Horvat, (1979a)

101. These may, in fact, be considered as preconditions for free exercise of involvement. As to rotation and involvement, see discussion in the next chapter.

102. Let us denote this proportion by $C$. If the number of newly appointed officials can only equal the number of retiring incumbents, and given $n$ posts to be manned, the picture after $t$ rotation rounds would look as follows:

$$R_t = n(1 - C)^t$$

Where, as $t$ approaches infinity, $R_t$ approaches zero. Paradoxically, the shorter the renomination/rotation intervals, the quicker the process.

103. The informal custom of "ceremonial refusals" in kibbutz nomination procedures (Talmon, 1972) may be seen as a way of weeding out candidates that are too keen on being elected, offering, at the same time a degree of insurance against loss of face, for the rejected aspirants.

104. As remarked in Stryjan, 1984b, such a state of affairs, if at all possible outside isolated aboriginal cultures, would rather be a case for organizational geriatrics.

105. The disruption caused by the appearance of the steel axe among Australian Aborigines is somewhat of an anthropological cause celebrée. For a short resumé, see Hernes, 1977, quoting Sharp and Lauriston, 1952.

106. Paraphrased from Weick, 1969:36.

107. Such as varying forms of legal incorporation, various ways of achieving tolerable levels of economic performance, and so on. Ancilliarity does not imply that the requirements such characteristics are to meet are in any way unimportant in themselves, merely that they can be met in a number of ways by one and the same organization.

108. Barnard, 1938; see also Perrow, 1979:70ff.

## Chapter 4

109.    Either a departure from the "right" model or an adherence to a flawed model. The notion of built-in failure as it has been developed early in in the study of producer-cooperative (Webb, 1891), democratic (Michels, 1970), and other "normatively legitimated" organizations (Selznick 1949) belongs to the second type.

110.    See the typology suggested by Scott, 1981.

111.    Or in the most "radical" versions, of a new management called in to replace the old one (Hedberg, 1974).

112.    The definition of what is to be considered "a product" (that loses quality), is left intentionally vague and loose. A product can in fact, be anything the member or customer may perceive himself as partaking of, from a toilet-soap brand to the general quality of life in a given country or the political line of a party of which one is a supporter.

113.    It is the combination of elements that is novel rather than the elements themselves. Monitoring and (aggregation of) "everyman inputs" are fairly common in economic theory and model building, but largely absent in organization theory. The opposite applies as far as the second element (qualitative criteria) is concerned.

114.    Somewhat in keeping with the less ambitious approaches to commitment, such as Hrebiniak and Alutto's (1972) or, in self-management contexts, Long's (1978b).

115.    The idea was first explored in Hirschman, 1981.

116.    Attitudes, too, are defined mostly negatively. Loyalty is thus seen as an internalized threshold to exit, involvement as a phase between two disenchantments (first with the private, and then with the public sphere). His somewhat hesistant excursion into positive motivations in *Shifting Involvements* (1982) notwithstanding, even Hirschman's theoretical work is to a considerable extent bound by a traditional economic view of humans, being, as he himself poined out (1977), an aggregation of vices tempered by reason.

117.    In fact, Hirschman himself hardly employed his own concepts when dealing with South American cooperatives (in a development context) in *Getting Ahead Collectively* (1984). A somewhat perfunctory application of Hirschman's initial framework(1970) was attempted in Hammer et al., 1982.

118.    The same argument, though in a somewhat weaker form, would apply to a large number of fairly common relationships between individuals and organizations, such as employment, being a client of an educational service, or prolonged hospitalization (Aldrich, 1979; Scott, 1981).

119.    To stretch the point further: for a member in a collective, "non-input" activities would be an exception rather than a rule.

120.    Hirschman dealt, under the somewhat clumsy label of "loyalist behaviour", only with particular circumstances for non-exit and for activation of protest mechanisms.

121.    Explicitly in *Exit, Voice and Loyalty* (1970), but also in *Shifting Involvements* (1982) the stress is on protest action.

122.    As suggested in the diagram, overlap or hybrid areas exist (some were, in fact, suggested by Hirschman, 1970:82ff). The intention here, however, is not to engage in a taxonomy of such forms.

123.    A point that is wholly missed by Birch, 1975.

124.    Giddens (1984) observed that absolute coercion rests on the coercion agent's independence of his or hers victim's performance. Loyalty is neither needed nor required.

125.    As Rokkan (1974:39) stated: "At all levels of life we can identify structures and processes ensuring some minimal maintenance of established systems /. . / In Hirschman's model these would be the *loyalty* mechanisms: the structures forcing the component parts to *stay* within the system".

126.    In a sense, this definition lies close to Becker's definition of commitment (see section 3.2 in this book).

127.        One hidden assumption in such an approach is, generally, that the rank and file member may be innovative, but such innovativeness would usually serve the member's own, rather than the organization's, ends. (See Perrow 1979:151).

128.        Buchanan, 1974. The statement deals, in fact, with commitment. As mentioned (ibid.), the various definitions of commitment easily tend to spill over to other forms of positive relation to the organization.

129.        Kanter, 1972:66: "Commitment thus refers to the willingness of people to do what will maintain the group because it provides what they need".

130.        Kaufman presupposed that such irritants should be eliminated by action from above.

131.        Besides its other tasks, dealt with in the previous chapter, namely, of equalizing the distribution of skills (Leviatan, 1978) and power. Such equalization may, in fact, be considered as a precondition for free exercise of involvement.

132.        It may be suggested that the involved innovator's and the protester's stance could be located near the respective ends of a continuum stretching between "saving the organization" and "saving one's own soul". Whereas the involved member would primarily see an effect to his or her action, the protester would, first and foremost, have his *right* proven — whatever the personal consequences may be. The description here closely resembles Weber's account of the value-rational mode of action: "the actions of persons who, regardless of possible cost to themselves, act to put into practice their convictions of what seems to them to be required by duty, honour, /. . / or the importance of some 'cause'" (1978:25). In a sense, it also makes evident the difficulty inherent in constructing an organizational model based on (thus perceived) value rationality. The mode of involvement, occupying a central place in our discussion, could probably be awarded the (non-existent) label of affect-rational action.

133.        This phenomenon is accounted for in slightly different ways in Stryjan, 1985 and Hirschman, 1970. In the cases included in my study, the rising intensity of activity was generally accompanied by a sharp decrease in the activity's effectiveness.

134.        Requoted from Hirschman 1970:92. See Hirschman's interesting discussion (ibid., note 8), on the phrase's pedigree.

135.        An insight into the problems involved is provided in section 5.3.

136.        Compare with Thibault and Kelley's (1959) comparison level concept.

137.        Thus Rhodes and Steers found, in their study of a plywood cooperative, that "the set of procedures around share-ownership serves /. . / as a 'turnover control policy'".

138.        Kibbutzim have a number of institutionalized alternatives that may be offered to (or sought by) a member in crisis; a sabbatical year or a temporary assignment outside the kibbutz (or even abroad) being the most typical (Stryjan, 1985).

139.        The question of "inverse selection" is well discussed in the kibbutz movement. The possibility of such selection occurring among kibbutz-born members has been refuted (in a quantitative comparison between "stayers" and "leavers") by Leviatan, 1975. For the case of externally recruited members (Stryjan, 1985a), accounting for a bigger part of the new member turnover (Leviatan, 1975, Leviatan et al., 1977), it has neither been refuted nor (at least on technical grounds) appears to be refutable (Stryjan, 1985a).

140.        Dealing with scenarios for decline of his "self-evaluating" organization.

141.        The Swedish *föreningstradition* of indirect democracy can be seen as an interesting example of this trend.

142.        See Bachrach and Baratz' (1962) and Lukes' (1976) respective discussion of power.

143.        For a virtually identical formulation, see Aldrich, 1979:235.

144.        In itself, a mapping of Allport's (1934) "J-curve" onto our "Hirschmanian" set of coordinates.

145.    Otherwise, a crisis of the sort may lead to the cooperative form being abandoned instead.

146.    Profit sharing in French worker cooperatives is equal to members and non-members. Return to capital (member shares) is strongly limited and paid first after return to labour, which it may not exceed (Jones, 1983; Jones and Estrin 1987; Oakeshott 1978:141). Members may, as long as they constitute a minority, reap an advantage through securing themselves management positions or other jobs that are in demand. This advantage (and, with it, the instrumental incitement to become a member) diminishes as the percentage of members in the workforce rises.

147.    See, for example, Oakeshott's (1978) description of the old "cloth-cap" British cooperatives. The differential in "recruitment costs" may have a more important role to play in "degenerative" shifts to hired labour than a labour costs differential, suggested as an explanatory factor by Miyazaki (1982) and Ben-Ner (1982).

148.    The history of the kibbutz provides an example of an unusual strategy, namely, recruitment of *Garinim*, i. e., youth groups, assembled and presocialized within the respective kibbutz movement's youth movements. Such a strategy may counteract the problems described above. At the same time, it gives rise to other problems, most notably, demographic discontinuities and potential cohort conflicts on one side and processes of contagious group exit on the other side.

## Chapter 5

149.    The division above is not meant to be exhaustive. The category of material resources in particular is treated here in an intentionally loose way and could, in principle, be subdivided further. Competence is seen in broader terms than those initially discussed by Webb (1891) and Horvat (1974). The importance of recruitment possibilities has been somewhat neglected in SM research. For organizations in general, it has been noted by Pfeffer and Salancik (1978).

150.    This feature may be presented as a lead in a process of macro reproduction (Sjöstrand, 1985) or in a process of institutionalization (Meyer and Rowan, 1977), depending on the theoretical standpoint chosen.

151.    One element of importance is deliberately left out as being the least relevant to organizations, our object of study, namely, the direct linkage between individuals and their actions and the structuration of macro systems.

152.    Rooted, in his opinion, in a mounting reluctance to recruit new members.

153.    A convenient example to consider would be the case of a user of electronic equipment in a country or region with an erratic electricity supply. Such a user would have to develop reliable backup routines, acquire a generator, or, at the least, establish a way of getting early warning from electricity suppliers pending expected electricity breaks.

154.    Thompson, as well as Scott, dealt explicitly with organizations' *technical core*. Their line of reasoning is followed here with one important modification, suggested in chapters 3-4, namely, that the technological core of the self-managed organization is defined in terms of social technology rather than production technology. Additional buffering techniques enumerated by Scott that would not be directly dealt with here are (a) forecasting: prediction of future problems in resource flow; fluctuations in prices of resources (expressed in monetary terms or as institutional demands) may facilitate choice of adaptation strategies. However, due to our organizations' marginal position and their dependence on unstable supplies, the benefits they would draw from forecasting would be limited; (b) growth: increased size both provides "a cushion or slack" (Pfeffer and Salancik, 1978:139), and thus a way of stockpiling resources, and increases an organization's power versus its environment, thus facilitating leveling strategies. However, our model would expect growth to be motivated by internal rather than environmental (or economic) considerations. Although often having buffering effects, in line with those predicted by Thompson, it can hardly be

considered a technique proper. Federative substitutes for organizational growth are dealt with in the next chapter, together with some broader applications of leveling techniques in the context of a broader environmental perspective.

155. Just as the influx of new employees may be for any industrial plant or office. Some of the research literature quoted below deals, in fact, with conventional organizations. It is important to keep in mind that a failure, intended or unintended, to recruit new employees would, if taken to the extreme, lead to the demise of the given plant, not necessarily of the firm or organization.

156. Since the burden of recruiting new members would usually fall on younger members, the effective long-range operation of such a recruiting strategy would presuppose an even, or pyramid-shaped, age distribution within the organization.

157. The internal manning of a vacancy at the top of a strictly hierarchic organization would entail at least as many steps as the number of hierarchy levels the organization supports. Since some of the vacancies created in the chain may be filled by lateral mobility, the number may be even higher.

158. Pfeffer and Salancik (1978) illustrated the case of resource dependence by the example of monastic orders, engaging in recruiting of prospective novices. A fact missed in their analysis, and self-evident to any superficial student of monasticism, is that such recruitment activities (to the extent they were undertaken at all) built on the fact that a corpus of would-be monks was continuously recreated by society at large.

159. The Shaker communities (Kanter, 1972) present an extreme example of a refusal to adjust recruitment to environmental change. The fact that the recent trend toward family housing in the kibbutz movement is often legitimated by enhancement of the kibbutz' attractiveness for would-be joining families is a (somewhat problematic) example of an adjustment orientation.

160. The recruitment possibilities in the Soviet Union were abruptly terminated in the 1920s.

161. Parallel efforts to recruit lower class "problem youth", in so called youth-communities (Hevrot No'ar) were at best half-hearted, with the focus set often on education rather than absorption. As a kibbutz educator once confided to me (unpublished report, Kolar and Stryjan 1980): "there's a paradox in working with youth communities: you are not supposed to be too successful".

162. Which, even in the movement's heyday, averaged 50 percent at most; see Rayman, 1981.

163. The importance of natural growth has been consistently underplayed in the kibbutz ideology. The nativity rate in the earliest, and materially most difficult, period appears to have been low. There is some documentary evidence as to opposition to establishment of family units and some anecdotal evidence of attempts to restrict the birth rate in hard times. At the same time, a great deal of resources was uncontestedly expended on outward-oriented activities. At present, the situation appears to be the reverse.

164. We should distinguish here between policies and random size fluctuations. If committed to growth, the organization would not contract its operations when it loses members.

165. A tendency to maximize return per workday has been noted, in the case of cooperatives, by a long line of theorists. However, as the case of the kibbbutz clearly shows (Barkai, 1977; Ben Ner and Neuberger, 1979a), such a drive need not be interpreted as aiming at maximization of individual revenue. It may also constitute an integral part of a growth strategy.

166. In one case of reconstruction negotiations, under negotiation in a cooperative in central Sweden in February 1987, the bank involved blandly stated that "the enterpreneurial idea is good, but the condition for debt rescheduling is that the company (i.e, the production assets) should be sold to a competent enterpreneur". Since no enterpreneur was found, the affair was concluded by selling the assets to a joint-stock company established by some of the former cooperative's leading figures.

167.    In those cases in which companies of the EDLA sample had external board members, they were as a rule nominated at the direct stipulation of creditors. The JUNO case (presented in some detail in an appendix to Stryjan and Hellmark, 1985) is a particularly extreme example of external control, labeled by the authors as permanent receivership. In this case, the company's two successive managers have been recruited by the creditors as well. An additional way of influencing a company's internal structure encountered in the sample is that of imposing consultants.

168.    Due to French cooperative legislation, members largely lack economic incentive for barring wage labour from membership. Becoming a member is to a great extent a question of the worker's initiative (see also note 146). The percentage of members can thus, to some extent, serve as an indication of the prevailing ésprit. The degree of the workforce's homogeneity may nonetheless have some independent effect on the propensity for solidary decisions.

169.    Saving and debt policies of kibbutzim present a somewhat complex problem. Stern (1965) criticized the kibbutzim's heavy indebtedness. Both tendencies seem, in fact, to have existed side by side. The reason for this paradoxical situation ought to be sought in the special structure of kibbutz debt at the time, consisting, to a considerable extent, of long-term advantageous loans from committed sources, and in the fact that the policy of absorbing whole groups at a time clearly entails periodical disparities between size of population and sources of income that would require bridging measures. At any rate, even Stern did not find the debt/equity ratio unreasonable.

170.    Or to avoid loss of face. The Skandinaviska Enskilda bank's involvement in the SYDOR takeover (EDLA sample) seems to have been motivated by a will to moderate the negative local publicity the bank's majority owner group has gained in the plant closedown (Bucht et al 1976, and confidential interview transcripts).

171.    See also Scott, 1981:183.

172.    Dealing with the British "cloth-cap" cooperatives, Oakeshott (1978:64) spoke of "a deep rooted suspicion of anyone with other than the most authentic 'cloth cap' credentials".

173.    An interesting twist to this procedure is reported by Niv (1976): a commune forced to send members for schooling "outside" would send them in groups, and arrange for lodging with sympathizers, so as to maximize social control and restrict environmental contact.

174    Since, in such cases, the would-be professional would first be able to manage his assignment after a considerable time lag, such a practice clearly presupposes a degree of internal slack. This issue is returned to in the next section.

175.    Internally recruited managers would, in such cases, be exposed to a secondary socialization in the business community that they would have to interact with. Problems of life-style and, inevitably, expense accounts that such resocialization may entail, can be deeply divisive (see Rosner and Shur, 1982). Problems of this sort provide certain merit to the claim, advanced by Gunn, that managers should be hired rather than permitted to become members. It should also be noted that the recruitment of managers to worker-owned enterprises would normally be fairly skewed, due to lack of advancement perspectives. To some degree this would moderate the effect of professionalization.

176.    Managers are barred from membership, and their high pay serves as an indirect disincentive for applying. The social distance is self-evident, and Greenberg (1986) quoted a deal of derogatory statements addressed at "that turkey in the office".

177.    Somewhat similarily the task of formulating a new policy in Japanese corporations is often assigned to the newest worker in the department in question (Ouchi, 1981)

178.    Kanovsky (1966) found that the greatest part of aid to agriculture during the period in question was directed to branches in which the kibbutzim were underrepresented. The massive expansion in the number of new kibbutzim has also imposed a heavy financial burden on the movements (ibid.). Finally, the *Ichud* and

*Meuchad* movements (especially the latter) were still suffering of the disastrous consequences of the great schism in the *Meuchad* movement in the early 1950s (see Rayman, 1981:130; Lieblich, 1983).

179.    Compare Wilkins and Ouchi, 1983:474.

180.    *Haartzi, Ichud* and *Meuchad*. The last two have since merged into one joint movement (*TaKaM*, an acronym for united kibbutz movement). For a brief summary of the movements' respective ideologies see Ben Ner and Neuberger, 1979b, Stern, 1965.

## Chapter 6

181.    Habermas' statement (1976), originally applied to macro systems, has a clear relevance here: "when systems maintain themselves through altering both boundaries and structural continuity, their identity becomes blurred. The same system modification can be conceived of equally well as a learning process and change or as a dissolution process and collapse of the system. It cannot be unambiguously determined whether a new system has been formed or the old one has merely regenerated itself" (Habermas, 1976:3).

182.    By *physical* is meant here preserving or increasing a workforce, a machine park, a budget slate and so on. In its narrowest formal interpretation, the concept may even be restricted to the continued occupancy of a register post in the company register.

183.    The issue of identity comes, naturally to the fore in cases of extreme change. As Gustavsen remarked, in a somewhat oversimplified manner: "It [the company] can exist as a legal entity while the members change /. . / Its existence is, however, also independent of of specific, physical resources: a company can sell all its production equipment and buy completely new equipment without any change in identity" (n.d.: 5). Pfeffer (1982:188-189), acidly stating that "unfortunately, organizations do not die as neatly as humans", illustrated the evasiveness of the issue by a short sketch of the fates of Penn Central Corporation: Created by merger of two major railroad companies, subsequently gone through bankrupcy, and reconstruction, it shed all of its railway assets (to Conrail) and is now back in profitable trade, though in different fields.

184.    Meyer and Rowan (1977:346) stated that, in the ongoing processes of institutionalization "organizations tend to disappear as distinct and bounded entities".

185.    Compare to Hannan and Freeman's statement: "The latter [normative order] offers particularly intriguing possibilities. Whenever the history of an organization, its politics and its social structure are encoded in a normative claim /. . / one can use these claims to identify forms and define populations for research" (1977:935). Deviance should, however not be *equated* with identity. To illustrate this point by a fictive example: A non-cannibal group in a society where cannibalism is the norm may be distinguished by its deviant behaviour. The label of "non-cannibals" would hardly be informative, though, as far as the group's identity is concerned.

186.    Selected here for their ability to systematize descriptions of the environment and not those of self-management, the picture of self-management that the application of ecological approaches tends to yield is *deliberately* skewed. In other words, the resulting picture should not be treated as a diagnosis of the state of SM but rather as a problem agenda. The reader ought to keep in mind that a great deal of the developments to be outlined below would require a breakdown of reproduction mechanisms in order to remain unchecked or to take place at all.

187.    Unwillingness to change is seen by Hannan and Freeman (1977) as a dysfunction of sorts (caused mostly by particular, vested interests) and not as a product of a conscious policy.

188.    As Aldrich stated: "The persistence of organizational forms does not depend on the fate of any particular organization" (1979:190).

189.    A third problem taken up by Horvat is the tendency of such enterprises to deny membership to workers recruited by its grounders under expansion. Horvat's claims notwithstanding, it is hard to relate this problem directly to the environment, though it would presumably disappear once private ownership is abolished.

190.    Pfeffer and Salancik (1978) proposed two distinct terms for denoting internal and external efficiency: *efficiency* and *effectiveness*, respectively.

191.    An environmental niche is defined by Hannan and Freeman as follows (1977:947): "that area in the constraint space (the space whose dimensions are levels of resources, etc.) in which the population outcompetes all other local populations".

192.    Kanter's notion of transaction costs centres on transactions with the environment. This application of the concept differs to a considerable degree from Williamson's (1975), Abrahamsson's (1986), or Ouchi's (1980). The latter refers exclusively to internal transactions.

193.    For Kanter's particular prescription for managing such pressures, see section 6.6. It is worth remarking that, despite some significant similarities, Kanter was not aware of Hawley's work.

194.    The choice of term consciously alludes to Weber (1930/1976).

195.    The three mechanisms can be grouped along a scale of directness-inobstrusiveness, with cases where practices are directly imposed on "deviant" organizations, on fear of explicit penalty (coercive isomorphism) at the top, through cases where they are "learned" from adjacent organizations in the field (mimetic), ending with cases where they are "independently arrived at" from within (normative isomorphism). Conceptually, this gradation parallels that of Luke's (1976) three dimensions of power. In an analytical sense, power is indeed being exercised upon the deviant organization, though it need not be directed by any coherent actor.

196    Coercive isomorphism in relations to other organizations would, as illustrated in the previous chapter, manifest itself most clearly under crises or during the organization's formation stage. Once the organization has been established, and as long as it fares well, manifestations of isomorphism in relations with other organizations would tend to become subtler, since no set penalty on refusal to conform exists.

197.    One of the enterprises in the EDLA sample has recently marked its 100th anniversary (as a company; worker takeover is a relatively recent event) by publishing a history of the enterprise. The publication focused on the founder, his family, subsequent owners, and so on, without devoting a single line to the present ownership form.

198.    In extreme cases, environmental imperatives may be evoked and blown out of proportion for manipulative ends, most typically, in cases where a management group that has a monopoly on external contacts filters the incoming information to advance its own interests.

199.    A not uncommon feature in such cases is the employment of consultants "which, like Johnny Appleseeds, spread a few organizational models throughout the land" (DiMaggio and Powell, 1983:152). As to consultants' role in spreading models and ideologies, see Himmelstrand et al., 1986. The extent to which consultants may be considered as independent agents in the process is questionable. Most typically, consultants are chosen by the enterprise, the choice being based on the consultant's record and image. Such choices may also be interpreted in power or policy-setting terms, especially in cases in which consultants are forced on the organization by creditors or by a power group within the organization.

200.    The range of problematic normative inputs is not necessarily restricted to the strict sphere of business functioning; we have already noted that an organization's boundary often cuts *through* its members. Areas adjacent to this boundary (e.g., members' leisure time or private social and economic resources) have been suggested as possible sources to draw upon in emergencies. This relationship has, of course, an obverse side; to the extent that an organization's mode of functioning places demands on (or presupposes stability in) additional

spheres of members' activity, besides work proper, such as members' leisure and consumption habits, it would necessarily be vulnerable to changes and normative pressures from these quarters as well.

201.     Labour legislation may also play an important role (Aspelin and Axelsson, 1982). Since variation between countries on the issues of labour legislation is – if possible – even more extreme, this issue will not be discussed here.

202.     Essential differences between tax systems make general conclusions (beyond the statement that each national taxation system elicits its own tax-specific behaviour) hard to draw. Since personal income, corporate income, and dividends may lie in entirely different tax brackets, tax-optimizing behaviour would differ widely between countries. Reviewing Gunn's (1984) recommendations, based on American experiences, Stryjan (1985a) remarked: "A great deal of the arrangements the author suggests, regarding profit distribution, wage setting and reinvestment, would appear superfluous, others — directly suicidal this side of the Atlantic".

203.     In a recent case, now on appeal, the county registrar for societies in a west Swedish county has refused to register a cooperative, since its articles of association state that the general assembly of members has the supreme executive authority over the organization (i.e., has the right to override executive decisions by the board). Such a prerogative is not provided for in Swedish cooperative legislation.

204.     This phenomenon has, to the best of my knowledge, never previously been recorded in any description of the kibbutz, presumably because of its total insignificance to kibbutz affairs. I became aware of this fact accidentally: As the chairman of my (then) kibbutz, I was supposed to sign the protocol of the (fictitious) council's annual meeting. It is possible that other kibbutzim may have solved the problem in some different fashion. It seems that the choice to abide by unsuitable, but largely toothless, legislation was motivated by the three kibbutz movements' interest in avoiding new legislation which they could not control.

205.     *Mimicry* would have been a much more fitting term for such behaviours. Since this term is too easily confused with to *mimetic change*, a term employed by DiMaggio and Powell to denote a somewhat different behaviour, it is not used here.

206.     One argument sometimes used to explain away such inconvenient exceptions (to the extent they are noted) is their apparent scarcity (Aldrich and Stern, 1983). The status of such organizational anomalies in an organization-ecological explanatory design reminds one, in a sense, of the role the fauna of Galapagos plays in the biological-evolutionary design. The logic underlying such explanations is somewhat flawed: basically, the ecological model consists of three elements: variation, selection, and retention (Aldrich, 1979). Research, however, centres predominantly on selection, as retroactively deduced from observed patterns of retention. Common to all authors is the lack of interest in the sources of variation. Thus the possibility that the composition of a population is largely determined before the selection process ever started operating on actual organizations is not even considered. When dealing with SM organizations, the possibility that the form's scarcity ought be traced to problems of "non-emergence" (Fanning and McCarthy, 1986; see also Jones, 1976), should not be excluded. In other words, the organizational environment, unlike the biological one, may not merely be selecting against certain forms, in a variety of spontaneously emerging variations. It may also be actively recruiting definite organizational forms. A broadening of the environmental perspective to encompass parameters that are relevant to organization formation could be extremely useful in explaining the scarcity of SM organizations.

207.     Not surprisingly, the organizational objectives identified by Pfeffer and Salancik are, as in Galbraight's analysis, growth, power, and predictability.

208     The nearest Pfeffer and Salancik ever came to the notion of principles, was in their discussion of restrictions on compliance. The sheer technical inability to comply, it is argued, can be considered a highly effective defense against

giving in to pressure. In the example given, the restrictions are lodged in an external regulatory agency.

209.    Not unsimilarily, family-owned business would incorporate in its strategies, if long-sighted enough, some considerations connected with inheritance tax legislation, which would be absent from institutionally owned corporations.

210.    To the extent such resources are acknowledged in economic thinking, they are usually placed under the nebulous term *goodwill*.

211.    The features stressed are (temporary) autonomy from technological development, due to an initial technological headstart; a relationship to an existing culture, which would cut down resocialization costs; and a source of "committed" financing. All of these conditions are met to a significant degree in the case of the kibbutz. See Stryjan, 1983b.

212    Or in Pfeffer and Salancik's (1978) terms, to maintain some degree of freedom in their resource dependence.

213.    A model of the kibbutz as an open organization, presented by Katz and Golomb (1974/1975) is, in fact, such an impure model. Premium is set on growth, but a particular emphasis is laid on commitment enhancing measures and on creative adaptation to environment change. Two central weaknesses of this model are (a) an atomistic view of the kibbutz, abstracting from the role of federations; and (b) a rosy assumption of harmony between the kibbutz and its environment, neglecting contradictions and defensive measures.

214.    As Selznick saw it, such strategies imply a degree of opportunism. This conclusion, though often justified, is not considered here as being inescapable.

215.    The organizations dealt with by Hedberg (e.g., 1974), and Starbuck et al. (1978), are, as a rule, big companies or multinational corporations, with Kalmar Carriage Works as the smallest case studied. Perrow (1979), applying a somewhat different perspective, dealt predominantly with giant corporations, though his outline of network analysis indicates an approach not unlike the one suggested here.

216.    The fact that organizations that differ in size would be competing for different resources (e.g., big organizations would seldom compete small ones out of the market) is recognized by Hannan and Freeman. Here, the point would be carried further: It is suggested that not only the relevant resources — but also the environmental texture would vary with size. Small organizations would tend to perceive environments as more rough textured than big ones that they seemingly share environment with.

217.    This state of affairs is by no means unique to SM. Within (conventional) industry it is most readily noted in cases where the "private" sphere impinges on the organizational one, as in the case of "Monday exemplars".

218.    My own unpublished interview material.

219.    In economic models of self-management, this conservative attitude to growth is noted, somewhat hastily, as one major mechanism of degeneration.

220.    It is possible that some recent developments within the Estonian cooperative movement can also be subsumed under this heading (own observations and interview material). The matter requires, however, some further research.

221.    See, for example, Elzinga, 1970; Telser, 1966.

222    The reference is to Freeman's article: "Organizational life cycles and natural selection processes", in Staw, B. M. and Cummings, L. L. (eds) *Research in Organizational Behaviour*, vol. 4 (JAI Press, Greenwich, CT).

223.    With the exception of Mondragon, at least under the Franco regime.

224.    The political and economic developments in Israel, during the past decade, seem to have turned this dependence into a major source of vulnerability. A banking crisis, a crisis in the labour-controlled economy, and, finally, the fact that kibbutzim cannot any longer count on the state as a de facto ultimate guarantor have all dramatically reduced the single kibbutz' creditworthiness.

225.    These procedures are carried on a service, rather than monopoly, base. Kibbutzim have full freedom of recruiting members and establishing youth groups by their own efforts. They may, however, use the respective federations' absorption departments to screen their own applicants. The movement provides also a point of reference for stray applicants: individuals without a kibbutz

connection that consider joining a kibbutz. A movement would, however, not start a general recruitment campaign.

226.    A reproduction circuit is defined by Giddens (1984:376) as "An institutionalized series of reproduction relations, governed either by homeostatic causal loops, or by reflexive self-regulation". The concept employed throughout this work was, instead, "reproduction loop" to denote the micro level and fragmentary character of the relations studied.

227.    The expression is taken from the subtitle of Catherine (not to be confused with Beatrice) Webb's work (1919).

228.    Jonnergård is referring to an earlier version of this work, submitted as a doctoral thesis in 1987.

229.    Empirically, Jonnergårds work is primarily based on material collected in established consumer cooperative federations. This has undoubtedly caused some narrowing of the findings' scope.

## Chapter 7

230    Herzberg's typology of motivators can, in fact, be seen as a handy methodology for weeding out problematic employees.

231.    See Morgan, 1986:243. Contrary to Morgan's opinion, I do not see such notions as invariably dysfunctional.

# REFERENCES

Abell, P. (1983): The Viability of Industrial Producer Co-operation. In *International Yearbook of Organizational Democracy*. John Wiley and Sons Ltd, London, pp. 73-103.

Abrahamsson, B. (1975): *Organisationsteori. Om byråkrati, administration och självstyre.* AWE/Gebers, Stockholm

————. (1977): *Bureaucracy or Participation. The Logic of Organization.* Sage, Beverly Hills, Calif.,London.

————. (1980): On Structural Criticism in Organizational Analysis. Working Paper. Arbetslivscentrum, Stockholm.

————. (1982): F. W. Taylor vs. the Peer Group. Paper prepared for the ISA World Congress, Mexico.

————. (1983): On Form and Function in Organizational Theory. Working Paper. Arbetslivscentrum, Stockholm.

————. (1986): *Varför finns organisationer?* Norstedts, Stockholm

Adizes, I.; Borgese E. M. (eds.), (1975): *Self Management: New Dimensions to Democracy.* Clio Press, Santa Barbara, Calif., Oxford.

Alchian, A. A. ; Demsetz, H. (1972): The Property Rights Paradigm. *Journal of Economic History*, 33, pp. 16-27.

Aldrich, H.; Pfeffer J. (1976): Environments of Organizations. In Inkeles, A.; Coleman, J.; Smelser, N. (eds.), *Annual Review of Sociology*. Vol. 2, pp79-105. Annual Reviews, Palo Alto, Calif.

Aldrich, H. (1979): *Organizations and Environments*. Prentice-Hall, Englewood Cliffs, N.J.

Aldrich, H.; Stern, R. N. (1983): Resource Mobilization and the Creation of US Producer Cooperatives, 1835-1935. *Economic and Industrial Democracy*, 4 no. 3 (August), pp 371-405.

Allport, F. H. (1934): The J-Curve Hypothesis. *Journal of Social Psychology*, 5, pp. 141-183

————. (1962): A Structuronomic Conception of Behavior: Individual and Collective. *Journal of Abnormal and Social Psychology*, 64, pp. 3-30

Andersson, A.; Lindroth, C. (1979): Styrelserepresentation för anställda i företag med 25-99 anställda. Småföretagsprojektet, Report No. 1979:6. Arbetslivscentrum, Stockholm.

Argyris, C.; Schön, D. A. (1978): *Organizational Learning. A Theory of Action Perspective*. Addison-Wesley, Reading, Mass.

Aspelin, S.; Axelsson, T. (1982): Löntagarägda företag- delägarnas dubbla sits. Mimeo. Faculty of Law, Lund University.

Bachrach, P.; Baratz, S. M. (1962): The Two Faces of Power. *American Political Science Review*, 56, pp. 947-952.

Bachrach, S. M. (ed.), (1982): *Research in the Sociology of Organizations*, vol. 1. JAI Press, Greenwich, Conn; London

Bager, T. (1988): The Rise and Development of Traditional and New-Wave Cooperatives in the Nordic Countries. Paper presented to the International Cooperative Symposium, Leningrad. Mimeo. Sydjysk Universitetscenter, Esbjerg.

Barkai, H. (1977): *Growth Patterns of the Kibbutz Economy*. North Holland; Amsterdam; New York; Oxford.

Barnard, C. (1938): *The Functions of the Executive*. Harvard University Press, Cambridge, Mass.

Barry, B. (1974): Exit, Voice, and Loyalty. A review article. *British Journal of Political Science*, 4 (January), pp. 79-107.

Bartölke, K.; Bergmann, T.; Liegle, L. (eds.), (1980): *Integrated Cooperatives in the Industrial Society: The Example of the Kibbutz*. Van Gorcum, Assen.

Batstone, E. (1982): France. In Stephen, 1982, pp. 99-121.

————. (1983): Organization and Orientation: A Life Cycle Model of French Co-operatives.in *Economic and Industrial Democracy*, 4, no. 2, pp. 139-162.

Baty, G.; Evan, V.; Rothermel, T. (1971): Personnel Flows as Interorganizational Relations. *Administrative Science Quarterly*, 16, pp. 430-443.

Baumgartner, T.; Burns, T. R. (1979): Institutional Conflict and Power: The Case of Capital and Financial Institutions in Relation to Self-Management. *Economic Analysis and Workers Management*, 13, pp. 582-602.

Baumgartner, T.; Burns, T. R.; DeVillé, P. (1978): Conflict Resolution and Conflict Development: A Theory of Game Transformation with an Application to the LIP Factory Conflict. in *Research in Social movements, Conflicts and Change*. JAI Press, Greenwich, CT.

Baumgartner, T.; Burns, T.R.; DeVillé, P. (1981): Autogestion and Planning. Dilemmas and Possibilities. *Economic Analysis and Workers Management*, 15, pp. 459-479.

Becker, H. S. (1960): Notes on the concept of commitment. *American Journal of Sociology*, 66, pp. 32-42.

Bellas, C. J. (1975): Industrial Democracy through Worker Ownership. An American Experience. In Vanek, 1975a, pp. 203-212.

Ben-Ner, A. (1982): Changing Values and Preferences in Communal Organizations: Econometric Evidence from the Experience of the Israeli Kibbutz. In Jones, D. C.; Svejnar, J. (eds.), pp. 255-286.

Ben-Ner, A.; Neuberger, E. (1979a): The Economics of Self-management: the Israeli Kibbutz and the Yugoslav Enterprise.in *Economic Analysis and Workers Management*, 13, pp. 47-70.

————. (1979b): On the Economics of Communalism and Self-Management: The Israeli Kibbutz. Paper prepared for presentation at the Walton Symposium: Labour management: Performance and Prospects, Glasgow. Draft.

Bergmann, T. (1980): The Kibbutz in the Continuum of Forms of Cooperation. In Bartölke et al., pp. 24-49.

Berle, A. A.; Means G. C. (1934): *The Modern Corporation and Private* Property. Macmillan, New York.

Berman, K. V. (1982): The United States of America: A Co-operative Model for Worker Management. In Stephen, 1982, pp. 74-98.

Berman, K. V.; Berman, M. D. (1978): The Long-Run Analysis of the Labor-Managed Firm: Comment. *American Economic Review*, 68, pp. 701-704.

Berger, P.; Luckmann, T. (1967): *The Social Construction of Reality*. Doubleday Anchor, Garden City, N.Y.

Beyer, J. M. (1981): Ideologies, Values and Decision Making in Organizations. In Nystrom and Starbuck, 1981, pp. 166-202.

Birch, A. H. (1975): Economic Models in Political Science: The Case of Exit, Voice, and Loyalty. *British Journal of Political Science*, vol.5 (jan), pp. 65-82

Blasi, J.R. (1982): Introduction. In Leviatan and Rosner, 1982, pp. v-x.

Blasi, J. R; Whyte, W. F. (1980): From Research to Legislation on Employee Ownership. *Economic and Industrial Democracy*, 1, no. 3 (August), pp. 395-414.

Blau, P. M. (1964): *Exchange and Power in Social Life*. Wiley, New York.

Bluedorn, A. C. (1978): A Taxonomy of Turnover. *Academy of Management Review*, 3, pp. 647-651.

———. (1982): The Theories of Turnover: Causes, Effects and Meanings. In Bachrach, 1982, pp. 75-128.

Bohman, B; Boter,H(1979): *Hur styrs mindre och medelstora företag?* Småföretagsprojektet, Arbetslivscentrum, Stockholm.

Bradley, K. (1980): A Comparative Analysis of Producer Co-operatives: Some Theoretical and Empirical Implications. *British Journal of Industrial Relations*, 18 (July), pp. 155-168.

Bradley, K.; Gelb, A. (1981): Motivation and Control in the Mondragon Experiment. *British Journal of Industrial Relations*, 19 (March), pp. 211-231.

———. (1982): The Mondragon Cooperatives: Guidelines for a Cooperative Economy? In Jones and Svejnar, 1982, pp. 153-171.

Broström, A. (1982): *MBLs gränser. Den privata äganderätten*. Arbetslivscentrum, Stockholm.

———. (1984): Loss of Shareholder Control and "The Managerial Revolution". *Economic and Industrial Democracy*, 5(1)

Brunsson, N.; Johannisson, B. (eds.), (1983): *Lokal mobilisering*. Doxa Ekonomi, Lund.

Buchanan, B., II (1974): Building Organizational Commitment: The Socialization of Managers in Work Organizations. *Administrative Science Quarterly*, 19, pp. 533-546

Bucht, J.; Hammarström, O.; Nording, L. (1976): Företag som tagits över av de anställda. Research report no. 39, Department of Sociology, University of Gothenburg.

Burnham, J. (1941/1960): *The Managerial Revolution*. Indiana University Press, Bloomington.

Burns, T. R. (1976): *Power and Control*. Sage, Beverly Hills, Calif.; London.

Burns, T. R.; Baumgartner, T.; DeVillé, P. (1985): *Man, Decisions, Society.* Gordon and Breach, New York.

Campbell, A; Keen, C; Norman, G; Oakeshott, R. (1977): *Worker-Owners: The Mondragon Achievement.* The Anglo-German Foundation for the Study of Industrial Society, London; Bonn.

Carnoy, M.; Shearer, D. (1980): *Economic Democracy.* M.E. Sharpe, New York.

Child, J. (1972): Organizational Structure, Environment and Performance: The Role of Strategic Choice. *Sociology*, 6, pp. 1-22.

Clarke, T. (1981): A Peaceful Revolution? The Politics of Workers Co-operatives 1800-1980. Paper prepared for the International Conference on Producer Cooperatives, Gilleleje, DK. Mimeo.

———. (1983): A Comparative Analysis of Range of Potential Orientations, Structures and Activities in Producer Cooperative Development. Mimeo.

Coates, K. (ed.), (1977): *The New Worker Co-Operatives.* Spokesman Books, Nottingham.

Cohen, R. (1972): *The Kibbutz Settlement.* Hakibbutz Hameuchad, Tel-Aviv.

Cohen, M. D.; March, J. G.; Olsen, J. P. (1972): A Garbage Can Model of Organizational Choice. *Administrative Science Quarterly*, 17, pp. 1-25.

Cornforth, C. (1982): *A Comparative Analysis of Decision Making and Control in Producer Cooperatives.*Mimeo. Milton Keynes.

———. (1983): Some Factors Affecting the Success or Failure of Worker Co-operatives. *Economic and Industrial Democracy*, 4, no.2 (May), pp. 163-190.

Conforth, C.; Paton, R. (1981): Participation and Power: the Case of the Jewellery Cooperative. Mimeo. Cooperative Research Unit, Milton Keynes.

Dahl, R. A. (1970): *After the Revolution?* Yale University Press, New Haven, Conn.

Daniels, G.; Redmon, G.; Mueller, C. (1986): A Lost Dream: Worker Control at Rath Packing. *Labor Research Review*, 6. Midwest Center for Labor Research, Chicago, pp. 5-24.

Darin-Drabkin, H. (1963): *The Other Society.* Harcourt, Brace & World, New York.

Demsetz, H. (1967): Toward a Theory of Property Rights. *American Economic Review*, 57 (May), pp. 347-359. (Reprinted in Furubotn and Pejovich, 1974).

———. (1983): The Structure of Ownership and the Theory of the Firm. *Journal of Law and Economics*, 26, no. 2.

DiMaggio, P. J.; Powell W. W. (1983): The Iron Cage Revisited - Institutional Isomorphism and Collective Rationality. *American Sociological Review.* 48, no. 2, pp. 147-160.

Domar, E. D. (1966): The Soviet Collective Farm as a Producer Cooperative. *American Economic Review.* 56, pp. 734-757.

Eidem, R. (1982): Risk och inflytande i företagetkapitalmarknadens funktioner i en ekonomi av Sveriges typ. Arbetsrapport II, EDLA 2:5. Mimeo. Arbetslivscentrum, Stockholm.

Ellerman, D. (1984): Workers' Cooperatives: The Question of Legal Structure. In Jackall and Levin, 1984b, pp. 245-257.

———. (1986): ESOPS & CO-OPS: Worker Capitalism & Worker Democracy. *Labor Research Review*, no. 6. Midwest Center for Labor Research, Chicago, pp. 55-70.

Elzinga, K. C. (1970): Predatory Pricing: The Case of the Gunpowder Trust. *Journal of Law and Economics*, 13, pp. 223-240.

Etzioni, A. (1961): *A Comparative Analysis of Complex Organizations*. The Free Press, Glencoe, N.Y.

Fanning, C. M.; McCarthy, T. (1986): A Survey of Economic Hypotheses Concerning the Non-viability of Labour-directed Firms in Capitalist Economies. In Jansson and Hellmark, 1986, pp. 7-50.

Fast, L (1986): Förslag till en inledande kartläggning av personalägda företag inom tjänstesektorn i Sverige. Mimeo. Linköping University, Linköping.

Fine, K. S. (1973): Worker Participation in Israel. In Hunnius et al., 1973, pp. 226-264.

Fleet, K. (1976): Triumph Meriden. In Coates, 1976, pp. 88-108.

Fletcher, R. (1976): Worker Co-ops and the Co-operative Movement. In Coates, 1976, pp. 173-215.

Furubotn E. G.; Pejovich, S. (eds.), (1974): *The Economics of Property Rights*. Ballinger, Cambridge, Mass.

Gabrielsson, Å. (1980): Löntagarägda företag. Kartläggning av förekomst och några problem och deras lösningar. In *Arbetskooperation*, Swedish State Report, SOU 1980:36, Stockholm, pp. 37-225.

Galbraight J. K.(1967): *The New Industrial State*. Houghton Mifflin, Boston.

Garfinkel, H. (1967): *Studies in Ethnomethodology*. Prentice-Hall, Englewood Cliffs, N.J.

Gavito, J.; Meza, JK.; Ravideneyra, I. (1986): Cruz Azul. In Ales Vahcic and Vesna Smole-Grobovsek, (eds.), *Workes' Self-Management and Participation in Practice*. ICPE, Ljublijana, 1986. Vol. 2, pp. 165-274.

Geeraerts, G. (1984): The Effect of Ownership on Organizational Structure in Small Firms. *Administrative Science Quarterly, 29*, pp. 232-237.

Giddens, A. (1978): *Émile Durkheim*. Penguin Books, Hammondsworth, Eng.

———. (1984): *The Constitution of Society. Outline of the Theory of Structuration*. Polity Press, Cambridge, Eng.

Glaser, B. G.; Strauss, A. L. (1967): *The Discovery of Grounded Theory*. Aldine, Chicago.

Goffman, E. (1974): *Frame Analysis. An Essay on the Organization of Experience*. Harvard University Press, Cambridge, Mass.

Golomb, N. (und): *Japanese Management Compared to American Management: A Challenge for Kibbutz Industrial Management* (Hebrew). The Ruppin Institute, Israel.

Gouldner, A. W. (1961): Metaphysical Pathos and the Theory of Bureaucracy. In Etzioni, A., (ed.), *Complex Organizations. A Sociological Reader*. Holt, Rinehart and Winston, New York, pp. 71-81

Gouldner, H. P. (1960): Dimensions of Organizational Commitment. *Administrative Science Quarterly, 4*, pp. 468-490.

Granrose, C. S.; Hochner, A. (1985): Are Women Interested in Saving Their Jobs Through Employee Ownership? *Economic and Industrial Democracy, 6*, pp. 299-324.

Greenberg, E. S. (1984): Producer Cooperatives and Democratic Theory: The Case of the Plywood Firms. In Jackall and Levin, 1984b, pp. 171-218.

———. (1986): *Workplace Democracy. The Political Effects of Participation*. Cornell University Press, Ithaca, N.Y. and London.

Grusky, O. (1966): Career Mobility and Organizational Commitment. *Administrative Science Quarterly,* 10, pp. 488-503.

Guion, R. M. (1981): Choosing Members for Organizations. In Nystrom and Starbuck, 1981, pp. 358-381.

Gunn, C. E. (1984): Worker *Management in the United States.* Cornell University Press, Ithaca, N.Y.

Gurdon, M. A. (1980): An American Approach to Self-Management. In Jain, 1980, pp. 295-309.

Gustavsen, B. (n.d.): A Decade With Employee Representation on Company Boards: Experiences and Prospects for the Future. Working paper, Arbetslivscentrum, Stockholm.

Habermas, J. (1976): *Legitimation Crisis.* Heinemann, London.

Hammer, T.H; Landau, J:C; Stern, R.N. (1980): Absenteeism When Workers Have a Voice: The Case of Employee Ownership. *Journal of Applied Psychology,* 66, pp. 561-573.

Hannan, M. T.; Freeman, J. (1977): The Population Ecology of Organizations. *American Journal of Sociology,* 82, no. 5, pp. 929-964.

Hawley, A. E. (1968): Human Ecology. In David L. Sills, ed,*International Encyclopedia of Social Sciences.* Macmillan, New York, pp. 328-37.

Hedberg, B.L.T. (1974): Reframing as a Way to Cope With Organizational Stagnation. Working Paper, IIM. Wissenschaftszentrum, Berlin.

———. (1979): How organizations learn and unlearn. Working paper. Arbetslivscentrum, Stockholm.

Hedberg, B.L.T; Jönsson, S. (1978): Designing Semi-Confusing Information Systems for Organizations in Changing Environments. *Accounting, Organizations and Society.* 3, no. 1, pp. 47-64.

Hernes, G. (1977): Structural Change in Social Processes. *American Journal of Sociology,* 82, no. 3, pp. 513-547.

Herskin, B. (n.d.): Aktivisten. På vej mod en ikke-ideologi. Handelshøjskolan i København, Copenhagen.

Herzberg, F. (1966): *Work and the Nature of Man.* World Publishing Co., Cleveland.

Himmelstrand, U.; Brulin, G.; Swedberg, R. (1986): Control, Motivation, and Structure. The "New Managerial Philosophies" vs. Industrial Democracy. *Economic Analysis and Workers Management,* 20, pp. 1-21.

Hindley, B. (1970): Separation of Ownership and Control. *Journal of Law and Economics,* 13, pp. 185-212.

Hirschman. A. O.(1970): *Exit, Voice, and Loyalty.* Harvard University Press, Cambridge, Mass.

———. (1974): Exit, Voice and Loyalty- further reflections. *Social Science Information,* 13, pp. 7-26.

———. (1977): *The Passions and the Interests. Political Arguments for Capitalism before Its Triumph.* Princeton University Press, Princeton, N.J.

———. (1981): *Essays in Trespassing. Economics to Politics and Beyond.* Cambridge University Press, Cambridge; London; New York; New Rochelle; Melbourne; Sydney.

———. (1982): *Shifting Involvements.* Martin Robertson, Oxford.

————. (1984): *Getting Ahead Collectively. Grassroots Experiences from Latin America*. Pergamon Press, New York; Oxford, Toronto; Sydney; Paris; Frankfurt.

Hochner, A. (1981): The Mentality of Worker Ownership: Reflections on Some Anomalous Research Findings. Paper presented at the International Conference on Producer Cooperatives, Gilleleje, Danmark.

Horvat, B. (1974): Varför har inte arbetarstyrda företag redan slagit ut de kapitalistiska? *Ekonomisk Debatt*, 2, pp. 288-293.

————. (1979a): Note on Participation, Hierarchy and Justice. *Economic Analysis and Workers Management*, 13, pp. 297-299.

————. (1979b): Self-Management, Efficiency, and Neoclassical Economics. *Economic Analysis and Workers Management*, 13, pp. 167-174.

Hostetler, J. A. (1977): *Hutterite Society*. The Johns Hopkins University Press, Baltimore; London.

Hrebiniak, L. C.; Alutto, J. A. (1972): Personal and Role-Related Factors in the Development of Organizational Commitment. *Administrative Science Quarterly*, 17, pp. 555-572

Hunnius, G.; Garson, G. D.; Case, J. (eds.), (1973): *Workers' Control. A Reader on Labor and Social Change*. Random House, New York.

Jackall, R; Levin H. M. (1984a): Work in America and the Cooperative movement. in Jackall and Levin, 1984, pp. 3-15.

————. (eds.), (1984b): *Worker Cooperatives in America*. University of California Press, Berkeley, Los Angeles, London.

Jain, H. C. (ed.), (1980): *Worker Participation. Success and Problems*. Praeger, New York.

Jansson, S. (1983): Svenska Personalägda Industriföretag. En faktasammanställning. Arbetsrapport 1983:2, Högskolan i Örebro, Örebro, Sweden.

Jansson, S.; Hellmark, A-B. (eds.), (1986): *Labor Owned Firms and Workers Cooperatives*. Gower, Aldershot, UK; Brookfield, Vermont.

Jobring, O. (1982): Arbetarproduktionsföreningarnas villkor 1897-1937. Mimeo. Företagekonomiska institutionen, Göteborgs universitet, Gothenburg.

————. (1988): *Kooperativ Rörelse*. BAS, Gothenburg.

Jobring, O.; Ottermark, K. (1982): Arbetarproduktionsföreningarnas villkor och möjligheter. in Kooperativ årsbok 1981. Kooperativa Institutet, Stockholm.

Jones, D. C. (1976): British Producer Co-operatives. in Coates, 1976, pp. 34-70.

Jones, D. C.; Estrin, S. (1987): Are There Life Cycles in Labor-Managed Firms? Evidence from France. Draft.

Jones, D. C.; Svejnar, J. (eds.), (1982): *Participatory and Self-Managed Firms. Evaluating Economic Performance*. Lexington Books, Lexington, Mass.; Toronto.

Jones, P. (1983): Developmental Choices for a Law of Workers Co-operatives. Mimeo. Faculty of Law, University of Toronto.

Jonnergård, K. (1988): *Federativa processer och administrativ utveckling. En studie av federativa kooperativa organisationer*. Lund University Press, Lund.

Jordan, J. (1986): A System of Interdependent Firms as a Development Strategy. In Jansson and Hellmark, 1986, pp. 105-116.

Kanovsky, E. (1966): *The Economy of the Israeli Kibbutz*. Harvard University Press, Cambridge, Mass.

Kanter, R.M.(1968): Commitment and Social Organization: A Study of Commitment Mechanisms in Utopian Communities. *American Sociological Review*, 33, pp. 499-517.

―――. (1972): *Commitment and Community*. Harvard University Press, Cambridge,Mass.

Katz, D.; Golomb, E. (1974/1975): Integration, Effectiveness, and Adaptation in Open Systems. A Comparative Analysis of Kibbutz Communities. *Administration and Society*, 6. (in two parts): part I in no. 3, pp. 283-315; part II in no. 4, pp. 389-491.

Kaufman, H. (1960): *The Forest Ranger*. Johns Hopkins University Press, Baltimore.

―――. (1973): *Administrative Feedback. Monitoring Subordinates' Behavior*. The Brookings Institute, Washington, D.C.

Klein, K. J.; Rosen, C. (1984): Employee Stock Ownership in the United States. In Stern and McCarthy (eds.) *The Organizational Practice of Democracy*, John Wiley and Sons Ltd, London, pp. 387-405.

Kowalak, T. (1981): Work Co-operatives in Poland. Basic information and critical review of the experiences of the last decade. Paper prepared for the international conference on producer co-operatives, Gilleleje (Copenhagen).

Kuhn, T.S. (1962): *The Structure of Scientific Revolutions*. University of Chicago Press, Chicago, Ill.

Laver, M. (1976): Exit, Voice, and Loyalty Revisited. in *British Journal of Political Science*, 6, pp. 463-82).

Lee, B. W. (1988): Productivity and Employee Ownership: the Case of Sweden. Doctoral thesis, Department of Economics, Uppsala University.

Leitner, K. (1980): *A primer on Ethnomethodology*. Oxford University Press, New York.

Leviatan, U. (1975): Factors That Determine Attachment of the Kibbutz-Born to Kibbutz Life and Reasons for Their Departure. Report no. 33. University of Haifa, The Kibbutz University Center.

―――. (1978): Organizational Effects of Managerial Turnover in Kibbutz Production Branches. *Human Relations*, 31, pp. 1001-1018.

―――. (1982a): Hired Labor in the Kibbutz: Ideology, History and Social Psychological Effects. In Leviatan and Rosner, 1982, pp. 64-75.

―――. (1982b): Individual Effects of Managerial Rotation: the Case of the "Demoted" Office Holder. In Leviatan and Rosner, 1982, pp. 153-169.

Leviatan, U.; Orchan, E.; Avnat, A. (1977): Increasing Retention among Kibbutz-Born Members. Report no. 37. University of Haifa, The Kibbutz University Center.

Leviatan, U.; Rosner, M. (eds.), (1982): *Work and Organization in Kibbutz Industry*. Norwood Editions, Darby, Pa.

Levin, H. M. (1984): ESOPs and the Financing of Worker-Cooperatives. In Jackall and Levin, 1984, pp. 220-245.

Lieblich, A. (1983): *Kibbutz Makom*. Am Oved Publishing House, Tel Aviv.

Lichtenstein, P. (1986): The Concept of the Firm in the Economic Theory of "Alternative" Organizations: Appraisal and Reformulation. In Jansson and Hellmark, 1986, pp. 51-72.

Lindmark, L. (1983): Den svenska industri- och regionalpolitiken - kontroll uppifrån eller samordning nerifrån? In Brunsson and Johannisson, 1983, pp. 81-91.

Lindqvist L. G.(1986): Arbetskooperativ och medlemsägda/styrda företag. Paper prepared for the Kooperativa Studier society's seminar, Lidingö.

Lindqvist, L. G.; Svensson, C. (1982): Worker Owned Factories in Sweden. *Economic Analysis and Workers Management*, 16, pp. 387-404.

Lissak, M. (1969): Images of Society and Status in Yishuv and Israeli Society. In Eisenstadt,S. N. et al.(eds.), *The Social Structure of Israel* (Hebrew). Academon, Jerusalem.

Livingston, C. (1986): Lessons from Three UAW Locals. *Labor Research Review*, no.6. Midwest Center for Labor Research, Chicago, pp. 35-40..

Long, R. J. (1978a): The Effect of Employee Ownership on Organizational Identification, Employee Job Attitudes, and Organizational Performance: A Tentative Framework and Empirical Findings. *Human Relations*, 31, no. 1, pp. 29-48.

———. (1978b): The Relative Effects of Share Ownership vs. Control on Job Attitudes in an Employee Owned Company. *Human Relations*, 31, no. 9, pp. 753-763.

———. (1982): Worker Ownership and Job Attitudes: A Field Study. *Industrial Relations*, 21, no. 2, pp. 196-215.

Lukes, S. (1976): Power. A Radical View. Macmillan, London; Basingstoke.

Lynd, S. (1986): Why We Opposed the Buy-Out at Weirton Steel. *Labor Research Review*, no.6, Midwest Center for Labor Research, Chicago, pp. 41-54.

Lysgaard,S(1976): *Arbeiderkollektivet*. Universitetsforlaget, Oslo; Bergen; Tromsö.

MAC-MAREV(1982): Det Kan Lade Sig Gøre. Mimeo (Issued 1983 in book form). Handelshøjskolen, København.

Maron, S. (1987): Changes in Kibbutz Society, 1980-85. *Kibbutz Studies*, May. Yad Tabenkin Institute, Efal, pp. 4-10.

———. (1988): Changes in Kibbutz, 1986. *Kibbutz Studies*, February, Yad Tabenkin Institute, Efal. pp. 2-5.

Marsh, R. M.; Mannari, H. (1977): Organizational Commitment and Turnover. A Prediction Study. *Administrative Science Quarterly*, 22, pp 57-75.

Meister, A. (1984): *Participation, Associations, Development, and Change*. Transaction Books, New Brunswick, N.J.; London.

Melman, S. (1970): Industrial Efficiency under Managerial versus Cooperative Decision Making: A Comparative Study of Manufacturing Enterprises in Israel. *The review of Radical Political Economics*, 2.

———. (1971): Managerial versus Cooperative Decision Making in Israel. *Studies in Comparative International Development*. 6, pp. 3-17.

Menconi, M. (1982): Labour Allocation and the Labour-Managed Firm. *Economic Analysis and Workers Management*, 16, no. 4, pp. 331-344.

Meyer, J. W. (1983): Institutionalization and the Rationality of Formal Organizational Structure. In Meyer and Scott, 1983, pp. 261-282.

Meyer, J. W.; Rowan, B. (1977): Institutionalized Organizations: Formal Structure as Myth and Ceremony. *American Journal of Sociology*, 83, pp. 340-363.

Meyer, J.W.; Scott, W. R. (eds.), (1983): *Organizational Environments. Ritual and Rationality*. Sage, Beverley Hills, Calif..

Mills, C. W. (1959): *The Power Elite*. Oxford University Press, Oxford; London; New York.

Miyazaki, H. (1982): On Success and Dissolution of the Labor-Managed Firm in a Capitalist Economy. *Journal of Political Economy,* 92, no. 5, pp. 909-931.

Morgan, G. *(1986): Images of Organization.* Sage, Beverly Hills, Calif.

Mowday, R. T.; Steers, R. M.; Porter, L. W. (1979): The Measurement of Organizational Commitment. *Journal of Vocational Behaviour,* 14, pp. 227-247.

Mygind ,N. (1986): From the Illyrian Firm to the Reality of Self-Management. In Jansson and Hellmark, 1986, pp. 73-104.

Nilsson, J. (1986): *Den Kooperativa Verksamhetsformen.* Studentlitteratur, Lund.

Niv, A. (1976): A Search for a Theory about the Survival of Communes. Doctoral dissertation, Harvard Business School.

――――. (1977/1978): The Survival of Social Innovation. The Cases of Commune and Kibbutz. *Hakibbutz* (Hebrew), nos. 6-7, pp. 115-130.

――――. (1980): Organizational Disintegration: Roots, Processes, and Types. In John R. Kimberley et al. (eds.): *The Organizational Life Cycle.* Jossey Bass, San Francisco; Washington, D.C.; London, pp. 375-394.

Nutzinger, H. G. (1982): The Economics of Property Rights--A New Paradigm in Social Science? *Economic Analysis and Workers Management,* 16, no. 1, pp. 81-97

Nystrom, P. C.; Starbuck, W. H. (eds.), (1981): *Handbook of Organizational Design.* Oxford University Press, Oxford; New York.

Oakeshott, R. (1978): *The Case for Workers' Co-ops.* Routledge & Kegan Paul, London; Henley; Boston.

Ouchi, W. G. (1977): The Relationship between Organizational Structure and Organizational Control. *Administrative Science Quarterly,* 22, pp. 95-108.

――――. (1980): Markets, Bureaucracies and Clans. *Administrative Science Quarterly,* 25, pp. 129-141.

――――. (1981): *Theory Z.* Addison-Wesley, Reading, Mass.

Ouchi, W. G.; Jaeger, A. M. (1978): Type Z Organization: Stability in the Midst of Mobility. *Academy of Management Review,* 3, pp. 305-314.

Pateman, C. (1970): *Participation and Democratic Theory.* Cambridge University Press, Cambridge.

Paton, R. (1978): Some Problems of Cooperative Organization. Mimeo. Cooperative Research Unit, Open University, Milton Keynes.

Peleg, D. (1982): An Economic Perspective on Kibbutz Industrialization. In Leviatan and Rosner, 1982, pp. 7-16.

Perrow, C. (1979): *Complex Organizations. A Critical Essay* (2d edition). Scott, Foresman, Glenview, Ill.

Perry, S. E.; Davis, H. C.(1985): The Worker-Owned Firm: The Idea and Its Conceptual Limits. *Economic and Industrial Democracy,* 6, pp. 275-297.

Pestoff, V. (1979): Membership Participation in Swedish Consumer Cooperatives. Research Report 1979:1. University of Stockholm, Department. of political science.

Peters, T. J.; Waterman, R. H. (1982): *In Search of Excellence.* Harper and Row, New York.

Pfeffer, J. (1982): *Organizations and Organization Theory.* Pitman, Boston; London; Melbourne; Toronto.

Pfeffer, J.; Salancik G. R. (1978): *The External Control of Organizations. A Resource Dependence Perspective.* Harper and Row, New York; Hagerstown; London.

Pollard, J. (1967): Nineteenth-Century Co-operation: From Community Building to Shopkeeping. In A. Briggs and J. Saville (eds.): *Essays in Labour History* Macmillan, London; Melbourne; Toronto; St Martin's Press, New York, pp. 74-112.

Porter, L. W.; Steers, R. M.; Mowday, R. T.; Boullian, P.V. (1974): Organizational commitment, job satisfaction and turnover among psychiatric technicians. *Journal of Applied Psychology*, 59, pp. 603-609.

Price, J. L. (1977): *The Study of Turnover*. Iowa State University Press, Ames, Ia.

Ranson, S.; Hinings, B.; Greenwood, R. (1980): The Structuring of Organizational Structures. *Administrative Science Quarterly*, 25, no.1, pp. 1-17

Rayman, P. (1981): *The Kibbutz Community and Nation Building*. Princeton University Press, Princeton, N.J.

Rhodes, S. R.; Steers, R. M. (1982): Conventional vs. Worker-Owned Organizations. *Human Relations*, 34, no.12, pp. 1013-1035.

Robinson, M. (1981a): The Identity of Human Social Groups. *Behavioral Science*, 26, pp. 114-128.

————. (1981b): Management and Self-Management: The Objective-Subjective Dimensions. *International Journal of Man-Machine Studies*, 14, pp. 151-167.

Rokkan, S. (1974): Entries, Voices, Exits: Towards a Possible Generalization of the Hirschman model. *Social Science Information*, 13, no. 1, pp. 39-53.

Rosner, M.; Cohen, N. (1980): Is Direct Democracy Feasible in Modern Society? The Lesson of the Kibbutz Experience. In Bartölke et al., 1980, pp. 193-219.

Rosner, M.; Palgi, M. (1982): Ideology and Organizational Solutions: The Case of Kibbutz Industrialization. in Leviatan and Rosner, 1982, pp. 17-33.

Rosner, M.; Shur, S. (1982): Structural Equality, the Case of the Kibbutz. Report no. 44, University of Haifa, The Kibbutz University Centre, Haifa.

Rothschild-Whitt, J.(1979): The Collectivist Organization: An Alternative to Rational-Bureaucratic Models. *American Sociological Review*, 44, pp. 509-527.

————. (1986): Who Will Benefit from ESOPs. *Labor Research Review*, no.6, pp. 71-82.

Rothschild-Whitt, J.; Whitt, J. A. (1986): Worker-Owners as an Emergent Class: Effects of Cooperative Work on Job Satisfaction, Alienation and Stress. *Economic and Industrial Democracy*, 7, pp. 297-318.

Rothschild, J.; Whitt, J. A. (1986): *The Cooperative Workplace*. Cambridge University Press, Cambridge; London; New York; New Rochelle; Melbourne; Sydney.

Russell, R. (1984a): The Role of Culture and Ethnicity in the Degeneration of Democratic Firms. *Economic and Industrial Democracy*, 5, no.1, pp. 73-96.

————. (1984b): Using Ownership to Control: Making Workers Owners in the Contemporary United States. *Politics and Society*, 13, pp. 253-294

Saglio, J.; Hackman, R. J. (1982): The Design of Governance Systems for Small Worker Cooperatives. Mimeo.

Schumacher, E. F. (1974): *Small is Beautiful. Economy as if People Mattered.* Sphere, London.

Scott, W.R. (1981): *Organizations. Rational, Natural, and Open Systems.* Prentice-Hall, Englewood Cliffs, N.J.

Selznick, P. (1949): *TVA and the Grass Roots.* University of California Press, Berkeley, Calif.

Sen, A. K. (1966): Labour Allocation in a Cooperative Enterprise. *Review of Economic Studies*, 33, No. 96, pp. 361-371.

———. (1981): *Poverty and Famines. An essay on Entitlement and Deprivation.* Clarendon Press, Oxford.

Sertel, M. (1980): A Rehabilitation of the Labor-Managed Firm. In *Workers and Incentives*. North Holland, Amsterdam.

Shapira, R.; Adler, H.; Lerner, M. (1977): The Youth Movement in Israel. A Model of a Youth Culture as an Agent of Socialization (Hebrew). In A. Nevo (ed.) *The Educational Practice* (Hama'aseh Hachinuchi). Yahdav, Tel-Aviv.

Sharp, M. and Lauriston, A. (1952): Steel Axes for Stone-Age Australians. *Human Organization*, 11, pp. 17-22.

Sheldon, M. E. (1971): Investments and Involvements as Mechanisms Producing Commitment to the Organization. *Administrative Science Quarterly*, 16, pp. 142-150.

Shepher, I. (1983): *The Kibbutz: An Anthropological Study.* Norwood Editions, Darby, Pa.

Shinar, D. (1987): Kibbutz Cable TV: A Case Study in the Promise and Performance of Community Media. *Kibbutz Studies*, no. 22, Yad Tabenkin Institute, Efal, pp. 19-29.

Shur, S.; Beit-Halahmi, B.; Blasi, J. R.; Rabin, A. I. (1981): *The Kibbutz: A Bibliography* of Scientific and Professional Publications. Norwood Editions, Darby, Pa.

Sjöstrand, S-E. (1985): *Samhällsorganisation. En ansats till en institutionell ekonomisk mikroteori.* Doxa Ekonomi, Lund.

Sørensen, B. A. (1968): *Når Arbejderne Styrer Bedriftet.* Pax, Oslo

Smelser, N. J. (1962): *Theory of Collective Behavior.* The Free Press, Glencoe, N.Y.

Spiro, M. E. (1970): *Kibbutz: Venture in Utopia*, Schocken Books, New York.

Sproull, L. S. (1981): Beliefs in Organizations. In Nystrom and Starbuck, 1981, pp. 201-224.

Starbuck, W. H.; Greve, A.; Hedberg, B.L.T. (1978): Responding to Crises. In C.F. Smart; W.F. Stanbury, (eds.), *Studies in Crisis Management*. Butterworth & Co., Montreal, pp. 111-137.

Starbuck, W. H.; Nystrom, P. C. (1986): Why the World Needs Organisational Design. In Rolf Wolf (ed.), *Organizing Industrial Development*. De Gruyter, Berlin; New York. pp. 3-17.

Steers, R. M. (1977): Antecedents and Outcomes of Organizational Commitment. *Administrative Science Quarterly*, 22, pp. 46-56.

Stephen, H. (ed), (1982): *The Performance of Labour-Managed Firms*. Macmillan, London; Basingstoke.

Stern, B. (1965): *The Kibbutz That Was.* Public Affairs Press, Washington, D.C.

Stodolsky, D. S. (1985): Information Systems for Self-Management. *Human Systems Management*, 5, pp. 39-45.

Stryjan, Y. (1983a): Review article of Rayman, 1981. *Economic and Industrial Democracy*, 4, pp. 409-413.

———. (1983b): Self-Management. The Case of the Kibbutz. *Economic and Industrial Democracy*, 4, pp. 243-283.

———. (1984a): A Reply to Prof. Rosner. *Economic and Industrial Democracy*, 5; pp. 401-408.

————. (1984b): Self Management and Community. Paper prepared for the European Conference on New Forms of Cooperation, Steinkjer, Norway (rev. version). Working Paper, Arbetslivscentrum, Stockholm.

————. (1985a): Leaving the Kibbutz. A study in Exit. Mimeo. Department of Sociology, Uppsala University.

————. (1985b): Review of Gunn (1984). *Economic and Industrial Democracy*, 6; pp. 385-388.

————. (1986): *Om Planering. En kort handledning i kooperativ planering.* Arbetslivscentrum and Kooperativa Institutet, Stockholm.

————. (1987): Att förnya medlemskapet. In *Kooperativ Årsbok 1987*, Kooperativa Studier, Stockholm, pp. 40-54.

————. (1988): Why does Established Cooperation Need New Cooperatives. Paper prepared for the ICA Research Party's Bologna Seminar.

————. (1989): Hunting and Gathering. The Self-Managed Organization and Its Environment. In *Traditions and Trends in Cooperative Development. Proceedings of the Stockholm Conference.* Forthcoming.

Stryjan, Y.; Hellmark, A-B. (1985): Beyond Ownership. On the Question of 'new' and 'old' cooperatives. Paper presented at the Seventh EGOS Colloquium, Saltsjöbaden, Sweden, June.

Stryjan, Y.; Mann, C-O. (1988): Members and Markets: the Case of Swedish Consumer Co-operation. In *Yearbook of Co-operative Enterprise*. The Plunkett Foundation, Oxford, pp. 121-131.

Talmon, Y. (1972): *Family and Community in the Kibbutz.* Harvard University Press, Cambridge, Mass.

Telser, L. G. (1966): Cutthroat Competition and the Long Purse. *Journal of Law and Economics*, 9, pp. 259-277.

Tetzschner, H (1981): Virksomhedsbeskrivelse Nr 1. Work Report from the MAREV project. Institut for Organisation og Arbejdssociologi, Handelshøjskolen i København

————. (1982): Struktur och Ledelseform. In MAC MAREV, 1982, pp. 161-227.

Thibault, J.; Kelley H. H. (1959): *Social Psychology of Groups*. Wiley and Sons, New York.

Thomas, H.; Logan, C. (1982): *Mondragon. An Economic Analysis*. George Allen & Unwin, London.

Thompson, J. D. (1967): *Organizations in Action*. McGraw-Hill, New York.

Toulmin, S. (1961): *Foresight and Understanding. An Inquiry into the Aims of Science*. Hutchinson, London.

Trevena, J. E.(1980): When All Else Fails, Read the Directions. Cooperative Future Directions Project, Working Paper no. 5. The Cooperative College of Canada, Saskatchewan.

Tsur, Z. (1987): The Kibbutz in Face of the Economic Stagnation. *Kibbutz Studies*, no. 23, Yad Tabenkin Institute, Efal, pp. 2-4.

U.S. General Accounting Office.(1986): *Employee Stock Ownership Plans*. Briefing report to the Hon. Russel B. Long, U.S. Senate. GAO-PEMD-86-4BR.

Vanek, J. (1970): *The General Theory of Labor-Managed Market Economies*. Cornell University Press, Ithaca, N.Y.

————. (1971): *The Participatory Economy*. Cornell University Press, Ithaca, N.Y.

———. (1975a): The Basic Theory of Financing of Participatory Firms. In Vanek, 1975, pp. 445-455.

———. (ed.), (1975b): *Self-Management: The Economic Liberation of Man.* Penguin, Hammondsworth, Eng.

———. (1978): Self-Management, Workers' Management, and Labour Management in Theory and Practice: A Comparative Study. *Economic Analysis and Workers Management*, 12, pp. 5-24.

von Otter, C. (1980): Swedish Welfare Capitalism. In R. Scase (ed.): *The State in Western Europe.* Croom Helm, London.

Ward, B. (1958): The Firm in Illyria: A Market Syndicalism. *American Economic Review*, 48, September, pp. 566-589.

Webb (Potter), B. (1891): *The Co-operative Movement in Great Britain.* Swan Sonnenschein & Co., London ; Charles Scribner's Sons, New York.

Webb, S.; Webb, B. (1897): *Industrial Democracy.* Longmans, Gren & Co., London.

———. (1920/1975): *A Constitution for the Socialist Commonwealth of Great Britain.* London School of Economics and Cambridge University Press; London; Cambridge.

Webb, C. (1919): *Industrial Co-Operation. The Story of a Peaceful Revolution* (eighth edition). The Co-operative Union, Manchester.

Weber, M. (1930/1976): *The Protestant Ethic and the Spirit of Capitalism.* George Allen & Unwin, London.

———. (1978): *Economy and Society*, (eds. G. Roth and C. Wittich). University of California Press, Berkeley.

Weick, K. (1969/1979): *The Social Psychology of Organizing.* Addison-Wesley, Reading, Mass.

Wildavsky, A. (1972): The Self-Evaluating Organization. *Public Administration Review*, 32, no. 5 (September/October), pp. 509-521.

Wilkins, A. L; Ouchi, W. G. (1983): Efficient Cultures: Exploring the Relationship between Cultures and Organizational Performance. *Administrative Science Quarterly*, 28, pp. 468-481.

Williamson, O. E. (1975): *Market and Hierarchies.* The Free Press, New York.

Wippler, R. (1986): Oligarchic tendencies in democratic organizations. *The Netherlands' Journal of Sociology*, 22, no. 1 (April), pp. 1-17.

Zamir, D. (1972): Hired Labour and the Structure of Industrial Plants in the Kibbutz Artzi Movement. Giv'at Haviva Publications (Hebrew), Givat Haviva..

Zucker, L. G. (1981): Organizations as Institutions. In S. M. Bachrach (ed.), *Perspectives in Organizational Sociology.* JAI Press, Greenwich, Conn., pp. 1-47

Zwerdling D. (1980): *Workplace Democracy.* Harper & Row, New York; Cambridge, Eng.

# INDEX

**About the Author**

YOHANAN STRYJAN is a research fellow at Uppsala University in Sweden. An Israeli citizen, he has degrees from Ben Gurion University and Stockholm University.